Medicine
and the
Mormons

Medicine and the Mormons

Robert T. Divett

An Introduction to
the History of
Latter-day Saint Health Care

COPYRIGHT © 1981 BY
ROBERT T. DIVETT

All rights reserved. Reproduction in whole or any
parts thereof in any form or by any media without
written permission is prohibited.

International Standard Book Number
0-88290-194-X

Library of Congress Catalog Card Number
81-84588

Horizon Publishers Catalog and Order Number
2050

Printed and Distributed in the
United States of America
by

**Horizon
Publishers &
Distributors**

50 South 500 West
P.O. Box 490
Bountiful, Utah 84010

Preface

My father was a book reader, and it just seemed natural that my sister and I grew up as readers. Dad's glass-fronted sectional bookcases held particular fascination for me, and two history books he had studied in high school were a particular delight to me. I don't remember when I first read them, but it was in the elementary grades.

I remember my teacher's astonishment at my knowledge of history and geography when I was a student in the firth or sixth grade. And I loved my junior high school history classes from "Doc" Archibald. Somewhere along the way I began to read every history book I could get my hands on. In high school a teacher who was primarily an athletic coach but taught a course or two in history found it convenient to regularly turn the class I was enrolled in over to me to teach while he went out and moonlighted selling insurance. I early found that you learned a lot if you had to teach others.

My mother was a very devout Mormon, and she instilled in me great interest in the teachings of The Church of Jesus Christ of Latter-day Saints. As a teen-ager, my own testimony of the gospel grew, and soon I found that my interest in history extended to the history of the Church, an interest that I have never lost.

In college at the University of Utah and the Salt Lake LDS Institute of Religion, and later at Brigham Young University, after a short abortive effort to learn architecture, I turned again to history and took a teaching major in the subject. I had wonderful general history teachers like Russell Swenson and S. Lyman Tyler, but I was strongly influenced to extend my interest in the history of the Mormons, Utah, and the American Frontier by T. Edgar Lyon, Alma Burton, and Richard Poll.

Upon graduation with a bachelor's degree, I found that there was a surplus of history teachers, and I hurriedly took nine quarter hours of librarianship to certify as a teacher-librarian and dashed off to Idaho to teach junior high school mathematics and social studies. My year as a teacher of junior high school youth convinced me that I should turn to librarianship as a profession.

At BYU, Hattie Knight had encouraged me to go to Peabody College to study under the great library science teacher Louis Shores, but when I got there Shores had moved on to another school. I stayed on at Peabody and took a couple of student library aid positions while completing a masters degree in library science. Before I graduated, having a wife and two little boys, I moved from a student aid to a professional librarian position, working at Vanderbilt University for one of the grand old dames of medical librarianship, Eileen Cunningham. It didn't take long to pique my curiosity about a medical school listed in the history section of the *American Medical*

Directory. I had never even heard of the Medical College of Utah at Morgan City, and I thought that I had a pretty good knowledge of Utah history.

It wasn't too long until I was invited to become the medical librarian at the University of Utah. There my boss was another librarian with a strong interest in the history of Utah, Mormons, and the American frontier. We soon became close friends, and for six delightful years L. H. Kirkpatrick was my mentor, always piquing my curiosity, encouraging my interests, and challenging me to write the results of my research.

When I pointed out the *American Medical Directory* entry for the Medical College of Utah, he made suggestions as to where to search for the history of the school, and eventually I found it, and he encouraged me to write the results, which won for me the Medical Library Association's Gottlieb Prize for the year's best article on the history of medicine. Kirk and I were continuously in a game of one-upmanship, trying to come up with bits of Utah and Mormon history that the other didn't know about.

When the university organized a speakers bureau, Kirk insisted that I list myself as a speaker on Utah medical history. For over a year no one requested my services. Then the Holladay Lions Club asked me to speak, and during the next couple of weeks, until the date to speak, I hastily pulled together and wrote out a talk on the subject. Kirk read my talk, passed it on to another medical librarian, and the two of them would not be content until it was polished and published. To my amazement, it won for me my second Murray Gottlieb Prize.

Kirk died a couple months before "Medicine and the Mormons" was published, but before his death he had strongly urged me to expand the material and to write a book on the subject.

After Kirk died, I left Utah and came to the University of New Mexico, accepting the challenge of building from scratch a medical library for a new medical school. Although my interest in the history of medicine and the Mormon people has never waned, the writing of the book had to be put off because of other pressures. Now the opportunity to write the book has come.

Although I am responsible for the contents of the book, I trust that it can be a satisfactory memorial to L. H. Kirkpatrick, who called himself a "dry-Mormon." Although he never joined the Church, he loved the young Mormon students whom he taught and with whom he associated. He challenged them to learn the history of their people so that they could better understand their heritage and thus themselves. If they were to be Mormons, he wanted them to have unshakable testimonies. May this book contribute to the understanding of the Mormon heritage.

Contents

Acknowledgments ... 8

Introduction ... 9

Chapter 1   Medicine in the U.S. in Joseph Smith's Day ... 14

Chapter 2   Health and the Smith Family to 1830 ... 21

Chapter 3   Medical Aspects of the Restoration ... 38

Chapter 4   Zion's Camp and Its Health Problems ... 53

Chapter 5   Nauvoo—The Beautiful Pesthole ... 60

Chapter 6   Doctor John Cook Bennett ... 67

Chapter 7   Joseph Smith and the Doctors ... 83

Chapter 8   Health and the Exodus ... 99

Chapter 9   The Trouble With Doctors ... 110

Chapter 10   Botanic Medicine in Zion ... 120

Chapter 11   The Changing Medical World During the Utah Territorial Period ... 129

Chapter 12   Brigham Young and Medicine ... 135

Chapter 13   Hospitals and Public Health in Utah, 1850 to 1910 ... 144

Chapter 14   Education of Mormon Health Professionals ... 159

Chapter 15   The Growth of the LDS Hospital System ... 169

Chapter 16   New Directions of the 1970s and 1980s ... 177

Notes ... 183

Bibliography ... 197

Index ... 211

Acknowledgments

A cursory count of persons who assisted me in this work in the last year of intensive work alone revealed a total of more than forty persons, and undoubtedly there were more whose names didn't come to mind during that hurried count. Therefore, it is impossible to name all who deserve thanks and acknowledgment, but the help of all is gratefully acknowledged.

Thanks go first to The University of New Mexico for granting a sabbatical leave in which to research and write the book. Thanks also go to Dr. Leonard Arrington for his interest and support, and for providing copies of articles in his personal files for my use.

The full cooperation of the Historical Department of The Church of Jesus Christ of Latter-day Saints made possible the work. Without access to the Church Library and Archives the work would have been impossible. All the staff of the Church Library were very helpful, but special thanks are due to Mary Schnichter who greeted me the first morning and led me to information, and figuratively held my hand through months of digging.

The librarians and staff at the University of Utah, Utah Historical Society, Brigham Young University, Utah State University, National Library of Medicine, Yale University, New York Academy of Medicine, and other libraries, were very kind, courteous, and helpful.

Ernest Hazelwood, Deputy Grand Master, New Mexico A&FM, read and made suggestions on the chapter about Dr. John Cook Bennett, also allowing me access to the library of the New Mexico Grand Lodge so that the masonic aspects of the chapter might be more accurate.

The help of Duane S. Crowther and Horizon Publishers & Distributors, Inc., is gratefully acknowledged. In the midst of sweats over pictures for the book jacket, my childhood buddy, Eldon Linschoten, came to my rescue, and his photography adds the cream to the cake.

My family deserves great thanks—for allowing me to be away from them so long, for enduring me in a pressing time. My son, Bill, and his wife, Pam, located valuable items for me in the Utah State University Library. My sister, Beth, and her husband, Don, read, criticized, and reread draft after draft, as did my father. To my parents, Robert W. Divett and Isabel H. Divett, go the greatest thanks. Dad's interest in the project has never waivered from the day it was conceived years ago. He has underwritten the expenses of a year on two-thirds pay, with months away from my household, and other costs so that the book could be written and published.

Robert T. Divett

Introduction

I have a two-fold purpose in writing this work. The first purpose is to provide for my fellow Latter-day Saints a tool to help understand a part of our heritage—a vital part that affects our day-to-day living.

Everyone desires to live a healthful life, and when that healthful life falters he takes steps to regain that healthful life. The things he does to keep his health, maintain, or restore it, are affected not just by the current practices and knowledge of the health professions, but by the culture of the society of which he is a part. He reacts in compliance with the values of his cultural heritage and his beliefs. If a person knows the historical antecedents of that heritage, he can be wiser in his actions. I have therefore attempted to outline, or introduce, the precedents that are reflected in the current health practices and concepts of the Latter-day Saints.

The second purpose is to provide a tool to those members of the health professions who are called upon to provide health care for Latter-day Saints so that they may better understand the actions and responses of their pa- so that they may better understand the actions and responses of their patients.

A study of the historical antecedents of health care among the Mormons is also a study of the history of health care on the American Frontier. Perhaps no other group of people resided on that frontier longer. The Mormon people moved with, or by their actions themselves moved the frontier from Vermont to upstate New York, Ohio, Missouri, Illinois, and to the Pacific Coast and the Rocky Mountain West. If the frontier began as civilization left the Atlantic Coastal Plain and moved west, and ended when the last part of the country was settled, the Mormons were there throughout the whole period.

The Mormons responded to the same health care needs and patterns of health care as did their neighbors on the frontier. The uniqueness of their response was only in religious doctrinal teachings and in their actions and response as a persecuted religious minority.

Today, as a 4½ million member world-wide church, that frontier heritage affects their response to health preservation and care efforts. Although Latter-day Saints for the most part accept and respond to health care much as do other contemporary people, there are differences quite frequently seen, and some that are occasionally seen, that come from their religious and historical milieu. They also have an outlook on health maintenance that is the result of their religious doctrinal heritage.

The physician, nurse, or other health-care professional involved in the care of a Latter-day Saint (Mormon) would on the surface very likely see very little difference between that patient and any other patient. There are, however, some significant differences in his religious beliefs that may very likely impact upon the way he reacts to the medical care received.

The first major difference is fundamental to the religious beliefs of the Latter-day Saint. He believes he is a literal son of God involved in a continuum of growth and development that preceded mortal life and which will continue beyond it. He believes that his present being is as a soul—a unified spirit and body. He believes that the spirit, as a type of matter called intelligence, has always existed, and was later clothed with a physical body which his spirit gradually learns how to control. At death his physical body will be temporarily laid down into the grave to later be reunited in a perfected form with the spirit body in the resurrection, thus creating an eternal soul.

In practicality, this means that in this mortal life if his spiritual body is properly attuned it may be able to control the physical body to the point of physical healing and even regeneration. The results of this belief may be seen in faith healing of various types.

The second major difference is in the way that he looks at illness. He sees some five or more causes of illness. Some of these causes parallel those of other Christians and of much of the world, but some are rather unique, at least in dogmatic emphasis.

Mormons believe that in the existance before present mortal life there was a great council in Heaven attended by all the spirits who were assigned to this world. Two concepts were presented at that council. One concept offered men the possibility of growing through mortal life into possible Godhood. The other concept, presented by Lucifer, called for saving all men by regimentation. Lucifer's proposal was received favorably by about one-third of those assigned to the world, while the majority accepted the first, the Lord's plan.

When the minority could not prevail, they rebelled and there was war in Heaven with Lucifer leading his followers and Michael, the archangel, leading God's followers. At the end of the war the losers, Lucifer and his angels, were cast out of Heaven and down to Earth to never have the privilege of obtaining physical bodies. These spirits have since wandered the earth, providing opposition to good. These unembodied spirits also have a keen desire to possess the bodies of the two-thirds who have been born over the course of the earth's entire existence, thus forming a majority at any one point of time, and these evil spirits have the ability to move into physical bodies upon occasion. The bodies thus become demon-possessed, and may show mental and physical illnesses as a result.

Mormons also believe that the earth was created, and that mankind exists, on the basis of eternal laws that have control of existence upon this earth. These laws have effect in all functions of existence including effect upon sickness and health. Thus illness may result as the consequence of operation of those laws. Mormons, for example, have no objection to the germ theory of disease. Their Word of Wisdom sets out guiding principles of ways to comply with God's laws and have better health.

A common belief throughout the world, especially in the time before the development of the germ theory of disease, was that God chastens man by means of diseases. If man does evil he may be afflicted. Mormons still accept, to a limited degree, this concept, as does much of the world. It is significant, however, that Lyman Wight, one of the early apostles of the Mormon Church, was rebuked by Joseph Smith, Jr., the first president of the Church, for teaching that "*all* diseases in this church are of the devil, and that medicine administered to the sick is of the devil . . ." [Italics added] Joseph Smith specifically stated that this was not in accordance with the laws of God.[1]

Another concept of disease which Mormons accept as one with limited occurrences is that some illnesses may happen so that God's powers might be demonstrated, similar in a way to Christ's explanation of the blind man's affliction.

Mormons believe that all healing ultimately comes from God. They believe that the physician using good medicine is utilizing knowledge which God has revealed to man for his benefit. They also believe in charismatic, or faith healing, from God. They believe that by operation of the principles of faith God will heal, and they believe that healing occurs primarily through operation of natural laws, some of them not necessarily presently understood by man. When man does good, he sets himself in compliance with those laws and God thus blesses him.

The Latter-day Saints also believe that God has given to man a special controlling force, the authority of the priesthood. This is delegated to man by the ordinance of the laying-on-of-hands, for ordination to office. A person so ordained has authority to lay on hands for the healing of the sick and to cast out devils, and he is utilizing God's higher laws, and God is willing to provide such a blessing, provided that faith is properly exercised by those using that priesthood and by the recipient of the blessing.

The health care professional caring for a Latter-day Saint will most likely encounter the ordinance of administration to the sick. This ordinance follows the pattern set forth in the New Testament: "Is any sick among you? let him call for the elders of the church; and let them pray over him, anointing him with oil in the name of the Lord: And the prayer of faith shall save the sick, and the Lord shall raise him up . . ." (James 5:14-15.)

In this case two elders, holders of the Melchizedek Priesthood (which is held by most adult male Church members), will anoint the crown of the head of the sick person with a few drops of consecrated oil (usually olive oil), and then lay hands upon the head of the sick person and pronounce a blessing upon him.

The health professional may also encounter Latter-day Saints who have been through a Mormon temple and "received his endowments." This educational ordinance is considered by Mormons to be of greatest sanctity. In receiving this ordinance they agree to always wear a sacred undergarment. They were taught that this garment would be "a shield and protection" to them throughout their life, and may believe that it has a healing influence upon them when they wear it while ill. It is therefore believed to be highly desirable that the temple garment be worn by the patient as soon as it will not interfere with other medical treatment or care of the patient. The garment should not, however, be open to view by those who might not understand its significance and would ridicule it.

The orthodox Latter-day Saint usually has strict standards of modesty. He or she will wish to have his/her genital and sexual organs modestly covered. Otherwise they may be embarrassed and have a psychologically traumatic and negative experience.

The health care professional may also encounter fasting, prayer, washings and anointings, and internal and external uses of consecrated oil which are in lesser use as faith-healing methods.

Another factor that may impact upon the care and treatment of a sick Latter-day Saint is the "Word of Wisdom." This health code was given as a revelation to the Prophet Joseph Smith on February 27, 1833. Most simply, it means that Mormons who live the Word of Wisdom will not use "hot drinks." These were defined by the prophet's brother, Hyrum Smith, as tea and coffee. Although their use as a prescribed medication is not prohibited, many will not use them if they are served to the patient as part of the prescribed meal tray. The Word of Wisdom also prohibits the use of any alcoholic beverage or any type of tobacco. The patient may become agitated if another patient in the room, or a visitor, smokes. The tea, coffee, alcohol, and tobacco prohibitions have become a "test of faith" to the Latter-day Saints, and any attempt to induce use of them in a patient may cause serious mental trauma.

The Word of Wisdom also advises the sparing use of meats, therefore a few Latter-day Saints are vegetarians and will not eat meat.

Although almost all Mormons accept and utilize modern medicine, a significant number of them are herbalists and have severe reservations about orthodox medicine. Some of the herbalists have gone so far as to maintain that Mormons who go beyond the use of faith healing or the use of herbs for healing are weak in the faith. However, these herbalists have been advised by the general Church leaders that use of the best medicine available does *not* indicate weakness in the faith and that such useage is desirable.

Regarding medication, Brigham Young's advice to Mormons was, "If we are sick and ask the Lord to heal us, and to do all for us that is necessary to be done, according to my understanding of the Gospel and salvation I might as well ask the Lord to cause my wheat and corn to grow without my plowing the ground and casting in the seed. It appears consistent to me to apply every remedy that comes within the range of my knowledge, and to ask my Father in Heaven, in the name of Jesus Christ, to sanctify that application to the healing of my body. . . . It is my duty to do, when I have it in my power."[2]

The reason for the strong herbal orientation is that the Word of Wisdom advocates the use of herbs for food and healing. Also, the Prophet Joseph Smith was an advocate of botanic medicine during his life and his successor, Brigham Young, was also until late in his life when he began to accept orthodox medicine.

A final point should also be made to health practitioners who may be called upon to care for Latter-day Saints. A revelation given to the Church in early 1831 directed that those that could not be healed by the laying-on-of-hands should be nourished by herbs and mild medications by those that are "not enemies." (D&C 42:43.) Unless friendship can be demonstrated to the patient, resistance to care by non-Mormons might occur. There may even be some Mormons who interpret this revelation to mean that they should be cared for only by Latter-day Saints.

Chapter One

Medicine In The U.S. In Joseph Smith's Day

The Church of Jesus Christ of Latter-day Saints was born during a time of great revolution in medicine, especially medicine in the new United States of America. The battles of that revolution took place not only among the providers of health care but among the consumers of that care. Since the members of the Church were among the consumers, and some of the members were among the providers of health care, the Church could not help but become embroiled in that revolution.

To understand what was taking place, we need to look at medicine in the United States from the time of the American revolution until the time of the organization of the Church.

At the time of the American revolution, American medicine was an amalgam of two major influences. The first was the historical train of western medicine descending from Greek medicine through Europe and especially Great Britain. The second was the impact of native-American medicine.

Western medicine, although also having roots in ancient Egypt and Mesopotamia, primarily came from the Aesculapean medicine of ancient Greece and the teachings of the great physician, Hippocrates, of the fourth century B.C. It was based on the Greek philosophy of the four elements—earth, air, fire, and water.[1] Hippocrates propounded the idea that there were four corresponding humors of the body—blood, phlegm, yellow bile, and black bile. His humoral theory of disease maintained that illness occurred when the body produced one of the four humors in excess. Then the body's defenses came into action. The patient's elevated body temperature, or fever, "cooked" the excess humor, separating it from the other humors so that the body could eliminate it.

The physician could help the patient by performing two procedures. First, to assist the body in cooking the excess humor, the physician could warm the patient externally or give medicines that would raise the body temperature. The second form of therapy available to the physician involved assisting the body to evacuate the cooked humor by purges that induced bowel movements, emetics that induced vomiting, sudorifics that induced sweating, or by bleeding.

The humoral theory of disease greatly simplified the practice of medicine by reducing major classes of drugs to those which warmed, cooled, purged, and so on, and by narrowing major therapies that did not call for medicines to the regulation of external temperature and to the removal of blood.[2] Although there have been minor variations, the humoral theory of disease was the basis of all Western medicine throughout the Middle Ages and the Renaissance, and remained so until well into the 1800s.

There was no nomenclature of diseases as we now look upon disease. The closest thing was the convenient names given based upon external appearance, etc., of types of diseases. For instance, small pox where a large number of pox developed on a sick person, and malaria for fevers supposed to be found in people where the air was bad. New names were being given to diseases with specific symptoms, but there was no formal nomenclature because all diseases were believed to be caused by imbalance of the humors.

Although there had been some two hundred doctors in America that had received formalized medical education in Europe and Great Britain prior to the time of the American Revolution, most medical care in America was provided by either self-taught practitioners or by those who had apprenticed under other doctors. It was only shortly before the revolution that America's first two medical schools were founded, the first in Philadelphia and the second in New York.

The greatest impact upon American medicine came from two Scottish professors of medicine, John Brown and William Cullen. Their medical school at Edinburgh had become the Mecca of aspiring American medical practitioners such as Samuel Latham Mitchill and Benjamin Rush. These men brought back the doctrines of their teachers and, especially in the case of Rush, they shaped American medicine for nearly a century. Their variations upon the humoral theory led to the development of "heroic" medicine in America.

Cullen declared that health and diseases were primarily a matter of "the motions of the system;" that fever, especially, was "a spasm of the extreme arteries" induced by the state of the brain. Therefore, this condition could be cured by that which would induce relaxation. Cullen did not exclude humors from the picture, but thought they were of minor significance. Once a fever appeared, Cullen held, a state of debility ensued. He assumed the existence of disease entities and believed it essential to identify and classify them as far as possible.[3]

John Brown, meanwhile, had taken the concept of debility, which in Cullen was just "the first consequence of fever," and made it the basic disease state. Or, rather, he postulated two such states, one of direct (asthenic) and the other of indirect (sthenic) debility.[4]

Benjamin Rush, pondering the tenets of both Cullen and Brown, decided that debility was neither a consequence of disease nor disease itself. It was, rather, a predisposing *cause* of illness. In a word, Rush reduced Brown's two states of disease to one. He maintained that the morbid excitement observed in fevers was "a spasm of the extreme arteries" or capillaries. In other words, fever lies in an excessive, convulsive, or wrong action of these vessels.[5]

Rush also took over from Cullen the advocacy of bleeding and purging as effective means for relieving vascular tension. He eventually carried his master's doctrine to extremes. Not only fevers but all types of illnesses were ascribed to capillary tension. He advocated, in extreme cases, the removal of as much as four fifths of all the blood in the body! Cullen had recognized the healing power of nature; but Rush banished nature from the sickroom altogether.[6]

Rush also repudiated the ontological concept in principle. There are no such things as disease entities, he held, so why search for them? The only reality, the only thing we can really see, is bodily reaction to adverse stimuli—to mental states within or to cold, miasmata, and the like without. It was effluvia or miasmata, arising from decaying materials, which Rush held responsible for epidemics.[7]

Benjamin Rush, upon his return from Scotland, joined the faculty of the first American medical school. He soon rose to social and political prominence and during the American revolution was active as a high-ranking medical officer for the Americans. He was also chosen a delegate to the Continental Congress from Pennsylvania, and was one of five physicians—the most prominent of them all—who signed the Declaration of Independence.

When Rush returned to the classroom, he did so as a Revolutionary War hero and a friend of such prominent persons as George Washington. Rush formulated his final views on bleeding and purging in 1793 when Philadelphia was struck by a decimating Yellow Fever epidemic.[8] When moderate treatment failed, Rush massively increased these two procedures. Patients were often "bled to faintness," losing as much as 1.5 liters (almost 50 ounces).[9] If they did not improve they were bled again. As his purgative, Rush devised a vigorous purge which contained 15 grains of Jalap, a tuberous root long used as a purgative, and 10 grains of calomel (mercurous chloride). He administered the purge orally, one every six waking hours.[10]

Cullen had recommended the use of calomel in his famous materia medica, describing it as a stimulant which could affect every secretory system of the body, from the salivary glands, bowels, and liver to the kidneys. Rush's major contribution to the use of calomel was teaching that it should be used in massive doses, up to 80 grains or more a day (a toxic dose).[11]

When some of Rush's critically-ill patients recovered despite his treatment, Rush hailed his own success and wrote a book about it. His approach became so popular with the medical profession that his concepts dominated medical care in America for nearly 100 years. Many physicians were equally copious with other treatments. If one dose was good, they reasoned, a dozen doses must be better. This was the basis of orthodox medicine during the lifetime of Joseph Smith. The great American physician and essayist, Oliver Wendell Holmes, would later derisively call it "heroic medicine."[12]

Not only the medical profession accepted heroic medicine, but many of the lay public as well. One of the most tragic cases of its acceptance by both the intelligent layman and the medical profession was the case of George Washington, Rush's friend.[13] Washington had been bled and had used calomel many times during his life, which was one of much sickness in spite of a general appearance of robust good health. Calomel loosens the teeth, and his tooth problems may well have stemmed from his use of calomel. In later life he also suffered from loss of hearing, another complication that could have stemmed from the use of calomel. On Thursday, December 12, 1799, Washington contracted what he thought was a cold. The next day he had his plantation foreman bleed him of 12 or 14 ounces of blood. The following day he consented to send for his friend, Dr. James Craik, who "employed two copious bleedings." Two consultants were called in, Dr. Gustavus Brown, and Dr. Elisha Dick, who had been trained by Dr. Benjamin Rush. A blister was applied to his neck, two "moderate doses" of calomel were given, and an injection (enema) was administered. Another bleeding of about thirty-two ounces was drawn. He then inhaled vapors of vinegar and water. This was followed by ten grains of calomel succeeded by repeated doses of emetic tartar (to make him vomit), amounting in all to five or six grains. Blisters were applied to his extremities, and a cataplasm of bran and vinegar applied to his throat. He died about 10:30 that evening. The doctors wondered why just before the end his blood had become thick and viscious. The doctors had applied the best medication they knew, according to the precepts of the heroic medicine of the day, and it most likely killed him rather than the "Quinsy" that was the diagnosis by the doctors.

A quarter of a century later the Smith family in upstate New York would have their experience with heroic medicine.

Now let us look at the other major impacting force upon American medicine of the time. Although it partially merged into orthodox medicine, it also spawned rival schools of medical practice.

When the British first settled in America they found a land that required modification of their erstwile living standards. They soon adopted many of the ways of the native Americans they found already living on the continent. As some of them moved away from the sea shore and lived among the natives, they found that the natives were using indigenous plants for medications. Long before the English discovery of the cause of scurvy, the French in Canada had had introduced to them an effective treatment for scurvy by the natives.[14]

Although there was an ethnic arrogance among the British educated orthodox medical profession that foreclosed any serious attention to the medical knowledge which the "savages" might have, the self-taught practitioner, especially those serving the frontier communities, readily adopted the medications of the natives. When they worked effectively for the frontier doctor, they gradually found their way into more orthodox acceptance. More than two hundred indigenous drugs which were used by one or more Indian tribes have at one period or another been official in the *Pharmacopeia of the United States of America* or in the *National Formulary* since the first of these therapeutic guides appeared in 1820. Among these have been the South American Indian contributions of coca, cinchona, curare, and ipecac.[15] A North American plant that was to have a major impact upon healing was lobelia.

The acceptance of native medications and herbs, especially by the lesser-educated practitioners of the frontier, ultimately led to the schism in medicine and the creation of the botanic and American eclectic schools of medical thought. It was these schisms that embroiled the Mormons in medical controversy during its early existence.

Although there were many self-taught doctors practicing in America, the one who undoubtedly had the most impact upon American medicine during the early 1800s, until his death in 1843, was Samuel Thomson.[16] Thomson was born in 1769 in Alstead, New Hampshire. He grew up in the woods country of New Hampshire, and early in life became interested in herbs, gaining information from his own experiments, an old woman neighbor who was a herbalist, and herb doctors.

Thomson made his major discovery at the tender age of four when, out of curiosity, he began to chew one of the plants in the fields near his home. The taste and effect were so remarkable that he never forgot them. The plant was *lobelia inflata,* a common emetic, and Thomson delighted in inducing other boys to chew it, "merely by way of sport, to see them vomit." When in his twenties, Thomson tested his emetic again, this time on a farm laborer. The usual vomiting resulted, but on this occasion it was followed by a rapid improvement in health, and the man felt better than he had for a long time.

Thomson began to treat first his family, then his neighbors, and finally acquired a major medical practice. Thomson had been raised a devout Baptist, and felt that the Lord had given him a special gift to heal the sick. He gradually formulated his own theory of disease which, despite his claim to originality, was simply a modification of the humoral theory of disease which dated from Greek times. Thomson, however, rejected blood-letting, and chose herbs instead of calomel for purging. In fact, he strongly condemned the use of calomel.

In 1809 he applied for a patent on his "system." The application, four years in process, was finally awarded in 1813. The first patent proved to be defective, but he received a second patent in January, 1823, and a third in 1835.

By patenting his system of medicine instead of freely sharing it with his fellow doctors, Thomson had violated one of the major tenets of medicine, and if there had been any chance of his being accepted by the orthodox medical profession before this, he was now anathema to them. Thomson, however, approached Dr. Benjamin Waterhouse, the Harvard professor famous for his role in bringing smallpox vaccination to America, and gained a letter of introduction dated 19 December 1825 to Dr. Samuel Latham Mitchill. Mitchill, an Edinburgh graduate, had founded America's first medical journal, the *Medical Repository*. He had been one of the founders of America's second medical school, and later was also one of the founders of another medical school. He was the owner of a great reputation as a politician and a research financier of various things (including Robert Fulton's steamboat). He was also known as America's greatest living encyclopedia. If Thomson could get Mitchill's endorsement, he might be accepted by the regular medical profession. Although Thomson claimed that he had received Dr. Mitchill's support, there is no written evidence of it, much as was Martin Harris' experience two years later.

In the winter of 1819, Thomson chose an agent, a Mr. Elias Smith, to promote his system of medicine. He had already published a small book that described his practice and was selling the book and rights to use his patents. Under Smith a major campaign was begun. In 1822, Thomson wrote an autobiography, *Samuel Thomson: Narrative of His Life and Medical Discoveries.*

During the period of the 1820s discerning patients, their families, and some medical practitioners, began to realize that heroic medicine, or as it was beginning to be called, the old school, was not saving too many lives, and in fact was causing many deaths, and a rebellion against the system began. Capitalizing on this growing rebellion, Thomson sold thousands of his patent use rights for $20 each, and with them a book, *Thomson's New Guide to Health; or Botanic Family Physician,* for $2. The book could not be purchased without previous purchase of the right, or license, to practice his medicine.

Thomson's sales campaign began in his native New England, but soon spread to western upstate New York where thousands were sold. Thomsonianism was very successful in Ohio where one agent sold five hundred rights to practice in eighteen months, and another agent, selling from Columbus, sold four thousand rights in Ohio and neighboring states in only three and one-half years.[17] By December 1833, there were forty-one agents selling patent rights in Ohio alone.[18] The spread of Thomsonianism covered the entire South and West of the United States, and contemporary observers claimed that in many states at least half of the practitioners and patients were adherents to the school. In Ohio it was claimed that more than three-fourths were Thomsonian oriented. A few years before his death, Thomson claimed to have sold more than 100,000 licenses over his lifetime.[19]

Thomson had one more concept that caused great upset among medical practitioners, even those who purchased his licenses. Thomson advocated a lay corps of medical practitioners. He thought that each father or mother in a home should be able to be the doctor for that family, and that no professional doctors were needed. He adamantly opposed the establishment of medical schools to teach his system, maintaining that even the unlearned could read his books and gain enough knowledge to practice his system; and he opposed the establishment of botanic (Thomsonian) medical journals. Instead, he advocated the organization of local botanic medical societies, where licensees could meet together frequently and share experiences and testimonies of the efficacy of his system.

Thomson was upset that he soon had little control of his system because of apostacies of his followers who established competing systems of the botanico-eclectic type. Schools sprang up and journals appeared, in spite of his opposition. Soon Botanic Medicine—Thomsonian, Neo-Thomsonian, or Eclectic Medicine—was the dominant school of medical thought in America.

Now, with whom did the majority of Mormon sympathies lie?

Chapter Two

Health And The Smith Family To 1830

The attitudes of early Mormons toward medicine were largely a reflection of those of their prophet, Joseph Smith. His attitudes in turn were developed by his environment—his own experiences, those of members of his family, and the conditions about them.

One family experience that happened more than three years before the prophet's birth made a significant impact. In fact, when his father, Joseph Smith, Sr., died in Nauvoo, Joseph Smith, Jr., included a report of it in his father's obituary. "At his marriage he owned a farm in Tunbridge. In 1802 he rented it and engaged in mercantile business, and soon after embarked in a venture of preparing ginseng to send to China, and was swindled out of the entire proceeds by the shipmaster and agent, he was consequently obliged to sell his farm and all of his effects to pay his debts."[1]

When Lucy Mack Smith wrote her reminiscences of her family, the story of this misadventure of the Smith family filled three pages.[2] It is apparent that the incident, which pauperized the Smith family, taking not only Joseph Smith, Sr.'s farm and savings, but also his wife's dowry, had a major impact on the family's finances, from which they never recovered. It became a major factor, which eventually led the family to western New York where the restoration of the gospel could take place.

Why did Joseph Smith, Sr., become involved in this trade, and what was so valuable about ginseng?

Ginseng was and is still considered as a medical panacea in China. Its use dates from the reign of Wenti, of the Sui Dynasty (A.D. 581 to 601). An ancient popular Chinese legend about man's first encounter with the ginseng root says that at Shanghai in Shensi, at the back of a house, a voice of a man was heard each night. When a search was made for the source of this sound, there was seen a remarkable ginseng plant. Upon digging into the earth to the depth of five feet the root was secured, and it had the shape of a man, with four extremities perfect and complete; and it was this that had been calling out in the night with a man's voice. It was called T'u-ching, "spirit of the ground."[3]

Ginseng is considered by the Chinese to be effective in curing nearly all illnesses. For this reason it is considered to be the best of medicines and is of great importance. They also believe that they should use the part of the root resembling a part of the human anatomy for treatment of afflictions in the corresponding area of the body. This "doctrine of signatures" concept is a very ancient idea common to many different regions of the world and among many people, and is also applied to several different plants. However, the Chinese also feel that ginseng has usefulness regardless of the "signature."

From early times, hunting for Ginseng became a respected profession. The hunters were called *va-pang-suis*.[4] Gradually, as years passed, the hills and mountains of China and surrounding countries were denuded of ginseng, until wild ginseng became rare and very valuable.

Although the Chinese gradually learned how to cultivate domesticated ginseng, they considered that the smoother ginseng thus produced was not nearly as valuable as the roughly shaped wild ginseng root. They gradually built up a heirarchy of efficacy of types of ginseng. Imperial, from the emperor's estate, was considered the best. Next was the wild ginseng from China, Manchuria, and Korea, then cultivated ginseng. Then came wild Japanese ginseng. Later they added wild North American ginseng in the heirarchy following their own wild ginseng, and before their cultivated ginseng.

There are numerous versions of how North American ginseng was discovered. A French missionary in Canada, Joseph Francois Lafitau, claimed that in 1709 a French Jesuit missionary, Father Jartoux, was in China doing a geographic survey and maps for the emperor.[5] During his travels, he noticed hordes of people scouring the region, apparently searching for something. An explanation of their activities opened the world of the herbal root to the missionary. Father Jartoux studied the plant and its folk use for the remainder of his survey, learning to use it as a remedy for his own fatigue and acquiring a deep respect for its importance and value to the Chinese. He wrote letters to other Jesuit missionaries describing his experiences. One of these letters, which described ginseng's appearance, habitat, and growth cycle, was sent to Canada because he believed that if the plant grew anywhere outside of China it would be in southern Canada and, possibly, in what was soon to become the northern United States, since the land lay between the same latitudes, had a temperate climate, and forested mountains. The letter was read in 1714 by Father Lafitau, who was then laboring near Montreal. With the help of the Iroquois with whom he was working, he spent many months looking for the plant in the forests. Lafitau finally stumbled across the plant growing at the site of a new house. The plant exactly matched Jartoux's description, and when it was shown to the Iroquois they recognized it as one of their most common medicinal herbs and were able to show him many other places where it was growing.

He gathered a small amount of the roots, dried them, and they were sent to China to see if they would accept this plant in lieu of their own native ginseng. The Chinese did accept the wild North American as being superior to their own cultivated ginseng. As a result, the demand for wild North American ginseng was very high. Although the market fell for some time because of improper preparation by the North Americans, the market had revived by 1802 when Joseph Smith, Sr., became involved in the trade.

North American ginseng is native to the New England area, Eastern Canada, and most of the United States east of the Mississippi River. In its wild or natural state, it grows mainly in mixed hardwood forests, although it is sometimes found among evergreens. It was originally found in abundance among maples, beeches, basswood, rock elm, and butternuts, and especially on the shady sides of deep gullies. It thrives in naturally-shady areas, and does not grow well in direct sunlight.[6]

At the time that Joseph Smith, Sr., entered the trade, most of the marketing of ginseng took place through local mercantile establishments within the growing area. The "sengers" (ginseng hunters) would sell their finds to the local general store. The store owner would dry or crystalize the root, and in turn sell it to the drummer who wholesaled store goods to him. The drummer, or his parent firm, arranged for the shipment to China.

Lucy Mack Smith says, "My husband . . . followed merchandising for a short period in the town of Randolph. Soon after he commenced business in this place he ascertained that crystalized ginseng root sold very high in China, being used as a remedy for the plague which was then raging there. He therefore concluded to embark in a traffic of this article, and consequently made an investment of all the means which he commanded, in that way and manner which was necessary to carry on a business of this kind, viz., crystalizing and exporting the root."[7]

Reading between the lines of her continuing narrative, it is apparent that Joseph Smith, Sr., probably was made acquainted with the ginseng trade by a Mr. Stevens of Royalton, who most likely was his drummer. It is also apparent that he was not willing to give the drummer his usual third cut of the profits on the China sale, but that he went to New York on his own to arrange for shipping the ginseng to China. Mr. Stevens apparently had no difficulty in ascertaining which ship Joseph Smith, Sr., had shipped his cargo on. It is probable that Father Smith was using information that he had gained from Mr. Stevens, since he had no previous experience in the ginseng trade. Mr. Stevens sent his son to New York with his own shipment of ginseng, and the son went on the voyage to China, handled the sale of his own ginseng, and evidently also handled the sale of the Smith's cargo for the ship's captain.

Had Father Smith been successful in cutting out the middle-man, he would have ruined the drummer's business because his other clients would have followed Smith's lead. It was to the advantage of both shipowner and drummer to see that Joseph Smith, Sr., received little or nothing. Thus it was that the Smith's received only a small chest of tea as payment for their shipment of ginseng.

It was unfortunate for the son of Mr. Stevens that he rented a building from Lucy Mack Smith's brother, Major Steven Mack, to process his next shipment of ginseng. Mother Smith's brother, aware of the fiasco of his sister's family, visited his building and found his tenant innebriated. In that condition the tenant confessed the swindle and showed Major Mack the real profits. Major Mack hurried to Randolf for his brother-in-law, but they returned too late. A sobered Mr. Stevens had abandoned the building and fled with his ill-gotten gains and what ginseng he already had prepared for his next shipment. He went across the border into Canada, where he was safe from extradition and pursuit. Stevens had not left the ginseng-producing area, and he undoubtedly continued in his profession.

Father Smith's greediness had cost him much. The chest of tea would not repay him what he had paid for the ginseng he had bought from the sengers, which was undoubtedly a substantial amount. He had financed the purchases by diverting funds from the store, and had used his credit to purchase store goods. He had, as a result, more than $3,000 debt (at that time a very large sum). He could have paid the debt and made a good profit had he not tried to cut out the middle-man, but now he was forced to close the store and sell his farm to pay his debts, and still he did not have enough money. Lucy Mack Smith took the check her brother had given her as a dowry ($1,000) to finish paying the debt. As a result they were debt free, but had nothing left. This was the financial condition of the family a few years later when Joseph Smith, Jr., was born.

A recently written pictorial history is entitled, "The Good Old Days—They Were Terrible." This title could well be taken to describe the health conditions in New England and western New York as Joseph Smith was growing up.

In comparison to today, the health conditions then were abhorent. There were endemic diseases that affected nearly everyone, and there were epidemics that swept through communities, in some cases wiping out entire families. A person who reached the ripe old age of forty years in all probability would have spent more than thirty of those years with one or more types of sickness. Sickness was so commonplace that the sick state was often looked upon as normal, and only in the case of acute episodes did people consider themselves to be sick, although they in all probability were chronically ill much of the time.

The germ theory of disease was yet a half century in the future. Its precursor, the possible causes of disease by tiny "animalacules" was still only a concept just being considered as a possibility by the most advanced thinkers, and had not reached the general public. Very few people had any idea of the causes of the spread of diseases.

Since people were unable to explain the causes of diseases, plague and pestilence were often considered to be a consequence of sin. If a person became sick, everyone "knew" that God was punishing that person for something that person had done. This even though the person may not know what he had done wrong. He was considered to have done something wrong, and his associates considered him to be a sinner.[8] It was frequently considered that a major cause of illness was demon possession.

Because water was essential—for transportation, for power, for human culinary purposes, etc.—most new communities were set up along water courses. There were very few wells dug, and most families dipped their water from nearby streams. It didn't matter that a neighbor might have flushed the manure out of his barn with that very water.

Daily baths were not even dreamed of, and the day of the Saturday-night bath was still in the future except in a few enlightened communities. A person more than likely got one or two baths a year. Often a person was sewn into his winter long-johns in the fall and didn't take them off until the warm days of the next spring, let alone take a bath in the interim. Habits of personal cleanliness simply did not exist for the majority of the populace.

Although glass was used, it was expensive, and the poor could not afford it. The idea of screening a house to keep out flies or mosquitos was unthought of. At most, only a bed would be screened to keep out the bothersome mosquitos. Flies multiplied unabated in tons of horse and cow manure.

The concept of bio-statistics was still a germ in the mind of a French doctor in Europe. No one kept statistics of accidents, but accidents were a major source of debility and took a large number of lives. They also had a significant economic impact. Consider the case of Solomon Mack, Lucy Smith's father. His financial status was seriously lowered as a result of an accident. He had earned "a large sum of money" during his service in the Revolutionary War and he invested in real estate in northern New York. He had, in fact, contracted to purchase the whole town of Granville. The purchase contract, in addition to the money involved, also stipulated that a number of log houses must be built within a specified time. He states, "I accordingly went to work to fulfil this part of the contract, but after laboring a short time, I had the misfortune to cut my leg, which subjected me that season to the care of the physician. I hired a man to do the work, and paid him in advance in order to fulfil my part of the contract, but he ran away, with the money without performing the labor, and the consequence was, I lost the land altogether."[9] This is but one example of hundreds of similar instances which impacted upon the young American frontier and upon the Smith family.

There was one disease that had more impact in early New England and on frontier America than any other. That disease, however, was not recognized then as one disease. It was considered to be numerous diseases—scrofula, consumption, phthisis, and many other diseases—but we know it today as tuberculosis. Consumption was endemic in New England, and it was a rare family that did not carry the tubercle bacillus. Without a knowledge of bacteriology or of means of prevention of spread of the bacillus, once one member of a family contracted consumption, usually the rest of the family sooner or later showed the symptoms of tuberculosis.

The Smith family was *not* one of the miraculous few that escaped from the ravages of consumption. Lucy Mack Smith's *Biographical Sketches of Joseph Smith, the Prophet, and His progenitors for Many Generations* contains numerous incidents of tuberculosis in Joseph Smith's progenitors, including especially his mother.[10]

Mother Smith early in her book outlines the lives and deaths of her sisters Lovisa and Lovina. She tells of Lovisa's marriage and sickness and the attendance by Lovina of her sister for more than two years. She states that Lovisa's sickness baffled the skill of the most experienced physicians. At the end of the two years Lovisa had a temporary remission of the disease. Meanwhile, however, Lovina acquired a case of consumption. Lucy Mack Smith, as a youth, was called upon to nurse Lovina, which she did until Lovina died. Shortly thereafter Lovisa also died.[11]

Mother Smith, in outlining her own life history, states that her mother "had a severe fit of sickness" when Lucy was eight years old.[12] Her description of the illness shows the high probability of the sickness being the acute stage of tuberculosis, even though her mother survived the acute attack.

Tuberculosis often grows slowly in an individual, remaining as a mild but chronic illness. Then it may flare up as an acute attack, and then may return to a chronic condition. The disease is infectious regardless of its stage, chronic or acute. Lucy had nursed her consumptive sister until her sister's death, and was well exposed to the disease. She remained in a chronic state, however, until about four years after her marriage to Joseph Smith, Sr. She was twice a mother, with children Alvin and Hyrum, and had lived in Randolph, Vermont, for six months when she "took a heavy cold, which caused a severe cough." Physicians pronounced her case to be consumption.

During her sickness she grew weaker and weaker until she could "scarcely endure even a foot-fall upon the floor, except in stocking-foot, and no one was allowed to speak in the room above a whisper." A Methodist "exhorter" came to see her to see if she was prepared to die. This left her meditating, when her husband came to her bed and took her by the hand

and said, "Oh, Lucy! my wife! my wife! you must die! The doctors have given you up, and all say you cannot live." After much prayer and pleading with the Lord that she would be allowed to live and raise her children, she made a solemn covenant with God that if he would let her live that she would endeavor to serve him according to the best of her abilities. Shortly after this she heard a voice say to her, "Seek, and ye shall find; knock, and it shall be opened to you. Let your heart be comforted; ye believe in God, believe also in me."[13] She then began to get better, regaining her strength, and was able to raise her children and to become mother to several others, including Joseph Smith, Jr., the prophet.

Although Mother Smith's acute case of consumption subsided, it is highly likely that she and the other members of her family, her husband and her children, continued to carry the tubercle bacillus throughout the rest of their lives. In fact, Father Smith's obituary, written by Joseph Smith, Jr., states that he died of consumption.

The Joseph Smith family lived during its New England period in various communities either in or close to the Connecticut River Valley. This river and its tributaries was polluted and carried various diseases up and down its length. One of these epidemics had a major impact upon the Smith family.

In later years, as Joseph Smith, Jr., was dictating the history of the Church, he recorded: "When I was 5 years old or therabouts I was attacked with the Typhus Fever, and at one time during my sickness, my father despaired for my life. The Doctors broke the fever, after which it settled under my shoulder and Dr. Parker called it a sprained shoulder and anointed it with bone ointment, and freely applied the hot shovel, when it proved to be a swelling under the arm which opened, and discharged freely, after which the disease removed and descended into my left Leg and ancle [sic] and terminated in a fever Sore of the worst kind, and I endured the most acute suffering for a long time under the care of Drs. Smith, Stone and Perkins, of Hanover. At one time eleven doctors came from Dartmouth Medical College, at Hanover, New Hampshire, for the purpose of amputation, but young as I was, I utterly refused to give my assent to the operation, but I consented to their Trying an experiment by removing a large portion of the bone from my left leg, which they did. & fourteen additional peices [sic] of bone afterwards worked out before my leg healed, during which time I was reduced so very low that my mother could carry me with ease. & after I began to get about, I went on crutches till I started for the state of New York where my father had gone for the purpose of preparing a place for the removal of his family...."[14]

Joseph's memory of his age was inacurate, but in the fall of 1812 and winter of 1813, when he would have been about seven years of age, a major epidemic of what we now call typhoid fever raged up and down the Connecticut River Valley. It is reasonably certain that this was the occasion that Joseph recalled.

At this time the Joseph Smith family was residing in Lebanon, New Hampshire, about five miles down stream from Hanover, New Hampshire, and its Dartmouth College. Little is said of the vocations of the family at this time, but it is recorded that Hyrum, the next to oldest of the children, was attending "an academy in Hanover." This academy was undoubtedly Dartmouth College, and the Smith family was directly affected by the activities of that school.

Some eighteen years before, a Dr. Nathan Smith, who was practicing medicine in Cornish, New Hampshire, a few miles downstream from Lebanon and Hanover, had made a radical proposal to the little college.[15] He proposed that they create, at that remote little college, America's fourth medical school. (The third school had earlier been organized in Boston at Harvard, and Dr. Smith had been its fifth graduate.)

As the trustees of the college debated the momentous decision, the impatient Dr. Nathan Smith went to Scotland for a year of advanced training. Naturally, he went to the great seat of medical learning of Europe, Edinburgh. But Nathan Smith was discontent with what was presented to him there.

In Great Britain, then as now, medicine and surgery were considered to be separate professions, and surgery was considered to be the lesser of the two professions. Smith, and the vast majority of his fellow Americans, had found the two professions to be inextricably intertwined, and in fact in America they became but one profession.

Scotland had produced several great surgeons, but most of them had gone to London, England, to greener pastures and more favorable acceptance. Among them had been the Hunter brothers, William and John. By the time Nathan Smith had arrived in Great Britain the Hunters were dead, but the great traditions and methods of training they had started lived on, and Smith partook of that training in London. He brought back to America the seeds for the foundation of surgery as a medical specialty.

Upon Nathan Smith's return to New Hampshire the Dartmouth trustees still had not made up their minds, so Smith went ahead anyway and in 1797 presented his first series of medical lectures at the school. The next year the trustees awarded him an honorary Doctor of Medicine degree and officially appointed him as the only faculty member of their medical school, neglecting to make any provision for his pay.

For some twelve years Nathan Smith was the sole faculty member of the medical school, occupying what Dr. Oliver Wendell Holmes (later also a Dartmouth faculty member) would call not simply a "Chair, but a whole settee" of professorships.[16] Finally, in 1810, the New Hampshire legislature and the Dartmouth trustees agreed to appoint Dr. Cyrus Perkins, a former student of Dr. Smith's, as Professor of Surgery and Anatomy to assist him. During this time, Dartmouth had graduated more doctors than any other American medical school. Nathan Smith had built a reputation as America's outstanding medical teacher and medical school administrator, besides that of a great surgeon. These were the "doctors Smith and Perkins of Hanover" that Joseph Smith, Jr., remembered as having come to treat him.

What could be called an amazing series of coincidences occurred that made Dr. Nathan Smith available and gave him just the exact skills needed to save the leg of young Joseph Smith, and probably also his life.

Dr. Smith had for some time been unhappy with the financial remuneration, or lack of it, which he had received from Dartmouth, and he had been approached by Yale College, which was planning to organize a medical school, and had accepted an appointment to Yale when the typhoid fever epidemic struck the upper Connecticut River Valley.

Nathan Smith at this time also had three sons, whose ages paralleled closely the ages of the Joseph Smith family's three sons.[17] One was very nearly the age of young Joseph Smith, and Nathan Smith's family, like the Joseph Smith family, came down with typhoid fever. In both families all the children came down with the disease, a fact now readily explainable since all in each family undoubtedly drank from each family's polluted water supply.

On 31 March 1813, Nathan Smith wrote to Professor Benjamin Silliman of Yale University an explanation for his delay in coming to New Haven: "Dear Sir . . . According to my promise to Dr. Cogswell, I intended to have visited you at New Haven last January, but before I was ready to set off on my journey, we were visited by a very fatal epidemic and instances of sickness and mortality became so frequent that I was afraid to leave my family in such perilous times; and my fears were not groundless . . . four of my children have lately been affected by the prevailing epidemic, but by the Divine Goodness have nearly recovered. I believe this country has never before been visited by sickness which has carried off so great a number of adult persons in so short a time. In some towns of this vicinity which contain perhaps from 1000 to 1500 inhabitants they have buried over fifty persons since the first of last January. The disease has not yet much abated either in its violence or frequency of attack. We hear of new cases every day, and almost every day brings me an account of the death of some friend or acquaintance. How long this dreadful calamity will be suffered to afflict us, no one can tell; but we hope and pray that when the winter is over the disease will disappear . . . The winter here has been long and severe . . . Your obedient servant, Nathan Smith."[18]

In 1786 William Heys, of Leeds, England, had published an account of his surgery in three cases of what is now called osteomyelitis.[19] It is not known if Dr. Nathan Smith ever knew of this paper, but it is very unlikely. In 1798, the year he officially began the Dartmouth medical school, Dr.

Nathan Smith had developed independently the same type of operation. It was this operation which was used by him upon young Joseph Smith some fourteen years later.

The fact that Nathan Smith had developed this operation as early as 1798 is further evidence of the repeated epidemics of typhoid fever that blanketed the upper Connecticut River Valley. Osteomyelitis is very frequently a complication of typhoid fever and occurs when the typhoid bacillus attacks the tissues of the bones. Smith, like everyone else then, had not yet been able to differentiate between typhus, a disease transmitted by fleas from rats and small animals, and typhoid, a disease usually transmitted by polluted water supplies.

Nathan Smith was a very busy doctor and did not have much time for writing until near the end of his life, but during his Dartmouth years he became the most knowledgeable individual on the disease he called Typhous Fever and which in 1838, ten years after his death, was identified as a distinct disease from typhus and labelled typhoid fever. He died in 1828, but four years before his death he published his book, *Practical Essay on Typhous Fever,* which is still recognized as America's great classical description of typhoid fever and methodology for treatment of the disease without antibiotics. He also had a great deal of experience with that very common complication of typhoid fever, then known as necrosis, and now known as osteomyelitis. A year before his death he published a paper, "Observations on the Pathology and Treatment of Necrosis," in a Philadelphia medical journal. This paper was years ahead of its time and preceded by five years a similar work published in England by Sir Benjamin Brodie.[20] Both papers were forgotten for another fifty years, and were rediscovered after another independent discovery of Nathan Smith's techniques described in this paper and used many years earlier on Joseph Smith and numerous other victims of osteomyelitis.

Nathan Smith's students at Dartmouth recorded in their lecture notes descriptions of Smith's treatment of necrosis, and in letters home to their parents told of trips when the entire class accompanied Dr. Smith to treat cases of necrosis. The notes and letters of 1812 and 1813 were particularly copious about necrosis, which was to be expected because of the typhoid epidemic. Unfortunately neither these notes, letters, or Dr. Smith's ledgers record the treatment of Joseph Smith, Jr., of Lebanon, New Hampshire.[21]

Of the typhoid epidemic as it impacted upon the Joseph Smith family, Lucy, the mother, writes that all the family with the exception of herself and her husband came down with the disease.[22] She lists the order of illnesses as first Sophronia, then Hyrum, who was taken sick while at school in Hanover and who came home sick, then Alvin, and finally Joseph, Jr. She records that Sophronia "had a heavy siege." The physicians attended her for eighty-nine days and she was so far gone that on the ninetieth day the doctors gave her up and ceased medicating her.

Had Sophronia had typhoid fever any place but in New Hampshire she most likely would not have survived so long. Dr. Nathan Smith had taught his students that they should not bleed typhous cases, nor give them calomel, and most of the doctors practicing in the vicinity were his graduates. In other parts of the country where more heroic medicine was the practice, she would have been bled and treated with calomel.

As the doctors gave up on Sophronia the family turned to prayer for her healing, and Mother Smith wrapped a blanket about the child, took her in her arms, and commenced walking the floor. Finally Sophronia sobbed, and Mother Smith records what she felt was the miraculous healing in answer to the family's prayers. But the trials of the Smith family were not over, and the greatest was yet to come.

Joseph's case appeared to be a mild one, and he was considered to have recovered after only two weeks of illness. Then one day while he was sitting in a chair he screamed in agony with a pain in his shoulder.[23] A doctor was sent for immediately, but he pronounced the pain as only a shoulder sprain, and anointed the shoulder with bone linament. Joseph suffered for two weeks before the doctor concluded to make a closer examination. Then the doctor found a "fever sore" gathered between his breast and shoulder. The doctor lanced the necrotic cyst and drained off "a quart of matter." The pain left the shoulder necrosis, but "shot like lightning" down his side into the marrow of the bone of his leg, and soon became very severe.

In his classic article on necrosis,[24] Nathan Smith says that the etymological definition of necrosis is the death of some part of the bony structure, but that as technically employed at that time, it designated a form of disease characterized by peculiar symptoms often or generally terminating in the death of a portion of the bone in which it is located. In New England it was known as a "fever-sore" because it is generally accompanied with a high degree of symptomatic fever.

He goes on to say that necrosis commences with an acute inflamation, either in the bone itself or its investing membrane, accompanied with an acute pain, not always at first in the part affected, but often felt most severely in the joint nearest the disease. This may be why Joseph Smith describes his pain as in his "ancle."

Mother Smith says that "His leg soon began to swell and he continued to suffer the greatest agony for the space of two weeks longer."[25] At the end of three weeks they sent again for a surgeon who came and made an incision of eight inches on the front side of the leg between the knee and ankle. This afforded some temporary relief, but the pain again became "violent." Nathan Smith had taught that perhaps in the very early stages such an incision as Joseph received might be enough, but since he had never been called that soon he wasn't certain. The surgeon was called again, and an incision was made down to the bone; but the bone was not removed or perforated to allow egress of pus, and bone death occurred. It healed for a short time but then it began to swell again. Obviously Nathan Smith did not perform either of these timorous procedures.

As Joseph became worse and was wracked with pain, a surgical consultation was obtained ("council of surgeons"). A Dr. Stone was apparently the principal surgeon up to this point. Although Stone is not further identified, it is possible that he had studied under Nathan Smith at Dartmouth since the two procedures performed suggest familiarity with Smith's teachings, although they were timidly and inadequately applied.[26]

After the council, they reported to the Smith family that they had done all they could and considered his leg incurable, and advised amputation as absolutely necessary to save his life. Mother Smith recalls that she appealed to Dr. Stone, saying, "Can you not make another trial? Can you not, by cutting around the bone take out the diseased part, and perhaps that which is sound will heal over, and by this means you will save his leg? You will not, you must not, take off his leg, until you try once more. I will not consent to let you enter his room until you make me this promise."

It is very likely that Mother Smith and other members of the Smith family had heard of the necrosis operations which were being performed throughout the area by Dr. Nathan Smith, although they were obviously still experimental and not standard surgical procedure. Also, Mother Smith's memory may have been hazy after thirty years and exact conversations poorly remembered. It is uncertain just when Dr. Nathan Smith, Dr. Cyrus Perkins, and the entourage of Dartmouth medical students were called in, but Dr. Stone was obviously too timid and inexperienced to perform such an operation which only one person was at that time performing.

Joseph was offered brandy as a sedative prior to the operation, but he refused it. Thus it was that there were no anesthetics for the procedure. The operation was carried out on a wide awake young man restrained by his father. Mother Smith remembers, "The Surgeons commenced operating by boring into the bone of his leg, first on the one side of the bone where it was affected, then on the other side, after which they broke it off with a pair of forceps or pincers. They thus took away large pieces of the bone."[27] She said that Joseph screamed out loudly as they broke off the first piece of bone. According to Dr. LeRoy S. Wirthlin, a surgeon who has studied this case, the sawing of the bone and the drilling of the bone probably was not painful in itself; but the dislodgement of the fragments with ends attached to living tissue must have produced acute pain.[28]

After the operation, Mother Smith remembers that Joseph immediately commenced getting better, and from then on continued to mend until he became strong and healthy. He was sent off to Salem, Massachusetts, with his uncle, Jesse Smith, in hopes that the sea-breezes would help him to recover his health. He thereafter retained fond memories of Salem. He continued, however, on crutches until the family moved to western New York state.

A bit further must be said about this remarkable doctor whose path crossed that of the founder of Mormonism at precisely the time when he could save the life and limb of the future prophet. He has been called a giant of American medicine. It has been said that, as a surgeon, Nathan Smith ranks among the greatest America has produced.

Recently the president of the New England Surgical Society chose this man as the subject of his presidential address because Nathan Smith had an impact upon every New England state.[29] He was born in a part of Massachusetts that would later become a part of Rhode Island, part of greater Providence. He was raised in Chester, Vermont. He attended school and received his medical degree in Boston at Harvard. He practiced medicine in New Hampshire and was the sole founder of Dartmouth Medical School. He was one of the founders of Yale Medical School. He also founded Bowdoin Medical School in Maine. He assisted his son, Nathan Ryno Smith in the founding of the University of Vermont Medical School, and also Jefferson Medical College in Philadelphia.

In addition to his development of the operation for necrosis, he performed the first ovariotomy in Connecticut in 1821, not knowing that McDowell had done it not long before in Kentucky. He was the first to perform staphylorrhaphy for cleft palate. He operated successfully on cataract. He was among the first to vaccinate in this country, losing out to Dr. Benjamin Waterhouse for first honors by only forty-eight days.[30]

Other early American doctors, such as Benjamin Rush, who initially outshone him, gradually diminished in status as time went on, but not Nathan Smith. Dr. William H. Welch eulogized him as "Famous in his day and generation, he is still more famous today for he was far ahead of his times, and his reputation unlike that of so many medical worthies of the past has steadily increased as the medical profession has slowly caught up with him. We now see that he did more for the general advancement of medical and surgical practice than any of his predecessors or contemporaries in this country. He was a man of high intellectual and moral qualities, of great originality and untiring energy, an accurate and keen observer unfettered by tradition and theories, fearless, and above all blessed with an uncommon fund of plain 'common sense.' "[31]

Some three years later the Joseph Smith family, which had continued to have financial problems in New England, moved from there to western New York state in a major attempt to recoup the family's finances. With this move the family, medically, moved from under the shadow of Dr. Nathan Smith to that of another early American medical leader.

Two years younger than Dr. Nathan Smith, Dr. Samuel Latham Mitchill was a native of Long Island, New York, where his parents were farmers and adhered to the Quaker religous beliefs.[32] He received his first medical training as an apprentice to his uncle, Dr. Samuel Latham. He also served a three-year apprenticeship to Dr. Samuel Bard. Finally, with the backing of his two mentors, he went to Edinburgh in Scotland to study. He returned to America to become involved in practically everything but a steady practice of medicine. Mitchill had been a pupil of Cullen and Brown and the Munros in Edinburgh, as had his rival Dr. Benjamin Rush, but did not carry bloodletting and the use of calomel to quite the same heroic extent as Rush.

Mitchill attempted to romanticize the mecical profession and to extend its influence beyond the field of medicine.[33] As far as his own personal career went, he was eminently successful in his efforts. During his lifetime he was the first Professor of Natural History, Chemistry, and Agriculture at Columbia College; one of the founders of the Society for the Promotion of Agriculture, Manufactures, and Useful Arts; physician of New York Hospital; Assemblyman to the New York Legislature; member of the U.S. House of Representatives; United States Senator from New York; Surgeon-General of the militia of the State of New York; and one of the founders of the College of Physicians and Surgeons in New York City, now part of Columbia University, and America's second medical school. He also was one of the founders of the *Medical Repository,* the first medical journal in the United States.

Mitchill, like Rush, was embroiled in the medical care of victims of Yellow Fever during the epidemics of the 1790s. But Mitchill took a different tack and attempted to convince public opinion that Yellow Fever was not imported from foreign cities and countries, the view then almost universally accepted. He rejected the prevailing theory of contagion and became interested in sanitary reform. He believed that the inhabitants of New York City were poisoning the city as a result of primitive sanitary conditions. He insisted that sewers should not be permitted to drain into shallow water, and claimed that sinks and privies were so contaminated as to make disease inevitable. Permitting waste to collect over days, weeks, and months was just asking for disease.

Mitchill had a great interest in the red man of America, the native Americans. He did researches on their ethnological characteristics, and his translations of Indian war songs gave him increased celebrity.[34] He was admitted as an associate of several Indian tribes. Finally, he was a member of the commission at the treaty of Fort Stanwix by which the Indians surrendered much of their land and opened much of western New York to settlement.

Dr. Mitchill has been called, "emphatically, our greatest living ichthyologist." This was because of his interest in fish. Among the fish that he identified and cataloged was the striped bass. Fishermen were always bringing him new species of fish. He was also responsible for extensive studies of the native vegetable materia medica of the United States.

He was the politician par excellence, with his elections to the New York State Assembly, the U.S. House of Representatives, and the U.S. Senate. He did just the right things to develop his national prominence, like underwrite and encourage Robert Fulton in developing the steam boat. He was one of those who took the first ride in a steam boat. He backed DeWitt Clinton's plans, including the Erie Canal, and was a guest in the first boat to officially transit the canal from Albany to Buffalo. As a result, Dr. Samuel Latham Mitchill had a fabulous reputation as a walking encyclopedia of information, and as a powerful politician who was accessible to the public.

He built his medical reputation by editing and writing articles for his *Medical Repository* and numerous other medical journals as they were established. As a professor in the College of Physicians and Surgeons, he was also involved in the education of many doctors. The graduates of his school tended to go northward and westward throughout the state of New York. Although his emphasis upon heroic medicine was less so than Benjamin Rush's, his support for it tended to establish heroic medicine in upstate New York where the Smith family had moved.

When the Smith family arrived in Palmyra, it was a booming town involved in the development of the Erie Canal, which was shortly to pass through it. There were three drug stores in town, and a number of doctors.[35]

Sometime after their arrival in Palmyra, the Smith family chose a family doctor: Alexander M'Intyre (or McIntyre), a local physician. Dr. McIntyre became a close friend of the Smith family and later defended them in confrontations with their neighbors, and warning them about planned mob attacks. It is apparent that one of the reasons the Smiths chose him was that he was moderate in his therapeutics. He was a nephew of Dr. Gain C. Robinson, who ran one of the drug stores, and had been his apprentice. Dr. McIntyre was also well respected by his fellow practitioners, as is evidenced by their election of him as the county's delegate to the Medical Society of the State of New York in 1827, and their election of him as vice-president of their county society in both 1829 and 1830.[36]

The Smith family began to purchase property just over the town line, in what was to become Manchester, not too long after their arrival in Palmyra. In 1820 occurred the first vision of Joseph Smith. There is ample evidence that the Smiths were not too well, with Mother Smith's recollections outlining several "fits" of sickness among her family. Much of this illness likely was because of the family's carrying of the tubercle baccilus.

The fall of 1823 became climatic for the Smith family for two reasons. Alvin Smith, the oldest son, had been employed in the neighborhood as a carpenter, and he had become involved in the building of a new home to replace the story-and-a-half log home the family had been living in. The home had not yet been finished when the angel, Moroni, appeared to young Joseph, the night of September 21, 1823.

The second climactic event began on November 15, when Alvin became sick with what his mother called bilious colic. This name was often applied to what was to be identified a half century later as appendicitis.[37] Therefore it is possible that that is what Alvin had. He became sick enough that an emergency call was sent out for Dr. McIntyre, but Dr. McIntyre was not available to take care of his patient. Instead, a Dr. Greenwood was summoned.[38]

Dr. Greenwood was more heroic in his medications than Dr. McIntyre, and over Alvin's protests he gave him a heavy dose of calomel. Alvin claimed that it "lodged in his stomach" and wouldn't go anywhere. We do not know if Dr. Greenwood administered multiple doses of calomel when the first dose failed to purge Alvin, but such treatment would have been in keeping with standard heroic medical practice. "All the medicine freely administered by four very skillful physicians" could not remove Alvin's dose(s) of calomel.

Three days later Dr. McIntyre returned to find a critical patient, and he summoned the help of four physicians. Alvin felt that the "calomel was still lodged . . . and that it must take his life." On November 19, 1823, Alvin died.

After Alvin's death, Dr. McIntyre performed an autopsy on Alvin's body and found the calomel lodged in gangrenous intestines, the same kind of findings that would be found numerous times some forty years later during the Civil War when the Surgeon General banned the use of calomel in the Union Army.

Alvin's body was interred in the Palmyra cemetery and lay undisturbed for nearly a year until vicious rumors began to circulate in the vicinity. About this time a new medical school had been established in Geneva, New York, and it was known that the school was searching for cadavers for their students to disect. On 29 September 1824, and for several weeks thereafter, the following notice was published in the *Wayne Sentinel,* Palmyra's newspaper.

> Whereas reports have been industriously put in circulation that my son Alvin had been removed from the place of his interment and dissected, which reports, every person possessed of human sensibility must know, are peculiarly calculated to harrow up the mind of a parent and deeply wound the feelings of relations—therefore, for the purpose of ascertaining the truth of such reports, I, with some of my neighbors, this morning repaired to the grave, and removing the earth, found the body which had not been disturbed.

This method is taken for the purpose of satisfying the minds of those who may have heard the report, and of informing those who have put it in circulation, that it is earnestly requested that they would desist therefrom, and that it is believed by some, that they have been stimulated more by a desire to injure the reputation of certain persons than a philanthropy for the peace and welfare of myself and friends.

JOSEPH SMITH
Palmyra, September 25, 1824.

Is it any wonder that the Smith family became members of the massive part of the American public that turned against heroic medicine?

Chapter Three

Medical Aspects Of The Restoration

During the first four thousand years of existence of the world (by traditional religious time), those who were the healers and physicians were religious leaders—the priest, the shaman, etc. It has only been since Roman times that Galenic and modern medicine have been divorced from religion. Even that divorce was not complete until the past quarter of a millennium.

Throughout these aeons of time, faith healing has been the principal means of making the sick well. This faith healing has been supplemented by the use of herbs and occasional primitive surgery. These facts are attested to by all of the earliest written records—the clay tablets of Ur, Nineveh, and Ebla, Egyptian papyri, and the Bible.

Adam laid hands upon the heads of his children to bless them, as did his successors. So began faith healing. Throughout the Old Testament this healing was attributed to God; and when the last prophet of the Old Testament, Malachi, wrote, he described the coming Messiah as the sun of righteousness who would come with healing in his wings (Malachi 4:2). In the New Testament, more than one-fifth of the writings of the gospels record the numerous incidents as Jesus went about Galilee healing all types of illnesses and disease among the people (Matthew 4:23). He healed by laying-on-of-hands, he healed when his clothing was touched, and he healed by command to be made well or for evil spirits to depart. He gave to his apostles and seventies power against unclean spirits, to heal the sick, cleanse the lepers, and raise the dead (Matthew 10:1, 8). And they cast out many devils and anointed with oil many that were sick, and healed them (Mark 6:13). When he left the New Testament Church, the healing of the sick by his disciples was firmly established. As the church expanded, his brother, James, would write: "Is any sick among you? let him call for the elders of the church; and let them pray over him, anointing him with oil in the name of the Lord: And the prayer of faith shall save the sick, and the Lord shall raise him up . . ." (James 5:14-15).

After the close of the New Testament history, healing ordinances continued to spread in the early Christian church. By the Third Century,

Christian churches had come to be regarded as healing shrines competitive with the shrines of the Greek god of healing, Aesculapius. In many places, the Christian church took over the function of those Aesculapian temples as the pagan religion died out, and a Christian shrine often appeared on the site of a former pagan temple.[1]

Meanwhile, the field of medicine was in headlong decline after the death of Galen of Pergamon in 200 A.D., and as the practice of medicine came into the hands of monks, theory was sacrificed to facility of practical treatment. Originality went out of Western medicine for hundreds of years. Faith healing developed to fill the void. As a result, it has been said that faith healing enjoyed its greatest vogue during the medieval period.[2]

As time went on, however, in the Roman church the service of unction for healing was gradually transformed into extreme unction for death. As healings became less frequent, and distressed priests were unable to heal, they began to dedicate the sick to God in preparation for death.[3]

Then began the awakening and reformation preparatory for the restoration of Christ's church. Some protestant churches developed outright hostility toward faith healing, but as the reading of Bibles began, first among the clergy and then among the members, they read of the healings of the New Testament church, and faith healing began to spread. By the time of the restoration of the church through Joseph Smith, faith healing was comparatively common among those religions looking forward to reformation of a New Testament-like church and those looking forward to the millennium.

As Joseph Smith translated the Book of Mormon, he found incidents of healing in that record, and he observed passages which confirmed to him the existence of spirit bodies (1 Nephi 11:11; 2 Nephi 9:12; Mosiah 2:28; Alma 11:45; Ether 3:16; Moroni 10:34) and this strengthened his belief in the possibility of evil spirits being able to take over human bodies and thus create illness. He continued to receive revelations relating to the human soul—a united spirit and physical body. This culminated in the King Follett funeral address given just a few months before his own death.

Within the same month of the organization of the Church (6 April 1830), Joseph commanded evil spirits to depart from the body of Newell Knight and the spirits came out of Newell, and his body was even levitated.[4] This action confirmed to the investigators of the Church at Colesville, New York, the realization of the power of Joseph's priesthood. Shortly after this, Newell was baptized. Thus the first recorded charismatic healing within the new Church was performed by use of a command by a priesthood holder.

A few months later, as Joseph was living in Harmony, Pennsylvania, he and Oliver Cowdery received a revelation stating: "Require not miracles, except I shall command you, except casting out devils, healing the sick, and against poisonous serpents, and against deadly poisons; And these things ye shall not do, except it be required of you by them who desire it, that the scriptures might be fulfilled; for ye shall do according to that which is written." (D&C 24:13-14.)

In December, 1830, after Oliver had gone on his mission to the Lamanites, Sidney Rigdon joined Joseph Smith as his scribe, and another revelation on healing was given: "And whoso shall ask it in my name in faith, they shall cast out devils; they shall heal the sick; they shall cause the blind to receive their sight, and the deaf to hear, and the dumb to speak, and the lame to walk." (D&C 35:9.)

One of the first recorded priesthood healings by a Church member took place in April, 1831. The Knight family and other members of the Colesville Branch had been asked to move west to Ohio. They had grouped at Ithaca, a port on Cayuga Lake. From there the branch was to take boats across the lake and down a canal to the Erie Canal, and from there to Buffalo. On the way to Ithaca, Newell Knight's aunt, Electa Peck, had broken her shoulder "in the most shocking manner." A doctor had stated that if she could travel before many weeks it would be a miracle. Sister Peck sent for her nephew as soon as he arrived in camp. He "stepped up to the bed and in the name of the Lord Jesus Christ rebuked the pain with which she was suffering and commanded her to be made whole; and it was done, for the next day she arose, dressed herself, and pursued the journey with us."[5]

Shortly after his arrival in Kirtland, Ohio, on 9 February 1831, the Prophet Joseph Smith received instructions for the Church's elders through a revelation. Included in the revelation was: "And whosoever among you are sick, and have not faith to be healed, but believe, shall be nourished with all tenderness, with herbs and mild food, and that not by the hand of an enemy. And the elders of the church, two or more, shall be called, and shall pray for and lay their hands upon them in my name; and if they die they shall die unto me, and if they live they shall live unto me. . . . And again, it shall come to pass that he that hath faith in me to be healed, and is not appointed unto death, shall be healed. He who hath faith to see shall see. He who hath faith to hear shall hear. The lame who have faith to leap shall leap. And they who have not faith to do these things, but believe in me, have power to become my sons; and inasmuch as they break not my laws thou shalt bear their infirmities." (D&C 42:43-44, 48-52.)

Less than a month later, on 6 March 1831, he received a revelation on the gifts of the spirit, which said, "And again, to some it is given to have faith to be healed; and to others it is given to have faith to heal." (D&C 46:19-20.)

Not long after this, the family of John Johnson began to investigate the Church, and the father, John, and his wife, Elsa, went to Kirtland to see the prophet and to find out more about the new religion. During the visit, a healing occurred which caused a great stir in the area. Elsa Johnson had had a rheumatic arm for many years, and for two years had not been able to raise her hand to her head. As the Johnsons and others from the Hiram, Ohio, area visited with the prophet in the Newel K. Whitney home, they discussed the gifts of the spirit as held in the New Testament church. Someone asked whether God had given power to men today to heal people like Elsa Johnson. After the conversation had turned to another subject, the prophet walked up to Elsa and said, "Woman, in the name of the Lord Jesus Christ I command these to be whole," and then he walked out of the room. Mrs. Johnson was instantly healed and the next day she did her washing "without difficulty or pain."[6]

At the beginning of a conference at Orange, Ohio, Joseph received a revelation in part directed to his brother Samuel Harrison Smith. One verse instructs him to "Lay your hands upon the sick and they shall recover." (D&C 66:9.)

It had long been known that apostles were to be called in the infant Church, and in September, 1832, in preparation for that calling, the prophet received another revelation which included: "In my name they shall cast out devils; In my name they shall heal the sick; In my name they shall open the eyes of the blind, and unstop the ears of the deaf; And the tongue of the dumb shall speak; And if any man shall administer poison unto them it shall not hurt them; And the poison of a serpent shall not have power to hurt them; But a commandment I give unto them, that they shall not boast themselves of these things, neither speak them before the world; for these things are given unto you for your profit and for salvation." (D&C 84:67-73.)

During the winter of 1833-1834, the saints in Jackson County (Zion), Missouri, were driven out of the county, and many miraculous healings took place among the refugee camps. Years later, after the saints had moved to the Rocky Mountains, George A. Smith, the prophet's cousin, would recall that the non-Mormons of Jackson County had charged the saints with blasphemy because they "professed to heal the sick with holy oil." It was considered to be a crime, and was one of the principal charges on which the Latter-day Saints were expelled.[7] Among the healing incidents was an occasion when Newell Knight fearlessly walked through a mob to administer to his friend, Philo Dibble, who had been shot in the abdomen and was not expected to live. As soon as Newell placed his hand on Brother Dibble's head, the wounded man "felt the spirit of the Lord rest upon him and pass gently through his body and before it pass all pain and soreness so that he felt perfectly easy in a few minutes."[8]

During the ensuing years, many healings took place in the Church in Kirtland and Far West, Missouri, and wherever the gospel was preached. Concerning this period John Whitmer, then Church Historian, wrote:

"About this time some were sick of various diseases, and were healed by the power which was in them through Jesus Christ. There was a tradition among some of the disciples, that those who obeyed the covenant in the last days, would never die; but by experience they have learned to the contrary. . . . The disciples increased daily, and miracles were wrought such as healing the sick, casting out devils, and the church grew and multiplied in numbers, grace, and knowledge."[9]

In the fall of 1837, Heber C. Kimball, who had been sent to England to open that land for missionary work, wrote home to his wife: "A singular circumstance occurred before morning, which I will quote from Br. Hyde's journal, as he wrote it down, he commences as follows, 'Elder Russel was much troubled with evil spirits and came into the room where Elder Kimball and myself were sleeping, and desired us to lay our hands on him, and rebuke the evil spirit: I arose upon the bed, and Br. Kimball got upon the floor and I sat upon the bed; we laid our hands on him, and brother Kimball rebuked and prayed for him but just before he had finished his prayer, his voice faltered, and his mouth was shut, and he began to tremble and reel to and fro, and fell on the floor like a dead man, and uttered a deep groan, I immediately seized him by the shoulder, and lifted him up, being satisfied that the devils were exceding angry because we attempted to cast them out of Br. Russel, and they made a powerful attempt upon Elder Kimball as if to dispatch him at once, they struck him senseless and he fell to the floor; Br. Russel and myself then laid our hands on Elder Kimball, and rebuked the evil spirits, in the name of Jesus Christ; and immediately he recovered his strength in part, so as to get up; the sweat began to roll from him most powerfully, and he was almost as wet as if he had been taken out of the water, we could very sensibly hear the evil spirits rage and foam out their shame. Br. Kimball was quite weak for a day or two after: it seems that the devils are determined to destroy us, and prevent the truth from being declared in England.' The devil was mad because I was a going to baptize, and he wanted to destroy me, that I should not do those things the Lord sent me to do. We had a great struggle to deliver ourselves from his hands; when they left Br. Russel they pitched upon me, and when they left me they fell upon Br. Hyde; for we could hear them gnash their teeth upon us."[10]

As the refugee saints settled in Commerce, Illinois (soon to be known as Nauvoo), they moved into an area where Malaria was endemic. Soon most of them were sick. Joseph Smith gave up his home to the sick and pitched a tent in which he lived, and he too fell to what were then called the "miasmas" of ague and fever. Heber C. Kimball tells what happened on 22 July 1839:

> July 22nd, the Prophet Joseph arose from his bed of sickness, when the power of God rested upon him, and he went forth administering

to the sick. He commenced with the sick in his own house, then visited those who were camping in tents in his own dooryard, commanding the sick in the name of the Lord Jesus Christ to arise from their beds and to be whole; when they were healed according to his words. He then went from house to house, and from tent to tent, upon the bank of the river, healing the sick by the power of Israel's God, as he went among them. He did not miss a single house, wagon or tent, and continued this work up to "the upper stone house," where he crossed the river in a boat, accompanied by Parley P. Pratt, Orson Pratt, John E. Page, John Taylor and myself, and landed at Montrose. He then walked into the cabin of Brother Brigham Young, who was lying very sick, and commanded him in the name of the Lord Jesus Christ to arise and be made whole. He arose, healed of his sickness, and then accompanied Joseph and his brethren of the Twelve, and went into the house of Brother Elijah Fordham, who was insensible and considered by his family and friends to be in the hands of death. Joseph stepped to his bedside, looked him in the eye for a minute without speaking, then took him by the hand and commanded him in the name of Jesus Christ to arise from his bed and walk. Brother Fordham immediately leaped out of his bed, threw off all his poultices and bandages, dressed himself, called for a bowl of bread and milk, which he ate, and then followed us into the street. We then went into the house of Joseph B. Noble, who was very sick, and he was healed in the same manner.

Joseph spoke with the voice and power of God.

When he had healed all the sick by the power given unto him he went down to the ferry boat, when a stranger rode up almost breathless, and said that he had heard that Joseph Smith was raising the dead, and healing all the sick, and that his wife begged him to ride up and get Mr. Smith to go down and heal her twin children, about three months old. Joseph replied, "I cannot go, but will send someone." In a few minutes he said to Elder Woodruff, "You go and heal those children, and take this pocket handkerchief, and when you administer to them, wipe their faces with it, and they shall recover." Brother Woodruff did as he was commanded, and the children were healed.[11]

By the end of that day, the most massive charismatic healing of the modern Church had taken place.

Nauvoo continued to be a sickly place, and in January, 1841, Joseph received a revelation for the new stake president in Nauvoo, William Marks: "If they live here let them live unto me; and if they die let them die unto me; for they shall rest from all their labors here, and shall continue their works. Therefore, let my servant William put his trust in me, and cease to fear concerning his family, because of the sickness of the land. If ye love me, keep my commandments; and the sickness of the land shall redound to your glory." (D&C 124:86-87.) Part of the same revelation called William Law to be Joseph's counselor, and said of him: "And these signs shall follow him—he shall heal the sick, he shall cast out devils, and shall be delivered from those who would administer unto him deadly poison; And he shall be led in paths where the poisonous serpent cannot lay hold upon his heel, and he shall mount up in the imagination of his thoughts as upon eagles' wings. And what if I will that he should raise the dead, let him not withhold his voice." (D&C 124:98-100.)

When the women's Relief Society was organized in Nauvoo, the minutes of the first meeting recorded Joseph Smith's approval for women to participate in healing ordinances. These instructions included guidance in the use of oil for anointing and blessing.

In 1834, when cholera struck the members of Zion's Camp, it had been found by them that immersing the sick in water for some time seemed to heal them. We now know the physiological basis for this effect.[12] In cholera cases, the body suffers from dehydration (loss of body fluids). When the body is immersed in water minute quantities of water enter the body through the skin, thus helping to restore the body's fluid balance. This healing effect might have been a precedent for a new type of faith healing that made its appearance in Nauvoo in 1845.

One of the ordinances to be performed in the new temple was to be the ordinance of baptism for the dead. To provide a place for this ordinance, a baptisimal font resting upon the back of twelve carved oxen was prepared. Very soon after baptisms for the dead were started, baptisms in the temple font for healing of the sick, primarily for chronic illnesses, began. This ordinance also reappeared when temples were completed in the West.[13]

Three other types of faith-healing actions also began in Nauvoo and were related to the temple ordinances begun in the room above Joseph Smith's store and in the Nauvoo Temple.

In the endowment ordinance, each person receiving it is authorized to wear a sacred undergarment. He is informed that this garment is to be a "shield and a protection" to him. There have been numerous documented incidents wherein wearers of the garment have not been injured where the body was covered by the garment when traumatic injury occurred to other parts of the body not covered by the garment, and when injury could have been expected to the shielded part. This garment has also been looked upon by many of its wearers as having healing abilities.

As a part of the endowment, participants are also taught a special high order of prayer which is understood to be more efficacious than ordinary personal or congregational prayer. This prayer ordinance invariably includes the placing of the names of sick individuals upon the temple altar and includes a special prayer for their healing. The use of prayer circles outside temples has also continued until recent times.

The temple ordinances also include a practice of washing and anointing and a promise of health to those participating in the ordinances who live up to the covenants and agreements made with the Lord in the temple. Very soon after Joseph Smith instructed the Relief Society sisters in how to anoint and bless, the sisters began, outside of the temple, to wash and anoint other sisters as a means of healing. This practice was also occasionally practiced by male priesthood holders upon other men, but the ordinance found its primary use in blessing sisters preparatory to childbirth. The ordinance was quite frequently practiced by midwives who had been set apart for that task by Church leaders.

Thus it was that by the time of the death of the Prophet Joseph Smith, the principles of faith healing were firmly established in the modern Church. The healing ordinances included fasting and the prayer of faith for healing. This prayer could be personal, congregational, or by the higher order of temple prayer.

Basic to all the healing ordinances was the instruction of James, the brother of the Lord, "Is any sick among you? let him call for the elders of the church, and let them pray over him, anointing him with oil in the name of the Lord: And the prayer of faith shall save the sick, and the Lord shall raise him up: and if he have committed sins, they shall be forgiven him." (James 5:14-15.) Sisters were anointing and confirming the blessing, while brothers holding the priesthood were anointing and sealing the blessings.

Healing blessings were also being pronounced incidentally to other priesthood blessings such as baby blessings, confirmation of membership after baptism, and ordinations to offices and setting aparts to callings. The Paulian use of healing tokens or relics such as a handkerchief[14] had appeared in the modern Church. And others, impressed by the consecration of oil for healing, had begun to utilize it not only for blessing ordinances, but for internal and external medication. Others were using simple commands by their priesthood authority to heal.

And finally, healing ordinances related in the minds of their users to the holy temple ordinances were taking place in the temple and in other consecrated locations. These were baptisms for healing, washing and anointing for healing, and the circle of prayer.

To the Latter-day Saint, the first and primary step toward healing the sick was faith healing. If healing through priesthood blessings and the faith of the individual or congregation failed to heal, then other steps requiring less faith could be taken.

As God created the world he created the herbs (Genesis 1:11), and when he pronounced all that he had made good (Genesis 1:31), those herbs were included. Since that time mankind has used those herbs, often "with thanksgiving," but much of the time without that thanksgiving, but with abuse. They have been used throughout history both as food and as medications.

On 9 February 1831, as He instructed the elders of the modern Church in faith healing, He recognized that not all would have faith to be healed. Therefore He said, "And whosoever among you are sick, and have not faith to be healed, but believe, shall be nourished with all tenderness, with herbs, and mild food, and that not at the hands of an enemy." (D&C 42:43.)

Although the Smith family had lost a son, Alvin, to the malpractice of heroic medicine, the family and the members of the new Church had until this time accepted health care treatment for those who had not been healed by charismatic healings. This verse of revelation was taken as an affirmation that their actions were proper, but that this treatment should not be by use of the heroic practices of "mineral" treatments such as calomel.

As new revelations were received by the Church, the saints found that they sometimes contained guidance on such temporal matters as diet. In March, 1831, a special revelation was given as a preparation for a group of missionaries who were soon to take the gospel message to the Shaker relgous community near Kirtland. They were told, "And whoso forbiddeth to abstain from meats, that man should not eat the same, is not ordained of God; For, behold, the beasts of the field and the fowls of the air, and that which cometh of the earth, is ordained for the use of man for food and for raiment, and that he might have in abundance." (D&C 49:18-19.)

The following summer the prophet journeyed to Jackson County, Missouri, where it had been revealed to him Zion should be established in the last days. While there he received a revelation for the guidance of those who should reside in Zion. After instructing them in the need of fasting and prayer, the revelation continued, "Verily I say, that inasmuch as ye do this, the fulness of the earth is yours, the beasts of the field and the fowls of the air, and that which climbeth upon the trees and walketh upon the earth; Yea, and the herb, and the good things which come of the earth, whether for food or for raiment, or for houses, or for barns, or for orchards, or for gardens, or for vineyards; Yea, all things which come of the earth, in the season thereof, are made for the benefit and use of man, both to please the eye and to gladden the heart; Yea, for food and for raiment, for taste and for smell, to strengthen the body and enliven the soul. And it pleaseth God that he hath given all these things unto man; for unto this end were they made to be used, with judgement, not to excess, neither by extortion." (D&C 59:16-20.)

When the Smith family had moved from New York state to Ohio, they had moved into a hotbed of the revolution against orthodox or heroic medicine. When they were new in Kirtland, Joseph and his wife moved into the home of Dr. Frederick Granger Williams, who was absent serving a mission for his newly-adopted church, with Oliver Cowdery and Parley P. Pratt in western Missouri.[15]

Some time after 1815, probably in 1821, when Samuel Thomson's namesake-son made his first visit to Ohio to sell patent rights and to promote Thomsonianism,[16] Frederick G. Williams purchased Thomson's book and a patent right. Williams, who had worked as a pilot on Lake Erie and as a school teacher and farmer, abandoned piloting and teaching, assumed the title "doctor," and began to practice Thomsonian medicine. He moved to Kirtland, purchased a large farm, developed an extensive medical practice, and was a man of considerable influence by 1830 when, at forty-four, he joined the Mormons. He then had followed the men who had converted him on the mission to western Missouri.

In August, 1831, about the time of receipt of the above revelation, Joseph and Dr. Williams first met. Dr. Williams covenanted with Joseph to serve the Church with all his possessions and abilities, and thus began an association that was to end only with the death of Dr. Williams eleven years later.

Dr. Williams accompanied Joseph Smith on the trip back to Kirtland. He also became Joseph's counselor in the First Presidency in early 1833, and it is reasonable to assume that he enlightened Joseph on the practice and teachings of Thomsonian medicine. Among those health doctrines were the use of herbs as medications and non-use of the so-called mineral medicines such as calomel (mercurous chloride), strichnine, and arsenic, which orthodox medicine was then utilizing. Thomsonianism also opposed the use of blood-letting (phlebotomy). It is likewise very interesting that Thomsonianism also strongly opposed the use of alcoholic beverages. Thomson was a strong temperance advocate. The use of tobacco in its most heavily used form at that time, chewing tobacco, as well as the smoking of tobacco in the form of cigars or in pipes, was also vigorously opposed by Thomson. Finally, Thomson taught his disciples that hot drinks should not be used, and defined those hot drinks as tea and coffee.

Thomson was not the only person advocating similar doctrines. In 1830, Sylvester Graham, a Pennsylvania temperance lecturer, had begun to expand his temperance teachings into a more generalized health code.[17] He decided that the way to a man's salvation was through his stomach. Gormandizing was one of the favorite indoor sports in America, and Graham came out in opposition to over-indulgence in meat and starches. He felt an abhorence for the practice that would cause an old cookbook to solemnly warn young husbands not to expect more than *three* sorts of meat in case they brought the boys home to dinner unannounced. How many could be anticipated in case of a premeditated orgy was left to the imagination. Graham felt that the American people were apparently headed straight for physical degeneracy. He also proposed the radical concept of frequent bathing. Finally, he began to advocate not only a vegetarianism that included whole wheat products but also the virtues of bathing, fresh air, sunlight, dress reform, sex-hygiene, and exercise. In the end, history was to remember him primarily for his graham flour and bread.

Alcohol was a major problem in America in the early 1830s.[18] Later fur trappers, miners, and cowboys were to be entrapped into problems of alcoholism, but in the 1830s only the native Americans and the pioneer farmers, the soldiers, and city dwellers were affected. The annual per capita consumption of distilled spirits in the United States had risen from 2.5 gallons in 1792 to 7.5 gallons in 1823, and fallen slightly to 6.0 gallons in 1830, as the awareness of the problems had spawned the birth of temperance movements.

Dr. Benjamin Rush, the famous Philadelphia medical teacher, had early propounded the concept of limiting use of alcoholic beverages. By 1826, 16 founders, 9 of them clergymen, had led out in the founding of the American Society for the Promotion of Temperance. The society grew rapidly and by 1832 claimed 500,000 members. Frontier clergymen were spreading the temperance gospel along with their other religious messages, frequently entwining the two and making temperance a fundamental doctrine of Christianity.

In contrast to this was the fact that whiskey was used so widely and frequently that it became an expected part of all social intercourse. Many Americans were in the habit of drinking throughout the day, from dawn to dusk. A foreign visitor discovered that "in the southern and western states it is that the custom of drinking is most prevalent" and he discovered that in the West it was literally "Stranger, will you drink or fight?" One could not decline a drink without giving serious offense. A Methodist minister was told by one man that "if I did not drink with him, I was no friend of his, or his family, and he would never hear me preach again."

Tobacco is a genus (Nicotiana) of the nightshade family (Solanaceae).[19] Many plants of the nightshade family have leaves that are deadly poisonous, like the common potato, also a member of the family. Tobacco leaves did not wholly escape the poisonous tincture of the family, and very early, after its introduction to Europe by Columbus' crew, it was noted that it had habit-forming qualities. Eventually it came to be recognized that tobacco had an addictive property. The earliest use of tobacco in Europe was as a medicine, and it was often thought of as a panacea that would cure all diseases. More than 260 diseases or other conditions have been thought to be treatable by using tobacco, at some time or other. By 1700, however, tobacco was being used more for pleasure than for its medicinal value, both in Western Europe and in the American colonies. There was a growing distrust of the efficacy of tobacco as a medicine.

In the 1700s, the primary use of tobacco came to be snuff, which was inhaled in a variety of ways. The wealthy devised beautiful containers from which the snuff could be inhaled, while the poor used anything they could find at hand. By 1800, chewing tobacco had been introduced and had taken over as the prime use statistic. A small number of cigars were still being used, as they had been since about 1500. Pipes were also a favorite way to burn tobacco. The cigarette had not yet been introduced by the 1830s.

In 1828, L. Posselt and F. A. Reimann at Lille, France, isolated the constituent of the tobacco plant now called nicotine. The name assigned to the poisonous alkaloid perpetuated the name of a French ambassador to Portugal who had done early studies on the plant.

Controversy surrounded the use of tobacco. Church pews, saloons, stores, offices, and homes, were festooned with spitoons for the convenience of tobacco chewers, and the spitoons were often missed by the less accurate spitters. The women who cleaned up after the men were the strongest opponents to the use of tobacco.

Tea, from the Far East—India, China—where it has been used from time immemorial, found its way to America very early, about the middle of the Seventeenth Century.[20] In 1821, about 5,000,000 pounds of tea were imported into the United States, and in 1836, the import was 16,382,114 pounds. It was the most frequently used hot drink of the 1830s.

Tea had other opponents than Thomson and Graham. A Dr. Burdell steeped a pound of young hyson tea in soft water, boiled it down to half a pint, then gave a three-month-old rabbit that had an empty stomach ten drops of the brew. The animal appeared to be "somewhat exhilerated" for the space of three or four minutes and then died. A Dr. John Cole wrote in 1832 or 1833 about tea, that "the mind does not escape injury, but partakes of the disorders of the body, as is seen by the temper becoming peevish and irritable, so as to render the suffering a torment to all about him."[21]

Coffee appears to have come from Abyssinia, the present Ethiopia, and from neighboring countries, especially Arabia.[22] Even in its early days, the use of coffee was controversial. Mohammed, in the Koran, forbade the use of coffee (and also alcohol). Coffee was often referred to as the Devil's brew. One legend told of it being baptized by Pope Clement VIII. Some priests were reported as having gone to the Pope to get it forbidden for Christian use, denouncing it as an invention of Satan. They claimed that the Evil One, having forbidden his followers, the infidel Moslems, the use of wine—no doubt because it was sanctified by Christ and used in Holy Communion—had given them as a substitute this hellish black brew of his which they called coffee. The Pope wanted to try the Devil's drink, and when he found it so pleasant exclaimed, "Why this Satan's drink is so delicious that it would be a pity to let the infidels have exclusive use of it. We shall fool Satan by baptizing it, and making it a truly Christian beverage."[23]

By the 1830s, the use of both tea and coffee was extremely controversial in the United States and was being debated on all sides.

In 1868, Brigham Young looked back to 27 February 1833, and told his listeners, "I think I am as well acquainted with the circumstances which led to the giving of the Word of Wisdom as any man in the Church, although I was not present at the time to witness them. The first school of the prophets was held in a small room situated over the Prophet Joseph's kitchen, in a house, which belonged to Bishop Whitney, and which was attached to his store, which more probably might be about fifteen feet square. In the rear of this building was a kitchen, probably ten by fourteen feet, containing rooms and pantries. Over this kitchen was situated the room in which the Prophet received revelations and in which he instructed his brethren. The brethren came to that place for hundreds of miles to attend school in a little room probably no larger than eleven by fourteen. When they assembled together in this room after breakfast, the first thing they did was to light their pipes, and, while smoking, talk about the great things of the kingdom, and spit all over the room, and as soon as the pipe was out of their mouths a large chew of tobacco would then be taken. Often when the Prophet entered the room to give the school instructions he would find himself in a cloud of tobacco smoke. This, and the complaints of his wife at having to clean so filthy a floor made the Prophet think upon the matter, and he inquired of the Lord relating to the conduct of the Elders in using tobacco, and the revelation known as the Word of Wisdom was the result of his inquiry."[24]

> A Word of Wisdom, for the benefit of the council of high priests, assembled in Kirtland, and the church, and also the saints in Zion—To be sent greeting; not by commandment or constraint, but by revelation and the word of wisdom, showing forth the order and will of God in the temporal salvation of all saints in the last days—Given for a principle with promise, adapted to the capacity of the weak and the weakest of all saints, who are or can be called saints.
>
> Behold, verily, thus saith the Lord unto you: In consequence of evils and designs which do and will exist in the hearts of conspiring men in the last days, I have warned you, and forewarn you, by giving unto you this word of wisdom by revelation—That inasmuch as any man drinketh wine or strong drink among you, behold it is not good, neither meet in the sight of your Father, only in assembling yourselves together to offer up your sacraments before him. And, behold, this should be wine, yea, pure wine of the grape of the vine, and your own make.
>
> And, again, strong drinks are not for the belly, but for the washing of your bodies.

MEDICAL ASPECTS OF THE RESTORATION

And, again, tobacco is not for the body, neither for the belly, and is not good for man, but is an herb for bruises and all sick cattle, to be used with judgement and skill.

And, again, hot drinks are not for the body or belly.

And, again, verily I say unto you, all wholesome herbs God hath ordained for the constitution, nature, and use of man—Every herb in the season thereof, and every fruit in the season thereof; all these to be used with prudence and thanksgiving. Yea, flesh also of beasts and of the fowls of the air, I, the Lord, have ordained for the use of man with thanksgiving; nevertheless they are to be used sparingly. And it is pleasing unto me that they should not be used, only in times of winter, or of cold, or famine. All grain is ordained for the use of man and of beasts, to be the staff of life, not only for man but for the beasts of the field and the fowls of heaven, and all wild animals that run or creep on the earth; And these hath God made for the use of man only in times of famine and excess hunger. All grain is good for the food of man; as also the fruit of the vine; that which yieldeth fruit, whether in the ground or above the ground—Nevertheless, wheat for man, and corn for the ox, and oats for the horse, and rye for the fowls and for swine, and for all beasts of the field, and barley for all useful animals, and for mild drinks, as also other grain.

And all saints who remember to keep and do these sayings, walking in obedience to the commandments, shall receive health in their navel and marrow to their bones; And shall find wisdom and great treasures of knowledge, even hidden treasures; And shall run and not be weary, and shall walk and not faint. And I, the Lord, give unto them a promise, that the destroying angel shall pass by them, as the children of Israel and not slay them. Amen." (D&C 89.)

Although "hot drinks" was a term in general use to define tea and coffee in the United States at that time, controversy arose almost immediately as to whether or not that was what was meant. Those who were habituated to these drinks were hoping against vain hope that it was not true. However, within a few weeks Joseph Smith had indicated that that was indeed what the Lord meant.[25] Some nine years later, his brother, Hyrum, had to reiterate the statement.

The introductory paragraph also caused controversy. Not long after the revelation was received the Kirtland High Council, then the highest council in the Church other than the newly organized First Presidency, a council, presided over by the prophet himself, met to discuss whether or not Church leaders could hold their posts if they did not abide by the Word of Wisdom. The decision was that they could not, and several leaders who did not live by the revelation were removed from their offices, and some disfellowshipped.[26]

During the life of the Prophet Joseph Smith, the record of enforcement of the provisions of the Word of Wisdom was spotty, as the social pressures of their American culture weakened the resolve of some of the leaders to live the revelation. At one time even Joseph Smith weakened to the point that he allowed the establishment of a bar in the Mansion House, his Nauvoo home, which also served as a hotel. Emma, whose pleas had instigated the inquiry that led to the revelation, soon put him in line, however. The revelation, particularly its don'ts, became the hallmark of the Latter-day Saint.

Chapter Four

Zion's Camp And Its Health Problems

When the Church moved from western New York to Ohio and western Missouri, it encountered new diseases in addition to those that had been prevalent in New England and New York. One of these diseases—the ague and fever of malaria—will be discussed later. Two other diseases had their most important initial impacts upon the saints as the expulsion of approximately 1,200 Mormon residents from Jackson County, Missouri, prompted Joseph Smith to assemble as many male members of the Church as possible to march to Zion "for the purpose of carrying some supplies to the afflicted and persecuted Saints in Missouri, and to reinforce and strengthen them; and, if possible, to influence the Governor of the State to call out sufficient additional force to cooperate in restoring them to their rights."[1] In May, 1834, Zion's Camp moved west to Missouri in two contingents, one from Ohio led by Joseph Smith and the other from Michigan led by his brother, Hyrum.

As the contingents of Zion's Camp moved west, they both traveled through areas where a disease known by many names, but most commonly as milk sickness, was endemic.

Fifteen years before their march, a little-known family had fled from Pigeon Creek in Spencer County, Indiana, just a few miles south of the route the camp was now taking.[2] The milk sickness had hung over the communities of this region for more than a decade, destroying man and cattle in large numbers. In 1815, in DuBois County, Indiana, half the human deaths occurring were said to have resulted from this disease. Now their eight-year-old son, Abe, mourned the loss of members of his family, Thomas and Betsy Sparrow, but most keenly his mother, Nancy Hanks Lincoln. Twenty-six years after the passing of Zion's Camp through the area, when little Abe became president of the United States, everyone knew about milk sickness, but the cause of the disease was still being debated.

Milk sickness appeared in North Carolina as early as the American Revolution, where a mountain peak was named Milk Sick, but the first published account of the disease was that of Thomas Barbee, who described the new disease in 1809 in *Notices Concerning Cincinnati* without naming it.[3] An 1811 article in Dr. Mitchill's *Medical Repository* had called it sick stomach. By 1821, the sickness which people in eastern America sometimes doubted the existence of because it didn't seem to occur in well-populated areas, was attributed to the same "miasmas" that caused yellow fever, malaria, and other illnesses, in an article in a Philadelphia medical journal.

Although the medical profession was not convinced as to its cause, by the time that Zion's Camp marched through the endemic areas of Ohio, Indiana, Illinois, and Missouri, the common farmer had realized that its primary cause was the drinking of milk from cows that had in it deadly poison, a poison no one could recognize or effectively guard against. They were also aware of the fact that it sometimes was transmitted to man and other animals when meat of cattle and other animals was eaten. They had also recognized that a sickness in their animals which they called the trembles usually was also present when milk sickness struck.

The symptoms of milk sickness in humans include loss of appetite, listlessness, weakness, vague pains, muscle stiffness, vomiting, abdominal discomfort, severe constipation, keto-acidosis, occasionally hypoglycemia and lipemia, and, at last, coma. The severe acidosis produces an acetone odor to the breath. In animals, chiefly cattle, it is characterized by loss of appetite, weakness, falling, trembling, and stiffness. Abdominal distention develops and the animals become unconscious. In both men and animals the disease may become chronic with periods of remission and exacerbation; or death can come quickly. In chronic cases exacerbations are brought on by fatigue, starvation, incurrent infection, or vigorous exercise.

Recovery from an attack is slow and may never be complete. The lethargy that characterizes the disease has helped give it one of its names, the slows. Lincoln, in removing McClellan from his Civil War army command, said, "I said I would remove him if he let Lee's army get away from him, and I must do so. He has got the slows!"[4]

The movement of Zion's Camp, a long distance on foot, through an area where thousands of people were dying of milk sickness, a disease that could strike anywhere without warning, was a highly dangerous activity. To add to the complexity of the problem was a recent revelation, the Word of Wisdom, received only a few months before, which forbad the use of tea and coffee and other beverages which otherwise would have been used as alternatives to milk. It is an amazement that both contingents and the unified camp covered the entire trip without a single occurrence of milk sickness, though it was a major concern of the Prophet during the march.[5]

Milk sickness continued to be a concern to Church members as long as the main body of the Church remained in what is now called the Middle West. It is still a potentially dangerous disease, although the cause has been identified.

The first person to identify the cause of milk sickness did it not long after Zion's Camp passed through. Anna Pierce Hobbs, called Dr. Anna by her neighbors and friends, was searching for the plant that caused the disease when she met an old Indian woman, called Aunt Shawnee, who led her to a plant that was to be called White Snakeroot.[6] Dr. Anna started a campaign to eliminate snakeroot from her vicinity, and was largely successful. For a time the disease disappeared in the area of southern Illinois where she lived. Somehow the word never got out of her vicinity, and five years later, in 1838, a farmer named John Rowe, of Fayette County, Ohio, discovered the same cause. He had even experimentally killed a calf and two cattle by feeding them the plant. But his report in a Washington, Ohio, newspaper was debunked by the famed Dr. Daniel Drake, who thought, although he had not tested his ideas, that the cause was poison ivy. This caused nearly a century more of indecision about the cause of the disease. The question as to what caused milk sickness was not settled until 1928 when Dr. J. F. Couch reported the isolation of three poisonous substances from white snakeroot. He named the most important one trematol. Trematol is also present in a plant of southwestern United States (another area where milk sickness was endemic) called rayless goldenrod.

In the spring of 1826, cholera broke out in the delta area of the Ganges River in India and began to spread over the country. Within two years, Asiatic Cholera ascended the river with its boatmen and passed over the northwest boundary on the Indian subcontinent. Within another year, cholera crossed the deserts with the caravans and reached the Caspian Sea. By 1830 it stretched deep into Russia and the Near East.[7] While the saints were congregating in Kirtland, Ohio, some 50,000 Mohammedan pilgrims met at Mecca. Cholera was an uninvited guest and nearly half of the pilgrims fell victim to the disease. As they fled the holy city, the pilgrims carried the disease to their homelands around the Mediterranean Sea.

From the Caspian Sea, the pestilence crossed by boat and caravan to the Black Sea, where it ascended the Danube into southern and central Europe. Meanwhile, it spread through Russia along the rivers from the Black and Caspian Seas and traveled along roads and trails to the Baltic Sea, where it took ship to other nations. Cholera first appeared in England in October, 1831, in the mining port town of Sunderland and then spread across England, Scotland, Wales, and Ireland. It reached Belfast and Dublin in time to catch the great wave of Irish immigrants to America in the spring of 1832.

Even before ice was cleared from the St. Lawrence River in the spring of 1832, immigrant-laden ships arrived at Gross Isle, the seaport for Quebec and Montreal. Within three months after the 1 May opening of navigation, the St. Lawrence River brought nearly 45,000 persons to Gross Isle and

Quebec. The first known cholera victim arrived in Canada in June, but there were undoubtedly many undetected cases before then.[8]

By mid-June cholera appeared at Plattsburg, New York, and at nearly every town on the waterway from the St. Lawrence to Albany, New York. The disease quickly spread along the waterways to New York City—though it may have been there sooner because of incoming ocean shipping—and traveled westward on the Erie Canal to Buffalo.

Meanwhile, war broke out with the Indians on the Mississippi frontier.[9] The warring tribes met federal troops that had been shipped through New York City, Albany, Buffalo, and via ship to Fort Dearborn (now Chicago). While on board ship, the troops had been attacked with cholera with a fantastic carnage. After what was thought to be an adequate quarantine period, the troops left for Fort Armstrong on Rock Island in the Mississippi River. On 26 August, without warning, the scourge violently broke out at the fort. From there it traveled down the Mississippi. While escorting captured warrior chiefs to St. Louis, nine Fort Armstrong guards died of cholera.

The troop transports that had carried the troops west turned back with crews sick and dying with cholera. The *Henry Clay* made an emergency stop at Cleveland. Six of her crew had cholera and one of them died. The sick were left behind to unknowingly infect Cleveland. From Cleveland, cholera followed the waterways and portages across Ohio to Cincinnati and then traveled up and down the Ohio River. Cholera by then was rampant in the west.

The Mormon settlements near Kirtland seem to have been relatively free from cholera during the 1832 pandemic despite their proximity to the cholera-infested pesthole of Cleveland. Latter-day Saints in other parts of the world were not immune to the disease, but as a people, the Mormons seemed to be protected by God's hand in being spared much of the affliction.

Cholera was terrifyingly unpredictable.[10] It ravaged some towns in a progressive sweep, yet entirely skipped or inflicted only a few in others. Health authorities tried to quarantine cholera cases, but the vagaries of its epidemic pattern eluded attempts to arrest its spread. Apparently no one thought to boil water to kill the disease. Instead, doctors theorized that cholera was spread by the miasmas of bad air and prescribed higher altitudes with plenty of cross breezes. But cholera struck there too.

The cause of Asiatic Cholera was totally unknown. It was not known that cholera was caused by accidental ingestion of bacteria spread by hands contaminated by feces, diarrheal "rice water," vomitus, or by contamination of drinking water. The bacteria itself is surprisingly benign, requiring massive ingestion to cause illness. Some individuals do not get the disease because of high stomach acid concentrations which kill the bacteria. In the first pandemic, the vast majority of the victims of the disease did not even realize they had it; most had only mild diarrhea. They were the unknowing carriers who infected others and contaminated water supplies. The diagnosed cholera victims were but a small fraction of the number who actually had cholera.

Since the cause was not known, doctors knew of no effective treatment for cholera. Many of the doctors of the heroic school of practice adapted the treatment of Dr. Benjamin Rush for yellow fever—after all, both diseases were supposed to be caused by miasmas. The treatment called for cleaning out the body by doses of calomel (mercurous chloride). A tablespoon dose was administered each hour until the patient got well or died. Also, the pressures within the body were reduced by bleeding the patient until he fainted. Needless to say, the mortality rate for cholera patients treated in this manner was extremely high.

The advocates of botanic medicine treated their cholera patients with a dose of lobelia and bayberry to induce vomiting. This was followed by an enema to clean out the bowels, and then the patient was alternately steamed and chilled. If there was no noticeable improvement within a day, a new round of the same treatment was given. We now know that cholera kills because of severe dehydration and upset of fluid balance that occurs in cases of extensive diarrhea. The botanic treatment tended to stem this dehydration and to replace some lost fluid. These patients were more likely to survive cholera and treatment. But neither method of treatment was very satisfactory. Both merely allowed the disease to run its course.

As the main contingent of Zion's Camp moved west, some of the members had trouble following the military-like discipline that was demanded of them by the prophet. They groused about food, quarreled among themselves, and in many cases would not follow the Prophet's counsel. As a result, before crossing the Mississippi River into Missouri, Joseph Smith warned the camp about incurring the Lord's wrath:

> I got up on a wagon wheel, called the people together, and said that I would deliver a prophecy. After giving the brethren much good advice, exhorting them to faithfulness and humility, I said the Lord had revealed to me that a scourge would come upon the camp in consequence of the fractious and unruly spirits that appeared among them, and they would die like sheep with the rot; still, if they would repent and humble themselves before the Lord, the scourge, in great measure, might be turned away; but, as the Lord lives, the members of this camp will suffer for giving way to their unruly temper.[11]

In early June both contingents of Zion's Camp arrived in Missouri. The one from Ohio, led by Joseph Smith, crossed the Mississippi River and camped on the banks of the river about a mile above the town of Louisiana,

Missouri. They were in a beautiful oak grove and undoubtedly drank water from the river, not knowing that it was polluted with choleraic bacteria.

The Michigan contingent crossed the Mississippi at Quincy, Illinois, and marched southward through Palmyra, Missouri, a town of 700 to 1,000 people before cholera struck the year before. More than a tenth of the population had died of cholera within two weeks. In accounting for the severe attack of cholera in Palmyra, it was explained that "rain followed by hot weather at a time when there was much new plowed soil gave rise to the pestiferous *miasmata* which resulted in congestive fever and cholera."[12] Cholera was undoubtedly still present in Palmyra when the Mormons passed through.

The united expedition, which met at the farm of John Allred on the Salt River in eastern Missouri, consisted of 205 men, 10 women, and several children. The camp reached Richmond, Missouri, on 19 June. They stopped for breakfast on a hill near a farm house. The farm's owner furnished the camp with a large quantity of milk. The milk was potentially a carrier of milk sickness, and was also a good carrier of choleraic bacteria. This was the camp's third exposure to cholera.

That night Joseph Hancock was stricken with cholera. Three days later Ezra Thayer and Thomas Hayes were also stricken. On the night of 24 June, cholera "was manifested in its most violent form. . . . Our ears were saluted with cries and moanings, and lamentations on every hand; even those on guard fell to the earth with their guns in their hands, so sudden and powerful was the attack of this terrible disease."

Elder John S. Carter was the first man to step forward to rebuke the disease, but upon doing so was instantly seized by the disease and became the first victim in the camp.[13] The prophet recorded in his history:

> At the commencement, I attempted to lay on hands for their recovery, but I quickly learned by painful experience, that when the great Jehovah decrees destruction upon any people, and makes known his determination, man must not attempt to stay his hand. The moment I attempted to rebuke the disease I was attacked, and had I not desisted in my attempt to save the life of a brother, I would have sacrificed my own. The disease seized upon me like the talons of a hawk, and I said to the brethren: "If my work were done, you would have to put me in the ground without a coffin."[14]

Since neither coffins nor lumber to make them could be obtained, the bodies of the dead were rolled in blankets and taken to the banks of a small stream that emptied into Rush Creek. The dead were buried at night in an attempt to keep secret the number of their losses and the fact that cholera was in their camp. By burying the bodies in the creek bank, they unknowingly insured the contamination of the creek.

On 25 June, the camp separated into small bands and dispersed among the local Church members, spreading the disease among the members. The news of the Zion's Camp outbreak of cholera spread despite attempts to suppress it. Joseph Smith recorded an incident of a woman refusing to give him a drink of water because of her fear of acquiring cholera. But the woman and three others in the family died of cholera within a week.[15]

In all, sixty-eight of Zion's Camp were stricken with cholera, and thirteen died, including the prophet's cousin, Jesse J. Smith, and one woman, Betsy Parrish. Of the 205 men of the camp, 33 percent had recognizable cholera and 19 percent of those who had cholera died. Overall, Zion's Camp's death rate of just over 6 percent was low in comparison to mortality rates in other groups such as the residents of Palmyra, Missouri, with more than 10 percent mortality rate.[16]

Among the local members of the Church that died after the Zion's Camp outbreak of cholera was Algernon Sidney Gilbert, one of the most prominent leaders. Joseph Smith had called Gilbert to preach the gospel, a task Gilbert greatly feared. Brother Gilbert allegedly had said he "would rather die than go forth to preach the Gospel to the Gentiles." Shortly afterwards he was granted his wish; he joined his brother, who had died some months before of cholera in St. Louis.

The affliction of Zion's Camp came near the end of the 1832 cholera pandemic. As 1834 ended, only isolated cases cropped up across the United States. The men who were later to become the leaders of the Church had had their baptism by one of the greatest pestilences to rage throughout the world in recorded history.

Chapter Five

Nauvoo— The Beautiful Pesthole

Malaria was not a native disease of America. It, with yellow fever, is now believed to be a legacy of the importation of slaves onto the American continent. It was to become endemic everywhere in North America that the Anapholes Mosquito existed (although the world before the beginning of the twentieth century would not recognize this relationship).

The massive area of the drainage of the Mississippi River and its branches, including the Ohio and Missouri Rivers, became infected with Malaria. The early French explorers of this river basin did not report the occurrence of malaria, but they did report massive numbers of pesky mosquitoes.

Malaria moved west from the slave-holding Atlantic colonies with the first frontiersmen. When they left the slave states the frontiersmen took the disease with them.

By the beginning of the nineteenth century malaria had already invaded as far west as the Mississippi River and as far north as the western Great Lakes. The American Bottoms in Illinois, near St. Louis, previously well settled, had been depopulated as people fled the disease. Early doctors in the West, like Dr. Samuel P. Hildreth (uncle by marriage to John Cook Bennett, who was to later become a Mormon), were fighting the disease for which the area was already notorius.[1]

The malariousness of the region was even such that in the 1820s serious observers doubted the possibility of settling it permanently. Travelers in the Middle West were struck by the "pale and sickly countenances, showing too clearly the traces of fever and ague." Many inhabitants carried voluminous "ague cakes" (spleen tumors) with them.[2] But strangely enough, malaria had become so common that many no longer regarded it as a disease. A common remark was, "He aint sick! He's just got the auger!" Malaria was to be the most prevalent disease in the Middle West until long after the Mormons left.

The Mormons that moved into the Kirtland area left little record of the occurrence of malaria there, and one wonders if they did not consider it a disease or if there was actually a relative freedom from the disease in the community.

There is likewise little record of malaria reported in Zion (Independence, Missouri), but non-Mormon medical historians report that the entire region along the Missouri River through Missouri at that time was being devastated with malaria. In the 1820s two Missouri River communities had even been abandoned because of malaria. Entire steamboat loads, passengers and crews, were stricken with the disease.[3] Communities in the area got to the point that they scheduled business and social functions for the days when townspeople didn't have the shakes.

The saints in Missouri undoubtedly came into contact with a most remarkable doctor who had moved to Arrow Rock, Saline County, Missouri, in 1820. This was near where the Santa Fe Trail then began. This doctor, John Sappington, although extremely controversial as a doctor, probably was as responsible as any other man for the successful settlement of the malaria-infested Middle West.

John Sappington was born in Maryland on 15 May 1776, the son of Dr. Mark B. and Rebecca (Boyce) Sappington. While he was a child, the family moved to Nashville, Tennessee. As a young man, he served a medical apprenticeship under the preceptorship of his father, and then practiced with his father and his brother. About 1800, he moved to Franklin, Tennessee, where he practiced alone. On November 22, 1804, he married Jane Breathitt at Russellville, Kentucky. They had seven daughters and two sons.

In 1814, Dr. Sappington, then thirty-eight years old, rode horseback to Philadelphia to attend the medical school of the University of Pennsylvania. At that time two sessions were required for a diploma, but Sappington quit after only one. Apparently the heroic medicine taught there conflicted with his own practical experience. He returned to private practice in Williamson County, Tennessee, remaining there until he moved to Howard County, Missouri, in 1817. In 1820, he moved to Arrow Rock.[4]

All of Sappington's professional life was spent in malarious areas, and he became adept at treatment of malaria. Orthodox medical treatment of malaria called for blood-letting and doses of calomel (mercurious chloride), and then, when the fever had subsided, possibly a dose of cinchona bark. Sappington used only treatment with cinchona bark, and that when the fever was high.

Cinchona bark, from South America, had been known for about 300 years, but its use was controversial because of side effects that frequently occurred—ringing in the ears, nausea, vomiting, etc. Because bark varied in potency, dosage could not be controlled. Sappington solved that by giving small doses only.

In 1820, two Frenchmen, Pelletier and Caventou, isolated the alkaloid, quinine, from cinchona bark. Very soon after this, just two years later, a

Philadelphia firm, Farr and Kunzi, began preparing quinine. Sappington began to be one of their largest customers.[5]

Quinine became equally as controversial as cinchona bark. Even twenty years later doctors were fighting about the use of the drug, and oddly enough the heroic medical practitioners of the "old school," as the non-orthodox medical practitioners called them, were opposed to the use of quinine unless it followed more heroic treatment.

Although Sappington did not totally renounce the old school of medicine, his methods of treatment were heretical, and he became a source of controversy. His old schoolmate, Dr. Daniel Drake, already prominent as a medical leader in the Middle West, closed the pages of his medical journals to publications by Sappington and snubbed him when visiting Sappington's vicinity. As an example of this lack of acceptance of Sappington by orthodox medicine, even in the twentieth century the renowned medical historian, Dr. Erwin H. Ackerknecht, who studied malaria in the Middle West, ignored Sappington's contributions.

There is no evidence that Sappington either liked or disliked the Mormons, and it is questionable how much direct contact they had. However, because many of Sappington's friends were strongly anti-Mormon, it is likely that Sappington was also. But nonetheless, Sappington impacted strongly upon the Mormons.

In 1830, Sappington took a partner into his practice, a Dr. George Penn. Sometime about then he began to manufacture pills for use in treating his malaria patients. In 1832, Sappington, then 56 years old, turned over most of his practice to Penn and began the wholesale manufacture and distribution of his fever pills.

It is possible that this venture arose through error. A story, which may be apocryphal, says that Sappington's son, instructed to buy 100 ounces of quinine, returned from Philadelphia with 100 pounds instead. At $15 an ounce it nearly bankrupt the old doctor, and he decided to commercially manufacture the pills in order to recoup his finances. He then taught his slaves how to make them, and used a building he had erected on his farm for the purpose.[6]

Sappington hired a crew of from fifteen to twenty-five salesmen to promote his pills. They were instructed to take their own pills as a prophylactic measure as they traveled throughout the most malarial areas. The pills contained 1 grain of quinine sulfate, ¾ grain of licorice, ¼ grain of myrrh, and oil of sassafras to flavor. The manufacturing cost was about 10 cents for a box of 24 pills, but it sold for about $1.50. Because of public and professional controversy over quinine, there was no mention of it as an ingredient of the pills by the salesmen.

As the Mormon settlements moved from Jackson County to Clay County, and to Davies and Caldwell Counties, they encountered malaria in each county. Even with fewer cases in sparsely settled Davies and Caldwell Counties, it is highly probable that Mormons bought and used these pills, which were sold both over-the-counter and by doctors. It was in Nauvoo, however, that Sappington's anti-fever pills became most important.

The Mormons fled from Missouri after its governor, Lilburn Boggs, had given them three options—to leave the church, leave the state, or be exterminated. Many of them gathered to Quincy, Illinois. The First Presidency of the Church, meanwhile, languished for six months in a Missouri jail. Bogg's extermination order forced a mid-winter evacuation without sufficient food, clothing, or shelter.

The evacuation was recorded in very few journals. They were too busy trying to save their lives to write much in journals. But their plight was sufficiently bad that it aroused the pity of the people of Quincy and other Illinois towns near Mississippi River crossings.

It is apparent that the refugees suffered with pneumonia, attacks of consumption, and other diseases. Mother Smith, Joseph's mother, was later to recall that she and her daughter had cholera in Quincy shortly after they arrived.[7] This may have been true, but since there was no recorded epidemic of cholera at that time, it is probable that they had a different disease. The refugees were, however, undoubtedly victims of "scorbutic disease" or scurvy, which occurred frequently in such occasions when fresh fruits or vegetables (later discovered to contain vitamin C) were not available. By April, Bishop Partidge, himself a sick and dying man, was despondent about the health and welfare of the refugee saints.

Meanwhile, Elder Isaac Barlow, in fleeing Missouri, had gone north to the village of Commerce, Illinois, where Elder Heber C. Kimball's cousins lived. There he met Dr. Isaac Galland, who offered to the Church most of Commerce and large tracts across the river in Iowa at comparatively low cost and long terms of repayment. Within a few days after Joseph Smith's escape from Missouri, he was at Commerce visiting Dr. Galland.[8]

Just above where the Des Moines River joins the Mississippi River, and for more than a dozen miles, an outcrop of rocks, the Des Moines Rapids, impeded traffic on the Mississippi. At low water only small boats could pass, and then only with difficulty. At the head of the rapids, the river made a sweeping half-moon circle around a peninsula, and there the town of Commerce had been platted.

Across the river the U.S. Army had built and abandoned Fort Des Moines, and in 1830, Missouri had unsuccessfully tried to annex the area in order to have access to the rapids, which were looked upon as a potential source of great water power.

Commerce had been platted in 1824, and was viewed as potentially a great city. It was the only place on the Illinois side of the river for many miles where the bluffs did not hug the river. Being located just above the rapids, it was the last river port above where traffic was impeded by the rapids. It was the natural place for the upper portage point around them. (The lower portage point was Warsaw.) But by the time of Joseph Smith's visit in late spring, 1839, there were still only half a dozen homes in the vicinity.[9]

The site of Commerce was beautiful, and Joseph Smith would soon rename it Nauvoo, which he said was a Hebrew word meaning beautiful. But it was also a pesthole! Commerce had failed to grow specifically because it was a place where malaria was endemic and particularly virulent.

There is no way that Joseph Smith could *not* have known that Commerce had a deservedly bad reputation as a malarial pesthole. And yet he chose to disregard this fact and chose it as the new gathering place for the saints. Some have likened this choice to his successor, Brigham Young's choice of Salt Lake City as a place to strengthen his followers. Flanders has claimed that the decision was made primarily because of Dr. Galland's offer, an opportunity to possess Galland's tract for no money down and long years to pay.[10] And thus it was that Joseph Smith led the Church, already suffering from the Missouri expulsion, into one of the most unhealthful places in the United States—a beautiful pesthole.

Joseph Smith described the place as "literally a wilderness. The land was mostly covered with trees and bushes, and much of it so wet that it was with the utmost difficulty a footman could get through, and totally impossible for teams. Commerce was so unhealthful, very few could live there; but believing that it might become a healthful place by the blessing of heaven to the Saints, and no more eligible place presenting itself, I considered it wisdom to make an attempt to build up a city."[11]

The bluffs that in other places followed the river, at Commerce continued north and south, while the river circled west around a lowland peninsula called "the flats." The flats were the boggy wilderness the prophet described, but their wetness did not come from the river, but from numerous springs in the face of the bluffs which discharged water onto the flats.

The saints followed Joseph Smith to Commerce in June, 1839. Soon nearly 5,000 persons were busily laying out the town and building log cabins, tenting, or otherwise industriously building a new city. But they faced problems. It was so swampy that when the first attempt was made to plow it the oxen mired. Brigham Young's lot was so boggy that he couldn't build upon it, so he moved across the river into a part of old Fort Des Moines.[12]

The saints arrived just in time for the dreaded "miasmas" to strike. Practically everyone became sick. A cemetery was begun above the bluffs, but there were not enough well persons to even bury the dead. Sidney Rigdon preached a mass funeral sermon for all the dead. It looked as if Commerce would have to be abandoned as the already-sick refugees fell victims to acute "ague" and fever (malaria). So it was on 22 July 1839 as Joseph

NAUVOO—THE BEAUTIFUL PESTHOLE

Smith rose from his own sickbed to begin a day of great faith healing of the sick. (See Chapter three.)

It was also under these circumstances that John Sappington, far away in Missouri, helped the saints by manufacturing his anti-fever pills. Dr. Calvin Pendleton, a young botanic physician, and several other botanic doctors, began to distribute Sappington's pills to the sick of Commerce, and the quinine in the pills lowered the raging fevers of the malaria victims. Dr. John Sappington had unknowingly made possible the continued settlement of what would soon be Nauvoo. These pills were extensively used in Nauvoo throughout the Mormon stay.

As the malaria crisis passed, it could be seen that other diseases were also present. In fact, the combination of the trials of the Missouri expulsion and malaria made the saints more susceptible to other diseases. Soon Father Smith, the prophet's father, died of consumption which had been aggravated by over exposure in the Missouri flight.[13] The prophet's brother Don Carlos Smith died of what may have been pneumonia. These diseases frequently struck.

Dysentery plagued the community. It is probable that typhoid (which may in this case have been confused with the ague) was also present. Brain fever (meningitis) was probably also present, as were measles, scarlet fever, and diphtheria.[14]

In 1840, another doctor, John Cook Bennett, came to Nauvoo. (See Chapter six.) By 1841, he was mayor of the city, and soon he had had a large drainage ditch dug to carry off the spring waters from the bluffs, before they reached the flats. The flats were drained, trees and underbrush cut out and burned. The source of the miasmas must be eliminated! The prophet had told him in a letter before Bennett came to Nauvoo, "like all other places on the river, it is sickly in summer." Nauvoo was fortunate to have John Cook Bennett.

We now know that one of the factors that keeps malaria virulent is the steady input of new humans into malarial areas, and that when a population becomes stable malaria has a tendency to become less so, and to even disappear.[15] Nauvoo did have a steady stream of new members that had to be "acclimated," and the ague and fever continued in spite of Bennett's efforts. Perhaps if he had stayed longer, things would have become even healthier.

If 1839 was bad, 1840 was worse. In January, 1841, the prophet sent out a proclamation stating, "This place has been objected to by some on account of the sickness that has prevailed in the summer months, but it is the opinion of Dr. Bennett that Hancock County, and all the eastern and southern portions of Nauvoo, are as healthful as any other portions of the western country, to acclimatized citizens; whilst the northwestern portion of the city has suffered much affliction from fever and ague, which, however, Dr. Bennett thinks can be easily remedied by draining the sloughs on the adjacent islands in the Mississippi."[16] To be acclimatized usually meant that a person had to have had malaria at least once. But in the summer of 1841, the disease was calamatous. It was 1842 before Bennett's efforts began to pay off in better health. But malaria never left Nauvoo, and each new settler from a non-malarial region became "acclimatized" with a dose of the shakes.

The botanic doctors of Nauvoo never were without an abundance of patients.

Chapter Six

Doctor John Cook Bennett

Like a streaking comet, one doctor flashed across the history of the Latter-day Saints in the early 1840s, leaving behind a comet's trail of turmoil and upset. Although a member of the Church only twenty months, he is undoubtedly the most controversial figure to ever join the Church.

The most charitable opinion of this doctor, John Book Bennett, came from Elder John Taylor, who was later to be president of the Church: "Respecting John C. Bennett: I was well acquainted with him. At one time he was a good man, but fell into adultery, and was cut off from the Church for his iniquity; and so bad was his conduct, that he was also expelled from the municipal courts, of which he was a member. He then went to lecturing through the country, and commenced writing pamphlets for the sake of making money, charging so much for admittance to his lectures, and selling his slanders. His remarks, however, were so bad, and his statements so obscene and disgraceful, that respectable people were disgusted."[1]

The famed non-Mormon historian, Hubert Howe Bancroft, says of him: "The role of traitor is not one which brings credit to the performer, either from one side or the other. However great the services he may render us, we cannot but feel that he is false hearted and vile. Many of the apostates, though they may not have written books, declare that they joined the sect only to learn their secrets and then expose them. These are the most contemptible of all. There may be cases, where a young or inexperienced person, through ignorance or susceptibility, has been carried away for a time contrary to the dictates of cooler judgement; but the statements of such persons are justly regarded more or less with suspicion. Far better is it, far more honest and praiseworthy, for him who, having unwittingly made a mistake, seeks to rectify it, to go his way and say nothing about it; for if he talks of writing a book for the good of others, as a warning, and that they may avoid his errors, few will believe him. 'If he has proved traitor once,' they say, 'he will deceive again; and if he is sincere, we cannot more than half believe him, for such an individual is never sure of himself.' John C. Bennett, general, doctor, methodist preacher, and quack, is from his own showing a bad man."[2]

That John C. Bennett was a help to the Church, during the period he was united with it, cannot be denied. Like Dr. Samuel Latham Mitchill, he strove to extend the influence of the physician beyond the field of medicine.

Bennett proved to be a very effective lobbyist, and as Quartermaster General of Illinois he was able to guide three bills to aid the Church through the Illinois legislature by unanimous votes. The most important of the three was the Nauvoo Charter, which provided for a city government. The second act provided for an independent militia unit under the city's control, the Nauvoo Legion. The third act empowered the city to establish an educational system and a university.

When the Nauvoo Charter went into effect, a grateful populace elected him Nauvoo's first mayor. When the Legion was organized, Joseph Smith was chosen its Commanding General with the rank of Lieutenant General, the highest military rank in the United States. Dr. Bennett added the rank of Major General, second in command of the Legion, to his Brigadier General rank as Quartermaster General. Finally, when the university act was implemented, Bennett also became chancellor of the university.

On February 3, 1841, Bennett delivered a laudable inaugural address that touched on proposed new laws and development of Nauvoo, including its Legion and university. He proposed that sale of spiritous liquors be limited to cases of sickness, upon recommendation of a physician or surgeon accredited by the chancellor and regents of the University. He also said, "The public health requires that the low lands, bordering on the Mississippi, should be immediately drained, and the entire timber removed. This can and will be one of the most healthful cities in the west, provided you take prompt and decisive action in the premises. A board of health should be appointed and vested with the usual powers and prerogatives."[3]

The public health measures were soon accomplished, eventually lowering the rate of occurrence of malaria significantly. Under Bennett, effective basic laws for the city were soon passed. He was, in fact, an able administrator. This led Joseph Smith to say "that he was about the first man he had about him who could do exactly what he wanted done, the way it should be done, and who would do it at once."[4]

On 8 April 1841, John C. Bennett, a member of the Church for only seven months, was present at General Conference "with the First Presidency, as Assistant President until President Rigdon's health should be restored."[5]

John Cook Bennett was born 3 August 1804 at Fairhaven, Bristol County, Massachusetts.[6] The town was then, with its neighbor New Bedford, a center for the whaling and shipping industries. In 1808, his parents moved the family to Washington County, Ohio, where his uncle by marriage, Samuel Preston Hildreth, was already building a reputation as the outstanding physician and surgeon of southeastern Ohio.

Little is known of his childhood and youth other than that he was raised in Marietta or Washington County. It is possible that during his teen years he attended what was to become Ohio University, at Athens, Ohio.[7] The first definitive information about his life now known is that he took a three-year apprenticeship to become a doctor under the tutelage of his renowned uncle.[8] Dr. Hildreth's wife was the sister of John C. Bennett's mother. There is some evidence that indicates that he might have been precocious. He later wrote of medical consultations he performed while still an apprentice.

On 1 November 1825, Bennett undertook a six-hour comprehensive examination before the licensing committee of Ohio's Twelfth District Medical Society.[9] The twenty-one-year-old candidate presented as a thesis: "All applicants for a diploma granting plenary powers to practice Medicine and Surgery according to the laws of this State, should be examined by the Censors and, if found qualified, be received into full membership without regard to the time of study."[10] This radical proposition failed. Nevertheless he was licensed and made a member of the society.

Sometime soon after his licensing as a doctor, Bennett married a young woman who was a native of Plymouth, Massachusetts.[11] In 1826, he was residing in and practicing medicine in St. Clairsville, Belmont County, Ohio, only about ten miles from the bustling metropolis of Wheeling, [West] Virginia. While there he was initiated an entered apprentice of the Belmont Lodge No. 16 of the Masonic Order.[12]

Just where he lived for the next couple of years is unknown, but later Bishop George Miller was to claim that he had lived in McConnelsville and Malta, Ohio, and Colesville, Pennsylvania. Perhaps he lived in some of those places then.

A new facet of his life emerged during this time. He later claimed to have been a Methodist preacher for three years. He must have begun his Methodist ministry during this period.

The year of 1829 found John C. Bennett residing in Circleville, Pickway County, Ohio, in the Scioto River Valley, some twenty-five miles south of Columbus. While at Circleville, he attempted to gain a charter for a Methodist university to be founded in the community, but was unsuccessful in his lobbying efforts with the Ohio Legislature.[13]

While Bennett was living in Circleville, he was a member of the Pickaway Lodge No. 23 of the Masonic Order.[14] The masonic historian, Joseph E. Morcombe,[15] claims that he was expelled from this lodge for unmasonic conduct, but the records of the Ohio Grand Lodge indicate that he "demitted" August 12, 1829. Since Bennett was later tried and convicted twice by different Church courts for adultery, it is possible that this may have been his problem if he was expelled. By this time, Bennett had begun to emphasize obstetrics and gynecology in his medical practice. Perhaps he fell to the temptations that other obstetricians have fallen to when treating attractive patients.

In 1830, Bennett left the Methodist faith and became a minister in the Disciples of Christ, led by Alexander Campbell. Another minister of this faith at that time was Sidney Rigdon. It has been claimed that Rigdon and Bennett knew each other as fellow Campbellite ministers.[16] If so, this acquaintance took place in 1830, before Rigdon's Fall 1830 conversion to Mormonism.

Some time in 1830, Bennett moved to Barnesville, Belmont County, Ohio, some fifteen or so miles from St. Clairsville, where he had lived in 1826. He became a partner of Dr. J. G. Affleck, a native of Scotland.

In 1830, he again attempted to found a university. This time it was to be a Christian university.[17] Again he failed in his lobbying efforts. He was of the wrong political party. He was a Jacksonian Democrat while the legislative majority were Whigs.

Just what happened in John C. Bennett's life in the fall of 1830 and early 1831 is a little confusing. He was supposed to have legally established residence in Wheeling, [West] Virginia, on 1 October 1830, and then immediately traveled to Montreal, Canada, to attend a medical school session at McGill University which lasted through early January, 1831.[18] But, on 3 December 1830, he was affiliated with the Friendship Lodge No. 89 in Barnesville, Ohio.[19] This was in spite of his alleged sentence of expulsion from the Pickaway Lodge. Either Bennett hid the fact of his expulsion and the lodge accepted him, remembering his previous membership with the neighboring St. Clairsville Lodge, or later Masonic historians, and Bishop George Miller who examined his background after his Nauvoo fiasco, were wrong about his expulsion. To increase the confusion, the records of the Grand Lodge of Ohio meeting at Columbus on January 3-5, 1831, record his presence as a representative of the Friendship Lodge of Barnesville.[20] He was appointed Grand Chaplain, but did not attend the next annual Grand Lodge communication because he no longer was a resident of Ohio. Therefore Bennett's claim to have attended McGill University becomes rather questionable unless another date can be established.

On January 27, 1831, the Virginia legislature in Richmond received a document in Doctor Bennett's handwriting.[21] It was a memorial bearing the signatures of eighty-eight men petitioning for the authority to incorporate Wheeling University, with authority to establish a medical school. It is not clear whether or not Bennett was a lobbyist for the measure, but it is probable that he was. On 23 March 1831, the Virginia General Assembly enacted a bill incorporating the university to be located in the city of Wheeling, which with a population of 5,000 whites was the second largest Virginia community, exceeded in size only by Richmond.

Bennett was not one of the incorporators or trustees, possibly because he had not resided in Virginia long enough to acquire citizenship. The St. Clairsville Gazette, however, proudly proclaimed, "Dr. Bennett has succeeded in establishing a college at Wheeling by an act of the legislature of Virginia." Ten weeks later, it reported that he had established the Wheeling Eye and Ear Infirmary. Seven weeks later is contained an announcement that "Dr. J. C. Bennett has been appointed Professor of Obstetrics and President of the Washington Medical College of Virginia." (The term "president" was then often applied in medical faculties to the office now occupied by a dean.) Dr. Frederick C. Waite, who was a fascinated student of the life of John C. Bennett, was unable to establish whether or not classes were ever held at the Wheeling medical school. Waite claimed that Doctor Bennett left Wheeling in late 1832, after Bennett's correspondence with Rev. Alexander Campbell had included Bennett's opinion that his efforts to found the institution were a failure.

As Bennett left Wheeling, he began an activity that was to brand him as one of the most controversial doctors of the first half of the nineteenth century. He moved to New Albany, Indiana, across the Ohio River from Louisville, Kentucky. In January, 1833, he was able to shepherd an act through the Indiana legislature that chartered a Christian College at New Albany. He was named as the first president of the institution.[22]

The incorporators organized as trustees in Bennett's home in New Albany. They proposed to organize seven departments and to authorize conferring eight different kinds of degrees on males and seven on females. Waite has noted that since their charter antedates that of Oberlin by more than a year, it was therefore the first chartered college in the United States that planned to be co-educational.

Sometime between 24 January and 5 March 1833, the college trustees decided to use a different name. A clipping from a New Albany paper states:

> University of Indiana
> At New Albany
> Ordinance No. 4
>
> Be it ordained by the Christian College that the Christian College is the name of the Corporation or Trustees of the University located at New Albany, Indiana only; and not the University itself; whereas the Institution under the supervision of the Christian College or Board of Trustees is recognized in the charter as "the University," that is "the University of Indiana at New Albany."[23]

Three forms of the new name are recorded: University of New Albany (Christian College); University at New Albany, Indiana; and University of Indiana. This institution has no connection whatever with the present Indiana University.

Another New Albany newspaper clipping, dated 31 May 1833, contained the following statement:

Medical College of Indiana
The lectures will commence in this institution in this place upon the first Monday in November next. Professor Riddell is expected to deliver a popular course of lectures in addition to his regular course in the college. Dr. Bennett is expected to go East in a few days to procure some anatomical preparations for the College and to make arrangements for the University in general.[24]

It was the activities of Dr. Bennett on that trip that made the school controversial.

On 5 March 1833, forty days after the charter had been granted, Dr. Bennett issued a degree of Doctor of Medicine. It is evident that no course of instruction deserving the earned degree of Doctor of Medicine could be given in forty days.[25] Even had Bennett been giving private lectures before 24 January, it is inconceivable that he could have given a sufficient number of them since his move to New Albany.

Bennett's 1825 licensing thesis had risen to the surface again. He had some radical ideas on medical education of his era. One was opposition to the traditional period of three full calendar years of study of medicine required before one might be licensed to practice medicine. He later wrote, "The requirement of a specified term of study is from purely mercenary considerations."[26] He evidently considered himself capable of independent medical practice before his three years of study under his preceptor had been completed. If he could do it, others could also.

As Dr. Bennett traveled East, he met with persons who desired medical degrees and awarded them to them. Later he would write the philosophy he now espoused: "Now no board of examinators [sic] have an equitable right to make more than one demand, and that is 'is the applicant qualified.' "[27] Bennett claimed that he "thoroughly examined all but those generally allowed to be qualified."[28] He awarded many diplomas based on those examinations.

Although he frequently conducted examinations alone, in New York City in the summer of 1833 he called two members of the county medical society to help him. The society later publicly censured these members for that action.

The names of only six recipients of the medical degree of the University of Indiana have been positively identified. Six more men are probably, although not certainly, identified as receiving this degree. Waite says that "seemingly reliable evidence shows the issue of a large number of diplomas, although a conjecture as to the probable number is not warranted by the meager evidence discovered."[29]

Although until this point Bennett's sole training had been in the heroic, or orthodox school, he was practicing in a hotbed of botanic medicine. One of his stops in New York was at the New York Reformed Medicine School. This school, founded by Dr. Wooster Beech, was the font of learning of one of the first and major offshoots from Thomson's botanic medicine. (That it was an offshoot from Thomsonianism was later to be vigorously denied by reformed medical practitioners and those of its successors—American eclectic medicine.) Bennett was to later proudly publish the wording of the M.D. Degree conferred on him by Beech 17 August 1833, but for now he kept the knowledge to himself.[30] The only difference was he began to sign papers John Cook Bennett, M.D. instead of Dr. John Cook Bennett. This was in compliance with the tradition in America that anyone could call himself doctor, but only those with a conferred degree used the initials "M.D."

On the diplomas issued by the New Albany school, Bennett invariably signed "John Cook Bennett, M.D., L.L.D., Chancellor." Waite, lacking any other evidence of a source for the medical and law degrees, has conjectured that Bennett arranged to award himself a doctor of medicine and a doctor of laws degree from New Albany.[31]

In 1834, the community of Chagrin, Ohio, only some five miles from Kirtland, had visions of rivalling its neighbor on the west, Cleveland, in size and commerce. One of the ways that it planned to establish itself was to establish a university in the community. Many of the town's settlers had come from the vicinity of Fairfield Medical College in central New York, where Doctor Wastel Willoughby was president. Hoping that by using his name they would be placed in his will, and that his name would draw support from Fairfield graduates, they sought and received from the Ohio legislature a charter for the Willoughby University of Lake Erie.[32] In December, 1834, the town changed its name to Willoughby.

On 16 August 1834, John Cook Bennett became president (dean) of the medical school faculty of Willoughby University. Finally Bennett had a school that taught a session, but Bennett's actions drew severe criticism and he was fired, along with most of his faculty, shortly after the end of that first session.

Since Chagrin was only five miles from Kirtland, he undoubtedly became better acquainted with the Mormons. If he knew Sidney Rigdon from 1830 when they were both Campbellite ministers, this allowed them to renew that acquaintance. If they did not know each other in 1830, they undoubtedly became well acquainted during Bennett's Chagrin stay. It is probable that he also became acquainted with Joseph Smith at this time.[33]

1835 and 1836 are another blank in the life story of John C. Bennett. Some time after he saw Sidney Rigdon in Chagrin, and before he moved to Illinois, he deserted his wife and children. Bishop Miller was to later say he deserted them in Pennsylvania, but just where is not now known. Another charge was that he had deserted his wife and children at McConnellsville, Ohio. Bennett showed up in Nauvoo sans wife and children.

In 1837, Bennett did two things, one of which was designed by him to draw attention to himself and flatter his vanity. That year, while he was residing in Big Hocking, Athens County, Ohio, he had a Buffalo, New York, printer produce a small thirty-two-page booklet, only 3½ by 5 inches in size, titled *The Accoucher's Vade Mecum*. This booklet attempted to describe the hows of child delivery. In it he began a practice he was soon to become a master of, the publication of solicited laudatory praise of himself. This booklet is now very rare, with known copies only in the Western Reserve Historical Society Library and the New York Academy of Medicine Library.

The second thing he did in 1837 he kept to himself for eight years before publishing.[34] On 4 February 1837, he purchased a patent to practice Thomsonian medicine, the grandfather sect of botanic medicine. In a period of bitter rivalry between schools of medical practice, it is very strange that John Cook Bennett tried to belong to all of the rival camps.

Sometime in 1838, Dr. Bennett made yet another move, this time to Fairfield, Wayne County, in southeastern Illinois. By 1839, he had become the commanding officer of the Invincible Dragoons, a multicounty brigade of the Illinois militia.[35] This appears to be his first military experience, but he began his military occupation as a brigadier general!

At this time Bennett wrote to Joseph Smith and Sidney Rigdon. Governor Lilburn Boggs of Missouri had issued his infamous extermination order and the saints were fleeing from Missouri while the prophet and Rigdon were languishing in Liberty Jail. As B. H. Roberts says, "John C. Bennett expressed himself very pronouncedly against the injustice suffered by the church at the hands of the officers and people of that state; and he 'proffered his military knowledge and prowess' to the saints . . . His proposal was to go to their assistance with all the forces he could raise in Illinois, as 'his bosom swelled with indignation' at the treatment the saints were receiving at the hands of the Missourians."[36] Bennett's offer was not accepted, however.

A year later, Bennett had apparently decided to set his star in the Mormon firmament. He dispatched two letters to Commerce (soon to be Nauvoo) from Fairfield, one on 25 July 1840, and the other two days later, on 27 July 1840. He followed up with still another letter dated 30 July 1840. He stated his desire to join with the Mormons, and informed them of his appointment as Quartermaster General of all the Illinois militia. He also reported his resignation as Brigadier General of the Invincible Dragoons, saying that it was so that he could be with them. Joseph Smith replied with a letter inviting him to Nauvoo, but painting a rather gloomy picture of his financial prospects should be come.[37]

In August, 1840, Dr. Bennett moved to Nauvoo, and on September 1 he was baptized as a member. Three weeks later, on 21 September, he received a patriarchal blessing from Hyrum Smith, who had only a few months before succeeded his father, Joseph Smith, Sr., as patriarch to the Church. A part of his blessing said: "Beloved brother, if thou art faithful, thou shalt have power to heal the sick; cause the lame to leap like a hart; the deaf to hear; and the dumb to speak, and their voices shall salute thine ears; thy soul shall be made glad and thy heart shall rejoice in God."[38]

In the October general conference of 1840, Bennett was assigned to a committee to draw up measures to be presented to the Illinois legislature in order to incorporate the city on Nauvoo.[39] Joseph Smith and Bennett drew up a charter based upon that of Springfield, which had passed the legislature the previous year. The major differences were provisions for the Nauvoo Legion and the University of the City of Nauvoo. In December, Bennett went to Springfield to lobby for the measures, where he secured the help of Secretary of State Stephen A. Douglas and other prominent politicians. The acts were passed unanimously, one of nine municipal incorporations passed that year by the legislature. Bennett came home to Nauvoo triumphant, and during the first few days of February, 1841, was rewarded by a grateful populace by being elected to three positions—mayor, major general of the legion, and chancellor of the university.

On 19 January 1841, shortly after Bennett's triumphal return from Springfield, Joseph Smith received a revelation which said, "Again, let my servant John C. Bennett help you in your labor in sending my word to the kings and people of the earth, and stand by you, even you my servant Joseph Smith, in the hour of affliction; and his reward shall not fail *if he receive counsel.* And for his love he shall be great, for he shall be mine *if he do this,* saith the Lord. I have seen the work which he hath done, which I accept *if he continue,* and will crown him with blessings and great glory." (D&C 124:16-17, italics added.)

On 8 April 1841, as the sustaining of general officers of the Church took place during general conference, Sidney Rigdon stood and proposed that John C. Bennett be sustained as "assistant president" in the First Presidency until Rigdon's health should improve. It has since been questioned whether or not the prophet Joseph knew in advance of Rigdon's proposal. Bennett was at the time boarding in the Rigdon home. There was no public objection by Joseph, and Bennett was unanimously sustained.

Concerning the situation which soon developed regarding Dr. Bennett, Joseph was later to say, "Soon after it was known that he had become a member of said church, a communication was received at Nauvoo from a person of respectable character and residing in the vicinity where Bennett had lived. The letter cautioned us against him, setting forth that he was a very mean man, and had a wife and two or three children in McConnellsville,

Morgan County, Ohio; but knowing that it is no uncommon thing for good men to be evil spoken against, the above letter was kept quiet, but held in reserve."[40]

Shortly after Bennett arrived in Nauvoo, he began to keep company with a young Nauvoo lady who knew nothing of his having a living wife. She began to expect him to marry her, and he gave her to understand that he would. Knowing of Bennett's marital situation, Joseph Smith called him in an privately counseled him, threatening to expose him if he did not desist. To outward appearance the counseling had the desired effect, and the acquaintance between Bennett and the young lady was broken off.[41]

In June, 1841, most of the Quorum of the Twelve returned to Nauvoo from their mission to Great Britain. Later, Bennett would claim that his Nauvoo troubles began then, and that Brigham Young, John Taylor, and Willard Richards were the source of them. It undoubtedly was a shock to the Twelve to return from their mission to find two new counselors in the First Presidency, and the one remaining old counselor almost totally inactive. At least one of the Twelve found a wife who had been taught a strange new doctrine of spiritual wifery by President Bennett.

It is not now known if Joseph Smith ever taught John C. Bennett anything regarding the doctrine of eternal marriage, which was not to be put down into writing for another two years, and was not to be announced to the world for twelve years. It is, however, in view of Joseph Smith's knowledge of Bennett's moral weaknesses, highly unlikely that he did. But Bennett was an astute observer, and in view of the nearly accurate (but significantly incorrect) exposes he would later make, he obviously had a garbled idea of what was taking place. It was this garbled idea that he propounded and secretively practiced, a doctrine that Church leaders had the right to free love with any Church female member.

Joseph Smith chose to introduce the apostles to the doctrine of eternal marriage shortly after their return. It was a hard pill to swallow, and the apostle whose wife had been taught the garbled teaching of Bennett choked on the doctrine, but he soon returned to the Church and the quorum.

Meanwhile Hyrum Smith and William Law, in July, 1841, wrote a letter to Joseph Smith from Pittsburgh, Pennsylvania, confirming the fact that Bennett did have a wife and children in McConnellsville, Ohio. When the letter was read to Bennett he acknowledged that it was true.[42] Shortly after he took a non-lethal dose of arsenic, feigning suicide. Apparently, however, his moral standards did not improve, and he continued to teach his style of spiritual wifery and free love, including copious use of brothels.

Bennett's Church assignments virtually disappeared. Part of the reason may have been the assumption of responsibilities by the Quorum of the Twelve. But Bennett continued full speed on his non-Church responsibilities. He had ditches dug to drain the swamps of Nauvoo and vicinity. He advocated the use of tomatoes as an anti-ague (malaria) medication.[43] He established public schools under the framework of the university, although the university itself would not teach classes while he was chancellor. And most apparent to the jittery non-Mormon neighbors of Nauvoo, he organized and effectively trained the most efficient military force then in the United States, the twenty-three company Nauvoo Legion.

In January, 1842, an order was issued that the Nauvoo Legion would have a parade, review, and sham battle on Saturday, 7 May 1842. For the next three months the militia prepared for the event. As the time neared for the event, General Bennett proposed that he command one cohort and General Smith the other cohort during the sham battle. Joseph Smith said that the spirit whispered a warning to him, and he declined the invitation. General Bennett then asked him to take his position behind the cavalry without having his staff with him. Captain A. P. Rockwood, commander of General Smith's life guard, counteracted that request. Joseph recorded in his journal, "And if General Bennett's true feelings toward me are not made manifest to the world in a very short time, then it may be possible that the gentle breathings of that Spirit, which whispered to me on parade, that there was mischief concealed in that sham battle, were false; a short time will determine the point."[44]

Matters developed rapidly after the sham battle. Ten days later Bennett resigned as mayor of Nauvoo. Two days later Joseph Smith was elected mayor in his place by the city council. Bennett's "evil and corrupt manner of life" had caught up with him and the town had risen in indignation. The day of his resignation, Bennett went before Daniel H. Wells, a non-Mormon alderman of Nauvoo, and made an affidavit in which he exhonerated Joseph Smith of Bennett's previous claims that the prophet was the source of Bennett's teachings.[45]

That day Bennett also asked Joseph Smith for permission to withdraw his name from the Church records, to which Joseph agreed, and a certificate to that effect was issued by James Sloan, General Church Clerk and Recorder.[46]

On May 19, a special session of the city council was held as Bennett tried to exhonerate himself before the council. In the midst of the session Bennett said, "I know what I am about, and the heads of the Church know what they are about, I expect; I have no difficulty with the heads of the Church. I publicly avow that any one who has said that I have stated that General Joseph Smith has given me authority to hold illicit intercourse with women is a liar in the face of God. Those who have said it are damned liars; they are infernal liars." Later in the meeting he was to say of Joseph Smith, "In all my intercourse with General Smith, in public and in private, he has been strictly virtuous."[47]

On Wednesday, 25 May 1842, the First Presidency, Twelve, and Bishops met as a court and disfellowshipped John C. Bennett, in compliance with his request to have his name removed from the records. Bennett was so notified, but publication of notice of the action was not made at Bennett's request.[48]

The next day the Nauvoo Lodge of the Masons, of which Bennett had been a major organizer, met to hear Bennett's case. Dr. Bennett acknowledged his wicked and licentious conduct toward certain females in Nauvoo, and begged the lodge that he might be spared chastisement. Joseph Smith recorded that he had plead for mercy for Bennett.[49] George Miller, the master of the lodge, was assigned to investigate Bennett's life before action was taken. That investigation confirmed the facts of Bennett's desertion of his wife and family, numerous cases of adultery throughout his life, and also reported that he had been previously expelled from the Pickaway Lodge in Circleville, Ohio.[50] He had thus been under sentence of expulsion from that lodge and therefore had not been a legal member of the Nauvoo Lodge. On 23 June 1842, Dr. John Cook Bennett was expelled from the Nauvoo Lodge as an illegal member and for unmasonic conduct. On 8 August 1842, the Illinois Grand Lodge confirmed the action of the Nauvoo Lodge.[51]

Although Joseph Smith and the Church had met Dr. Bennett's request for confidentiality regarding his actions and disfellowshipment, the Nauvoo Masonic Lodge and the Illinois Grand Lodge published announcements of his expulsion. Bennett could see no difference between the Church and Lodge since the highest ranking Church members were also lodge members. After the 26 May 1842 masonic hearings, even before Bishop Miller's investigation was completed, a bitter, angry Doctor Bennett fled Nauvoo determined on reprisal.

Bennett went first to Springfield and wrote a series of bitterly anti-Mormon articles that were published by the *Sangamo Journal.* Then he made a quick trip back to Nauvoo to gather anti-Mormon affidavits from apostates, disgruntled members, and his own followers. Then he started for New York, lecturing along the way about the so-called evils of Mormonism.

By the time he reached New York City, Bennett had nearly completed his *The History of the Saints, or An Expose of Joe Smith and the Mormons.* In this book he spent over fifty pages attempting to justify himself with narrative and copious solicited personal references, many of which dated back fifteen and sixteen years, to long before he became a controversial figure. He also published in the book, without acknowledgement, all of the notorius *Mormonism Unvailed* [sic] from Painsville, Ohio, and much of the apostate writings of John Corrill. He tried to gather together every anti-Mormon work published until that time.

Bennett continued on the lecture circuit, capitalizing on the notoriety of his book. Among the places he stopped were St. Louis and Independence, Missouri, where he tried to persuade ex-governor Lillburns Boggs to level charges against Joseph Smith. When the steam ran out of his anti-Mormon diatribes, and people stopped buying his book and paying for his lectures, he moved to Plymouth, Massachusetts, where his wife's parents lived.[52] Did he become reconciled with his wife? Why did he move to her parents home town? These are unanswered questions that future study may possibly answer. At any rate, Bennett used Plymouth, Massachusetts, as his home base until nearly 1860—with a few notable absences.

In the spring of 1844, Dr. Bennett began a new phase of his life. Some years before, Dr. Alva Curtis had broken with Dr. Samuel Thomson, the founder of the botanic medical school of practice. He had edited several Thomsonian journals. Curtis founded a botanic, or neo-Thomsonian school of medicine in Columbus, Ohio, which had moved to Cincinnati before 1844. Dr. Curtis hired John C. Bennett as Professor of Midwifery and Diseases Peculiar to Women and Children for his Botanico-Medical School of Ohio.[53] With that action, Bennett was once again to be considered a heretic by the old school of medicine (heroic or orthodox medicine). But Bennett's bitterest opponents were from the reformed school of medicine that Wooster Beech had created from botanic medicine, a school that was already beginning to be called America's school of eclectic medicine. In July, 1845, a dispute between Dr. T. V. Morrow of Cincinnati's Eclectic Medical Institute and Dr. Bennett was aired in the pages of the *Western Medical Reformer* and Dr. Curtis' *Botanico-Medical Recorder.* Morrow resurrected charges that Bennett had peddled worthless medical diplomas from his "diploma mill" at New Albany, Indiana. Bennett rejoined, "Now I never conferred the Degree of the Doctorate of Medicine ILLEGALLY in my life, and I am not aware that I ever conferred more than one that was UNDESERVED, and that one, WHICH IS YET UNPAID FOR!! was on THOMAS VAUGHN MORROW!!! Yes, it is true that I made *Thomas Vaughn Morrow* an M.D. of the OLD SCHOOL; and that is the whole secret of his OLD SCHOOL *Degree and Diploma! Sic transit gloria mundi.*"[54]

Bennett remained with the Botanico-Medical College until 28 March 1846, when he resigned because he had "received an offer from the north, under date of March 9th, of a highly honorable character, which, in justice to myself, I cannot refuse to accept."[55]

This "highly honorable offer from the north" was from James J. Strang to become a counselor in the First Presidency of the "Church of Jesus Christ of Latter Day Saints," which Strang was presiding over.

In the turmoil that followed Joseph Smith's and Hyrum Smith's assassinations, Sidney Rigdon rushed from Pittsburgh, Pennsylvania, to Nauvoo to claim the guardianship of the Church. On the way he evidently had stopped at Cincinnati and picked up John C. Bennett, for Bennett also appeared claiming that he had a sealed envelope that Joseph Smith had given him to care for, the letter to be opened only upon the prophet's death. The contents stated that Rigdon should be guardian of the Church. With the arrival of the Quorum of the Twelve, Rigdon's claims and Bennett's support were discounted. Bennett went back to Cincinnati.

Shortly after the Rigdon claims, a recent convert to the Church, who recently had been authorized to establish a stake of the Church in Voree, Wisconsin, interpreted this authorization to be a mandate to be president of the whole Church. James J. Strang soon gathered several hundred members of the Church that did not wish to follow the Twelve. Among them were two who had been apostles, John E. Page and William Smith, the prophet's brother. James J. Strang had become the major challenger to the succession of the Twelve to the leadership of the Church.

Just when Strang and Bennett began to correspond is not known, but seven letters from Bennett to Strang written in March, 1846, are in the archives of the Beineke Library of Yale University.[56] In one of them Bennett says, "You have inspired me with new life and vigor. . . . For about four years past I have not been myself, for my spirits have been depressed and gloomy, but I have felt like a young lion let loose ever since I heard of your glorious movement. While you will be the Moses of the last days, I hope to be your Joshua, my old position, your General-in-chief. . . . I have loved the Church for many years. I love it now. I shall devote all my energies to revive it."

Bennett went to Voree in late April and was there in early May, 1846. He returned to Plymouth in late May, but was back in Voree in July. In August he was in Burlington, Vermont. He had returned to Voree in time for the October, 1846, semi-annual conference.

The Beineke Library archives contain the minutes of a high council court of the Strangite church dated 4 October 1846. The court excommunicated Bennett for adultery and violation of the laws of chastity. However, Bennett continued to act as a counselor in the presidency of Strang's church. Evidently Strang overruled his high council court. In the next few months Strang and Bennett introduced the "Order of the Illuminati" in the church. Also started was a limited practice of plural marriage, which caused a measure of apostasy from the Strang church.

In the October, 1847, conference of the Strang church, Strang accused Bennett of apostasy. The charges were:
1. Suppressing letters addressed to President Strang.
2. Giving instructions to Saints, purporting to be by the authority of the First Presidency, which were entirely unauthorized, and directly contrary to their known instructions and settled policy.
3. Teaching unsound doctrines.[57]

Bennett was finally expelled from Strang's church.

After this excommunication, Bennett returned to Plymouth, Massachusetts, where he apparently lived until about 1860. He was involved in the manufacture of drugs and the practice of medicine. He began to raise exotic chickens and other fowl. In late 1849, he promoted what may have been the first poultry show in the United States. In 1850, Bennett published a 320-page book which claimed to be a *vade mecum* for poultry growers. It was titled, *The Poultry Book: A Treatise on Breeding and General Management of Domestic Fowls; With Numerous Original Descriptions, and Portraits from Life.* He also has been credited with developing the "Plymouth Rock" breed of chicken.[58]

Bennett began to specialize in dental medicine and invented the dental forceps. He also became an early user of ether anesthesia in his dental surgery.[59]

In December, 1849, Bennett renewed his correspondence with James J. Strang, and the letters read as though he had never been excommunicated. The correspondence continued until Strang was killed by a disgruntled follower.[60]

Just when Bennett moved to Polk City, Iowa, is unknown, but he was living there and practicing medicine and breeding poultry, sheep, and cattle when he took occasion to write to Joseph Smith III, who had just accepted the presidency of the Reorganized church. In that letter he stated that he was still adhering to the Gospel principles and believed strongly in the Church. He stated that he wanted to cooperate with Joseph and that he had lands to give the church. However, he wanted the transactions secret and Joseph objected to his overture.[61]

As the Civil War broke out in 1861, he promoted the organization of the 10th Iowa Infantry, but in this army he was only a major, not a major general. In 1865, he entered the army as Surgeon-in-Field with the staff of the 3rd United States Infantry.

He died 5 August 1867, and an eight-foot stone monument was placed on his grave at the Polk City Cemetery.[62] An 1868 issue of the *Juvenile Instructor* described his last days:

> ... For some years before his death he had fits, which were very violent; he also partially lost the use of his limbs and his tongue. [A classic description of a stroke victim.] It was difficult for him to make himself understood. He dragged out a miserable existance, without a person scarcely to take the least interest in his fate, and died a few months ago without a person to mourn his departure. . . .[63]

On 25 December 1869, Joseph Rich wrote to Edward Hunter (then Presiding Bishop of the Church) that Bennett had died a "vagabond on the earth."[64]

This remarkable man had his strongest impact upon the administration of the Church and city of Nauvoo. He unleashed the forces that led to the assassination of Joseph and Hyrum Smith, teaching into apostasy several of those who directly participated in that assassination. For several years he spearheaded the opposition in the world to the Church. But medically he made Nauvoo a liveable place, planned the organization of a board of health and worked to overcome other health problems that were to continue with the Church membership for many years.

It has been said that he was "ambitious and vainglorious in the most disturbing sense of the word. His inherent drive was for eagerly anticipated personal recognition, the plaudits and deference of those about him, and his elevation to high places of influence, authority and power . . . He was indescribably conceited and adept at name dropping . . . It is a pity that John Cook Bennett couldn't consistently and honestly direct his inherited talent and ability to positive and constructive ends."[65]

Chapter Seven

Joseph Smith And The Doctors

More than a dozen doctors had major impacts upon the life of the Prophet Joseph Smith, Jr. These doctors are nearly evenly divided between doctors of the old school (orthodox or heroic) and the botanic school of medicine. One of these doctors started out in the old school but also was affiliated with the botanic school at least part of his life.

Three of these doctors affected his life from a distance, and there is no evidence that he ever personally met them. But nonetheless they made an impact upon his life.

The first of these three was Dr. Samuel Latham Mitchill, whose closest relationship to the prophet was non-medical. He was the doctor to whom Martin Harris took the copies of the Book of Mormon characters. Because of Dr. Mitchill's reputation as a walking encyclopedia, and his knowledge of the American Indian, he was the natural person for Martin Harris to go to. He also had an indirect impact upon the prophet and his family in a medical way. Most of othe doctors in western upstate New York were disciples of the heroic medicine advocated by Mitchill. He may well have been partially responsible for the death of Alvin Smith, the prophet's oldest brother. (More about Dr. Mitchill is in Chapters One and Two.)

The second of these three is the botanic doctor, Dr. Samuel Thomson. Dr. Thomson was the father of botanic medicine and his teachings were in large part accepted by Joseph Smith. Many of the prophet's associates were Thomsonian practitioners, and the prophet utilized Thomsonian medicine during the last half of his life. (More about Dr. Thomson is in Chapter One.)

The third of these three that Joseph Smith never met personally, so far as is known, is Dr. John Sappington. Without Dr. Sappington, Nauvoo could not have existed as the gathering place of the Church. His anti-fever pills made possible settlement in the community when malaria might otherwise have destroyed the settlement. (More about Dr. Sappington is in Chapter Five.)

Two other doctors treated Joseph Smith and/or his family, but did not become associated with The Church of Jesus Christ of Latter-day Saints.

The first of these two was one of the great luminaries of American medicine, one of the first great surgeons of America, a founder of five medical schools. He was the only man in America, and probably the entire world, who could have saved Joseph's leg when he had osteomyelitis. Dr. Nathan Smith miraculously was only five miles away when he was needed. (More about Dr. Smith is in Chapter Two.)

The second of these two was Dr. Alexander M'Intyre (or McIntyre). A quiet small-town doctor, McIntyre is now almost completely unknown. His sole point of prominence is that, as the Smith family doctor, he was not available when Alvin Smith became sick, and he returned in time to helplessly watch Alvin die. He was thus at the event that turned the Smiths to botanic medicine. (The little that is known about him is written in Chapter Two.)

The other eight doctors all affiliated with the Church, although five of them left the Church before Joseph's death. One of the five returned to the Church before his and Joseph's deaths. The other three doctors remained faithful to the Church until their own deaths. Of the eight doctors who joined the Church, two became members of the First Presidency, and one became an apostle and chief scribe to the prophet. Another became a secretary to, and close associate of, the prophet; and another the prophet's personal physician. One became land agent for the Church with the prophet's power of attorney. Another organized a para-military organization to protect the Church. And one was given responsibility for the educational programs within Nauvoo. All of them received influential positions in the Latter-day Saint community, and most became at one time close friends of Joseph Smith.

The first, and most influential of them, especially during the first decade of the Church, was Frederick Granger Williams. This botanic physician maintained a close friendship with Joseph Smith until Williams' death. It was marred only by one disagreement in 1837, which soon was healed. Dr. Williams became a counselor in the First Presidency, which strengthened even more his relationships with the prophet. Although theirs was primarily a religious association, it is apparent that Dr. Williams taught Joseph much of the botanic medical beliefs. Although Dr. Williams was dropped from the First Presidency in 1837 and was excommunicated in 1839 while Joseph was in Liberty Jail, he was restored to full membership soon after the prophet escaped. (More on Dr. Williams is in Chapter Three.)

The second of the eight was Dr. Sampson Avard. He was born on 23 October, year unknown, in St. Peter's Parish, Isle of Guernsey, of the Channel Islands off the coast of France.[1] Sometime prior to 1835, he migrated to the United States and settled at Freedom, Beaver County, Pennsylvania. He there was engaged for a time as a Campbellite preacher. He also had acquired the title "doctor," probably through purchase of a Thomsonian patent and book, as thousands of others were doing.

It is entirely possible that Sidney Rigdon and Sampson Avard may have been personally acquainted prior to Avard's joining the Church, since both came from the same area of Pennsylvania and were Campbellite ministers.

On 14 October 1835, Elder Orson Pratt left Kirtland, Ohio, on a mission. His account of the mission states, "Started on a mission to the Ohio River, preaching by the way; tarried two or three weeks in Beaver County, Penn.; held sixteen meetings, baptized a few and raised up a small branch of the Church, and ordained Dr. Sampson Avard an elder, to take charge of them, and then returned to Kirtland." Elder Pratt, in a report published in the Church's newspaper, the *Messenger and Advocate* in November, 1835, said that he "baptized three in Freedom, Pennsylvania, one of whom (Sampson Avard) I ordained an elder . . . After parting with two Books of Mormon; four books of Revelations, and obtaining 14 subscriptions for the 'Messenger and Advocate,' I left them with Elder Avard to continue the work. There is a prospect of many embracing the gospel in these parts."[2]

After Elder Pratt left, Dr. Avard did some missionary work near his home with Elder Erastus Snow. About this time Brigham Young's brother, Lorenzo Dow Young, was also engaged in missionary work in that vicinity and came in contact with Avard, who was still presiding over the branch at Freedom, Pennsylvania. Elder Young became disturbed at some of Avard's teachings and wrote that he "did not like the spirit or the teachings of the man." Later he claimed that he had discovered that the doctor and Sidney Rigdon were on quite intimate terms, and that Rigdon was "considerably tinctured" with the ideas and spirit of Avard. When Lorenzo Young reported to the First Presidency on his mission, he spoke of his reaction to Avard, whereupon President Rigdon allegedly showed his displeasure and criticized him for his remarks. The Prophet Joseph Smith is said to have encouraged Lorenzo with his report. At the end of it he said, "Give Avard time and he will prove that he is a consumate hypocrite and wicked man."[3]

Avard moved to Kirtland late in 1836. He received a patriarchal blessing from Joseph Smith, Sr. One year later, during the troubled time of apostacy at Kirtland, Avard's license as a high priest was revoked. B. H. Roberts asserts that Avard had gone to Canada at the behest of the "apostates" in Kirtland who wished to replace John Taylor, who was presiding in Canada, with someone less loyal to Joseph Smith. Avard presented false credentials, claiming that he had been appointed president in Taylor's place. The prophet is said to have severely rebuked Avard for his action and that is why Avard lost his license. Whether or not the license was ever renewed is unknown.[4]

By June of 1838, Avard was in Far West. Shortly afterward, Sidney Rigdon gave his "Salt Sermon" in which he likened dissenters to "salt that has lost its savor." Over the next few months Avard, apparently with Sidney Rigdon's acquiescence, organized a para military secret society that came to be known as the Danites. Each member was required to take secret oaths and covenants. Joseph Smith once referred to the Danites as a secret combination, linking them to the satanic organizations mentioned in the Book of Mormon. Soon the Danites began to pilage the non-Mormon neighbors of the Church, thus helping to solidify the hatred against the Church, which led to the Missouri expulsion.

Avard surrendered to the Missourians shortly after the "Mormon War" of expulsion began, and he soon broke his Danite oaths and "told all." He alleged that Daniteism was an order of the Church and that he was merely acting under orders of the Mormon First Presidency. He also appeared before the Missouri courts as one of the primary witnesses against the Church and the prophet.

The Danites came to an end after only five months of existence.[5] But accusations of Danite horrors were to follow the Church for decades. Dr. Avard, himself, was excommunicated, with others who had apostasized during the Missouri troubles, by a Church court early in 1839.

Dr. Sampson Avard was one who brought great tribulation upon his fellow Latter-day Saints.

The third of those doctors that joined the Church was Dr. Isaac Galland. Isaac Galland, son of Matthew and Hannah Fenno Galland, was born 15 May 1791, in Somerset County, Pennsylvania. When he was born, his parents were enroute from Norfolk, Virginia, to Marietta, Ohio. Galland was raised in Marietta until he entered William and Mary College in Williamsburgh, Virginia, at age 13. About 1810, he and some friends traveled to the Spanish Southwest in search of gold and adventure. They found, instead, a year-long jail term in Santa Fe on charges of plotting against the Spanish government of Nuevo Mexico.[6]

Galland returned to Ohio and married Nancy Harris 22 March 1811. By 1816 he had married again, this time to Margaret Knight, and had settled in Washington County, Indiana. He was living in Owen County, Indiana, in 1820.[7]

In 1821, Samuel Thomson, Jr., came into the old Northwest peddling books and patent rights to use his father's medical system.[8] About this time Isaac Galland began to use the title "doctor" and it may be assumed that Galland purchased a Thomsonian right. Apparently Galland did not practice too much medicine in his life, only a few cases being remembered. His major medical accomplishment was to manufacture and market a medicine chest for home use—a chest stocked with mostly botanic remedies.

Soon Galland moved to Edgar County, Illinois, where Governor Thomas Ford later accused him of belonging to the "Massac gang" of outlaws. In 1824, he left his wife, Margaret, in Edgar County and moved to Horselick Grove (soon to be in Hancock County). On 5 October 1826, without having divorced Margaret, he married Hannah Kinney. He lived in several western Illinois and eastern Iowa communities until Hannah died on 17 March 1831. Two years later, 25 April 1833, he married Elizabeth Wilcox, sister of the commanding officer of the fort located where Warsaw, Illinois, would soon rise.[9]

In 1834, Galland ran unsuccessfully for the Iowa territorial legislature. He had already begun a notorious career as a land speculator. Many of his land dealings involved the Half Breed Tract, a 119,000-acre parcel of land lying between the Des Moines and Mississippi Rivers in the southeast corner of Iowa. This land had been set aside by Congress in 1824 as a reservation for the mixed-bloods of the Sac and Fox Indian tribes. In 1833, Congress allowed the half-breeds to sell tracts of their land, and land speculators rushed to buy the land for a pitance. Through a complex series of events, all the titles became legally clouded. Galland had acquired large interests in Half Breed Tract lands which he began to sell. He also acquired most of the plotted town of Commerce in Illinois, which was a largely unsuccessful development made so because of its malarial infestation. A more successful development of his was Keokuk, Iowa.

Galland's association with the Mormons began in late 1838 when he met, in Commerce, Israel Barlow, a Mormon refugee. Finding that the Mormons were looking for places to settle, he offered them parts of his Half Breed lands for very favorable terms.[10] In the coming months he dickered with them and wrote letters to Joseph Smith in Liberty Jail. Within less than two weeks of the prophet's escape from Missouri, he was in Commerce, Illinois, with a committee to choose a location for the Church to settle. Shortly thereafter the Church purchased $18,000 worth of Commerce property, and approximately 20,000 acres of Half Breed Tract lands, all on long-term contracts.

By June the saints were enroute to their new sanctuary, and on 3 July 1839, Isaac Galland was baptized and ordained an elder in the Church. The following day Galland and his family boarded a riverboat bound for Ohio. In his pocket was a power of attorney from Joseph Smith to transact land business for the Church. He purchased lands in the East, and also in Missouri, from Church members who were residing in or wanted to move to Commerce. The properties were taken as payment against the amount the Church owed Galland and Horace Hotchkiss, another Commerce land owner.

In March 1841, the prophet's brother, Hyrum, went East to assist Galland in making payments to Hotchkiss, but Hyrum took sick and had to return home before the business was consumated. Hotchkiss later claimed he was not paid. Meanwhile, Galland had taken in from members thousands of dollars worth of land. Galland was to leave Ohio for Nauvoo the latter part of July, 1841. Instead he went to Keokuk. There followed several letters between the prophet and Galland, Joseph seeking an accounting of the Church funds Galland had collected, but none was forthcoming. Finally, Joseph sent Brigham Young to retrieve his power of attorney, and Joseph published the fact that the power of attorney was no longer in force. In February, 1842, Galland finally met with the prophet.

No formal action was taken against Dr. Galland for any wrongdoing. Flanders says, "The conclusion of Galland's relations with the Church are left to conjecture. It is scarcely accurate to say that he 'fell from favor;' rather he seems to have been dropped from official cognizance . . . Galland soon withdrew his fellowship and boasted his conviction that Joseph Smith was a fraud."[11] After all, it was wisdom on the Church's part to not upset the man who held mortgages on much of Nauvoo and other places where the Saints were gathered.

Galland had been lauded by Joseph Smith as a benefactor of the Church. It had even been said by some that Galland was an instrument of the Lord sent when the Saints needed help. Certainly he still remains a question mark to the Latter-day Saints. Though he carried the title "doctor," there is no evidence that he ever practiced medicine among the Mormons.

Although Galland discontinued his life as an active Saint, he had constant association with Mormons, even visiting Salt Lake City in 1853. He died in Fort Madison, Iowa, at the age of sixty-seven, on 27 September 1855.[12]

In March, 1843, Dr. Galland wrote a letter to Joseph Smith, expressing his outrage at the actions of the fourth doctor in this group that had joined the Church and then left it. Galland was upset at the post-Church membership activities of Dr. John Cook Bennett.

John C. Bennett was a member of the Church for only twenty months, but during that time he became a counselor in the First Presidency, mayor of Nauvoo, second in command (as a Major General) of the Nauvoo Legion, and chancellor of the University of the City of Nauvoo. A brilliant man, as an apostate he turned his talents bitterly against Joseph Smith and the Church. He was a great help when he was a Saint, but he was considered to be a devil after he had left. (Chapter Six tells the story of Dr. John Cook Bennett.)

The fifth doctor in this group that joined, then apostatized from the Church, was one of the small group of men directly responsible for the deaths of Joseph and Hyrum Smith. Little is known about Dr. Robert D. Foster. He was a resident of Commerce in the fall of 1839 when he joined the Church, and may have lived there before the saints' arrival. He was ordained an elder during the October conference of the Church.[13]

Less than a month later, as Joseph Smith, Judge Elias Higbee, Sidney Rigdon, and O. P. Rockwell, their carriage driver, were traveling to Washington, D.C., to make appeals for redress of the Saints' Missouri grievances,

Sidney was sick. The party met Dr. Foster and he agreed to go along to medicate President Rigdon. While on the trip, the prophet found it necessary to rebuke Dr. Foster for his loose moral standards. Near Columbus, Ohio, the party split and Joseph Smith and Jodge Higbee went on ahead by stage coach, while Sidney Rigdon, Dr. Foster, and Porter rockwell went on at a slower pace as Rigdon's health allowed. They all eventually reached Washington, but the trip was to no avail.[14] Joseph asked Foster to keep a daily journal of the trip, but upon his return to Nauvoo Joseph was to record that "Dr. Foster failed me."[15] Foster, however, was made a member of the next April Conference's committee that prepared resolutions for conference vote regarding the trip.[16]

Foster was appointed to several community leadership positions in the next few months. He was made an "associate" on the board of the Nauvoo Agricultural and Manufacturing Association. He was also a regent of the University of the City of Nauvoo, and under direction of Dr. John C. Bennett, was placed in charge of the common schools of the community.

Foster, however, was soon charged before the Nauvoo High Council of use of abusive language to the Church's leaders. Five days before Christmas in 1840, Joseph Smith acquitted Foster of the charge. However, a year and a half later, Samuel H. Smith, another brother of the prophet, preferred the same charge against Foster.[17]

Foster had evidently been a major land owner in Nauvoo and vicinity from the beginning of the Mormon settlement, and by early 1843 he and his associates, William and Wilson Law, were prospering as their lands on the hill near the temple were selling well. The land owned by the Church on "the flats" was not moving because of the fear of "miasmas" that caused malaria. The Church was appealing for cooperation to help get it out of debt, but the real estate rivals ignored the appeals. That spring Joseph Smith refereed a land dispute involving Dr. Foster, and soon Foster proudly claimed to have given $1,000 toward construction of the Nauvoo House. Perhaps it was to slow down Foster's land sales and help the Church's financial position that in April Conference, 1843, Dr. Foster was called on a mission to Tioga County, New York.[18]

Dr. Foster had been a close associate of Dr. John C. Bennett prior to Bennett's excommunication and departure from Nauvoo to propagandize against the Church. It is evident that Foster had been taught the "spiritual wife" doctrine of Bennett, which allowed free intercourse by its adherents. The rupture of Dr. Foster's internal relationships with Joseph Smith and the Church occurred in April, 1844. The prophet called upon Foster to recant statements Foster had made against him. This confrontation, before the city council, was immediately followed by high council charges against Foster and the Law brothers. On 18 April 1844, they were excommunicated from the Church. John Taylor was to later say Foster was excommunicated for dishonesty, fraud, and falsehoods.[19]

One of the associates of Dr. Foster and the Law brothers was Augustine Spencer, who, after an argument, assaulted his brother, Orson Spencer. When the city marshall went to arrest Spencer he was with the Fosters and Laws, who, rather than assisting the marshall, assisted Spencer and prevented his arrest. This resulted in civil charges against Dr. Foster, and after a municipal court trial before Alderman William Marks, he was fined $100. On 10 May 1844, Dr. Foster, who had been Surgeon-in-Chief and Brevet Brigadier General in the Nauvoo Legion, was court martialed and cashiered from the Legion.[20]

Meanwhile, the Laws and Fosters had organized a "New Church" in opposition to the Latter-day Saints. Foster was made an apostle of the new church. They decided to publish a newspaper which would expose the so-called evils of the leadership of the Mormons. On the day Dr. Foster was court martialed the prospectus for the *Nauvoo Expositor* was published.[21]

Dimick B. Huntington made an attempt to reconcile the parties, especially Dr. Foster and Joseph Smith, and a visit was made by Dr. Foster and Huntington to the prophet, at which it appeared reconciliation might be possible, but the next day the prophet received a "saucy" letter from Foster, and the first issue of the *Nauvoo Expositor* was distributed.[22]

The ensuing destruction of the press of the *Expositor* under orders of the Nauvoo City Council, and resultant legal charges, led to the incarceration of Joseph Smith and Hyrum Smith in Carthage Jail, where they were assassinated by a mob. Willard Richards, who was in the jail when it was attacked, accused Dr. Foster of being a member of the death mob.[23]

Foster had the audacity to return to Nauvoo not long after the assassinations, but nine women met with him and requested that he leave the city. Over a year later, he came to Nauvoo on a boat and attempted to kidnap Jackson Redden, but failed.[24]

On 2 November 1845, Abraham C. Hodge stated that he had had a conversation with Dr. Foster about the Saints' move West. According to Hodge, Foster said, "Hodge, you are going west and I wish I was going among you, but it can't be so. I am the most miserable wretch that the sun shines upon. If I could relive eighteen months of my life I would be willing to sacrifice everything I have upon earth, my wife and child not excepted. I did love Joseph Smith more than any man that ever lived . . . I have not seen one moment's peace since that time."[25] Thus ends the Church chronicles of the doctor most nearly responsible for the death of the Prophet Joseph Smith.

Three doctors joined the Church and remained valiant members throughout their lives. Each became close friends of the Prophet Joseph Smith, and the three were with the prophet within hours of his assassination in Carthage

Jail. One of the three was actually in the jail and helped defend the prophet, witnessing the killing. Two of the three were brothers and cousins of the man who succeeded Joseph Smith as leader of the Mormons, Brigham Young.

The least known of these three was undoubtedly the best medically-trained and educated man of them. Joseph Smith respected this education and called upon him to live in his own home and be his confidant and advisor, as well as personal attache. After Smith's assassination, this doctor continued to play vital roles in the leadership of the Mormons, but strangely enough was never called to an ecclesiastical role after his close association with the prophet began.

John M. Bernhisel was born near Loysville, Cumberland County (later Perry County), Pennsylvania, of 23 June 1799. He was the oldest child of Samuel and Susan Bower Bernheisel. After his parents' deaths in 1817, John went to Philadelphia, where he studied medicine for two terms. He received a medical certificate in 1820 and moved to Harrisburg, nearer his home, to begin his medical practice. He did not remain there long, but began a series of moves that was to take him over much of America west of the Allegheny Mountains.[26]

By 1822, Bernhisel was practicing in Herculaneum, Missouri, on the Mississippi River, some thirty miles south of St. Louis. While there, he came down with a fever and had subsequent relapses. In all likelihood, it was the malaria endemic in this area. He spent time in Tennessee and Kentucky where he met Andrew Jackson and Henry Clay. He survived a steamboat sinking, and fought a yellow fever epidemic in Natchez, Mississippi.[27]

After more than four years in the West, Bernhisel returned to the University of Pennsylvania, where he studied medicine for two more years, graduating with a medical doctor degree in 1827. His thesis for the doctorate was on apoplexy. He was admitted as a member of the Philadelphia Medical Society the same year.[28]

By 1832, Bernhisel was living in New York City, where he was licensed by the Board of Physicians. He practiced there until the spring of 1843.[29]

It is not clear exactly when John Bernhisel became a Mormon, but serious L.D.S. missionary work in New York City began in 1837 under Parley P. Pratt's direction, and it is possible that he joined soon after the missionary work began. In April of 1841, Bernhisel was ordained a bishop in New York City. He was also appointed secretary of the New York Conference of the Church, which also included much of New England.[30]

In March of 1841, Bernhisel began a correspondence with Joseph Smith, with the intention of acquiring investment property for Bernhisel near Nauvoo. During the correspondence, Joseph Smith dropped broad hints that he hoped Bernhisel would move to Nauvoo soon. Finally, in the fall of 1842, members of the Quorum of the Twelve visited Dr. Bernhisel and convinced him that he was needed in Nauvoo.[31]

Bernhisel closed his medical practice in New York, and in April, 1843, moved to Nauvoo. The handsome bachelor was invited by the prophet to make his home with the Smiths in the newly-completed Mansion House. Bernhisel thus became a member of the Smith household, not just a guest in the hotel part of the Mansion House.[32]

Dr. Bernhisel did not enter into regular medical practice in Nauvoo, instead only occasionally treating a patient. He was asked by the prophet to become his personal assistant, to keep the prophet's daily journal, and to be his advisor. Soon after Bernhisel moved into the Mansion House, steps were taken by the prophet to create a new council, which was to be involved with the temporal affairs of the Kingdom of God. This council was not announced to the world, and its meetings were held in confidence by its members. Dr. Bernhisel was one of the charter members of this Council of Fifty, and remained a member of the council until his death.

As trouble brewed in Nauvoo among the apostates of the Church, Joseph Smith gave more and more responsibility to Dr. Bernhisel, who attended nearly all functions that the prophet did. Finally, when the *Nauvoo Expositor* was published and the press destroyed by city council order and Governor Ford wanted Joseph Smith to send representatives to Carthage to explain Smith's position in the controversy, Joseph sent Dr. Bernhisel and Apostle John Taylor. When Joseph went to Carthage to surrender, it was to Dr. Bernhisel that Joseph confided, "I am going like a lamb to the slaughter." Dr. Bernhisel was in the jail with the Smiths most of the time, but had been sent on an errand at the time of the mob assault upon the Smiths, and thus he was spared from the mob.

Bernhisel followed Brigham Young's leadership after the assassination and became a trustee handling sales of property in Nauvoo after the saints had fled West. He became Utah's first delegate to the U.S. Congress and served ten years in that position. He finally returned to the practice of medicine in Utah after his congressional years. He died in Salt Lake City 28 September 1881.

The other two faithful doctors, both botanic physicians, were the brothers Willard and Levi Richards. The two brothers were constantly together in their youth, and in adulthood, except when their various Church duties directed them in different paths. They were the children of Joseph and Rhoda Howe Richards. Their mother and Brigham Young's mother were sisters.[33]

Levi was the eldest by more than five years, and apparently accepted the responsibility of caring for his younger brother. Levi was born 14 April 1799, and Willard was born 24 June 1804. (There was another brother, William, born 2 May 1801, between them in age.)

When Willard was four he fell from a scaffold on the family barn, and landed on his head. One wonders if the palsy (paralysis) he suffered in adulthood might not have stemmed from this accident. Shortly after that, young Willard fell into a stream and would have drowned had not Levi saved him.[34]

It is apparent that in their youth Willard followed his older brother's lead. Levi was interested in mechanics and science, so Willard also became interested in that field. When Levi attended high school in Richmond, Massachusetts, and became certified as a science teacher at age 18, Willard had to outdo him. He attended the same high school and became certified in the same field when he was only 16 years old. Apparently he did not, however, follow Levi's lead in forcing himself to become proficient in music, manufacturing instruments, and learning to play several instruments, even becoming a clarinetist in the Massachusetts militia band.[35]

The first profession of both brothers was school teaching, and they taught for several years in various places in Massachusetts and New York. Willard, however, added a new wrinkle—he began to make side money by lecturing on electricity.

It is impossible to tell just when the Richards brothers became interested in medicine, but family folklore indicates that it was sometime before 1830, when sister Susan died of a mysterious malady that no one seemed to be able to diagnose or treat.[36] The brothers took up the study of medicine together, with a view to helping the family to better health. Later sister Rhoda and brother Phineas would also take up botanic medicine.

The medicine which the Richards brothers chose to study was Thomsonian or botanic medicine. By spending twenty dollars to purchase a right to use Thomson's patents, and by spending two dollars to buy Thomson's how-to-do-it book, they could become doctors. Both brothers were inquisitive and undoubtedly went far beyond what they could learn from the text book. In 1834, when he was thirty years old, Willard went to the Thomson Infirmary in Boston and spent seven weeks working with the old doctor. The old man was strongly opposed to medical schools, but since Willard had been practicing Thomson's medicine for some time, evidently the old man agreed to let the young doctor work with him to learn. Willard came out of the experience with a commission to serve as an agent for sales of Thomson's patent rights. He may have sold his other brother and a sister their rights.

Soon after this Willard went out on the sales circuit, lecturing on Thomsonian medicine, and stopped at Holliston, Massachusetts, for a sales pitch. He was implored to remain there and practice medicine, which he did until a copy of the Book of Mormon, which had been circulated among his relatives after being left behind by his cousin Brigham Young, fell into his hands.[37]

Typically, the two brothers studied the Book of Mormon together, and together got excited about this new religion. Willard declared that he felt that the Lord had something else for him to do besides practicing medicine, and he proceeded to sell off his supplies and medications. Levi, since he was not an agent for Thomson, didn't have so much to sell off.

But then illness struck Willard. He came down with an attack of palsy that was to leave him partially paralyzed for the remainder of his life. Finally, after more than a year of illness, the two brothers were able to make their planned trip to Kirtland to see Joseph Smith, their cousin Brigham Young, and to decide for themselves if the Church was of the Lord or of the Devil. Of course, they were predisposed to consider that it was from the Lord.

They arrived in Kirtland in October, 1836, and studied the church and its leaders for a couple months before Willard was baptised on 31 December 1836. Whether Levi preceded Willard into the baptismal waters or followed him is not known, but both brothers joined.

Not long after, Levi was ordained a High Priest and, on 6 March 1837, Willard was ordained an elder. A day or two later Willard accompanied Brigham Young on a mission to the East where they tried to teach their relatives about the gospel. Brigham returned to Kirtland, leaving Willard to make a last try to convert his family. The two had also transacted some Church business, and when Elijah Fordham, in New York City, wrote to Willard asking him to come and see him, Willard had a strong feeling that he must hurry back to Kirtland.

Willard arrived back in Kirtland just in time to attend an informal meeting in which plans for sending missionaries to England were being made. He wanted to go, but felt that he could not ask. The next day, Heber C. Kimball, who was to lead the missionary force, stopped him on the street and asked him if he would go. After getting Joseph and Hyrum Smith's assurances that he should go, he left for England with Heber C. Kimball on 13 June 1837. He was not to return for over four years.

Meanwhile, Levi had made himself useful about Kirtland by helping sick people, but only while he was waiting a Church calling, he thought. Gradually people began turning toward him for medical care. This was the time of the Kirtland schism, and Dr. Frederick G. Williams, who had previously had the lion's share of Mormon medical care business, was at the moment in disfavor, so loyal Church members were turning elsewhere for their health care. And after Levi had nursed Joseph Smith himself back to health he was not given a Church missionary calling, but left in Kirtland to help the people.[38]

By December 1837, the bitterness of the schism was such that the apostates were very indignant with anyone who sided with Joseph Smith, and since both Brigham Young and Levi Richards had sided with the prophet it became advisable for them to flee Kirtland to Far West, Missouri, to save their lives. There Levi watched helplessly as his beloved sister, Hepsibah, who had been his housekeeper, died of the ague (malaria), and heard of his mother's death in far away Massachusetts. Then, as the saints fled Missouri in early 1839, Levi was assigned to lead parties from the state to safety in Illinois. He wrote to Willard that he was nigh unto death himself from the dreaded ague in Quincy, Illinois.[39] It took him months to recover.

Meanwhile, Willard was serving a successful mission in England, impressing Heber C. Kimball and his fellow missionaries. On 1 April 1838, he was ordained a High Priest and left in England as a counselor in the mission presidency when Elder Kimball went home. After Heber arrived home, Joseph Smith received a revelation, on 8 July 1838, that Willard should be ordained an apostle.

Heber had baptized a young woman named Jenetta Richards, and proceeded to tell Willard that he had just baptized his wife to be. After getting Miss Richards to agree that she should not change her last name, Willard and Jenetta were married on 24 September 1838. The next July their first son was born, only to die five months later.

The Quorum of the Twelve had been called to England as missionaries. They came from pestiferous Nauvoo, and when Willard Richards met his cousin, Brigham Young, Brigham was so emaciated from illness that Willard did not recognize him. But Brigham soon demonstrated who he was by ordaining Willard an apostle on 14 April 1840. Shortly after, the word reached Willard that his father had died in Massachusetts. Then, on 11 October 1840, Jenetta again bore Willard a son, and they gave him the same name, Heber John, that they had given their first-born. Willard functioned with the Quorum, and when the Quorum decided to return to the United States, Willard and Jenetta went with them, home at last after four years.

Now it was Levi's turn. He had finally recovered sufficiently from the ague to move to Nauvoo, and he was called as a missionary to England. He left in 1840. Did he meet Willard in England? Levi was to serve an honorable mission of nearly three years time, and he finally returned to Nauvoo early in 1843, leading a company of British saints. On Christmas Day, 1843, the forty-four-year-old bachelor married Sarah Griffiths, one of those he had shepherded from England.[40]

When Willard and Jenetta arrived in Boston in May 1841, they visited Willard's relatives, and he left his wife and child to become acquainted with their relatives while he hurried on to Nauvoo.

Upon his arrival in Nauvoo, Willard was assigned by the Quorum to serve as a land agent in Warsaw to settle immigrants from Britain nearby. In October he was elected to the Nauvoo City Council in spite of the fact that he was living in Warsaw, but in December he moved to Nauvoo supposedly to take over the editing of the *Times and Seasons,* but Joseph Smith had other plans for him. Willard made a hurried trip to Massachusetts to get his wife, but otherwise he spent the next two and a half years working directly with the prophet.

Six months before this Joseph Smith had lost his right-hand-man, John C. Bennett, to apostasy, and he needed another one badly. Willard was elected. Instead of editing the newspaper, Willard was asked to become the prophet's private secretary. He went to work in Joseph's new red brick store building, in the office upstairs. He was soon keeping Joseph's journal. Joseph decided to have a history of the Church written, one he'd started several times before, only to stop; one that he had called others to write many times before, only to be frustrated by their apostasy. Willard was soon church historian, temple clerk, and general church clerk. He truly became Joseph's right hand, and Joseph appreciated what he was doing and praised him lavishly. On Willard's part the attachment became very close, and Willard was not to leave the prophet's side.

When Levi finally reached home early in 1843, the brothers were reunited and renewed their close friendship. Levi resumed his practice of medicine, and Joseph Smith, who had experienced Levi's healing touch back in Kirtland, chose Levi as his personal doctor.

By the spring of 1844, Joseph Smith had his coterie of three doctors, John M. Bernhisel and the Richards brothers, close about him, and close they were. The Laws and Fosters were excommunicated and cashiered from the Nauvoo Legion, and Levi was elevated in rank in the Legion until he became Surgeon-General in place of Dr. Foster. As most of othe Twelve were sent once again to preach, this time for Joseph's campaign for the presidency of the United States, Joseph kept Willard with him, and had Levi elected to fill Brigham Young's seat on the Nauvoo City Council. The three doctors worked closely with the prophet.

When the *Nauvoo Expositor* was published it was Levi who urged its destruction before the city council. And when indictments were issued from Carthage for the city council, Levi was one included therein.

When Joseph Smith and Hyrum decided to flee to the Rocky Mountains rather than go to Carthage to almost certain death, the three doctors accompanied them across the Mississippi, expecting to go to the mountains. When they yielded to pleas from Emma Smith and other Nauvoo citizens, and returned to Nauvoo and went to Carthage to surrender, the three doctors were with them. They were apparently inseparable.[41]

Then Joseph decided to separate them. When Levi was excused until the next term of court instead of being held a prisoner, Joseph sent him back to Nauvoo with the charge to calm its citizens, and keep the lid on no matter what happened, a responsibility he felt to be very important to the safety of his people.

Bernhisel, as we have seen, was sent on various errands, and was not present when the attack came.

Some months before, Joseph had told Willard that the time would come when he would be placed in a situation where bullets would be whizzing about his body, but that he would be unharmed. The prophecy was fulfilled as Willard battered down the rifles and bayonets of the mob with his cane as they attacked the jail.[42] He, with John Taylor, another apostle, filled their apostolic calling as witnesses as they watched the deaths of their beloved leaders.

As the only able bodied apostle in Nauvoo after the death of the prophet, it fell to Willard to temporarily lead the Church and calm the members, which he did very effectively.

The three doctors had served Joseph Smith well, and they continued in their service. Willard was in the Pioneer Company into the Salt Lake Valley, and in December, 1847, he became counselor to Brigham Young in the First Presidency. He died from a renewed attack of palsy on 11 March 1854, himself a victim of poor health most of his life.

Levi, his wife, and infant son, Levi Willard, accompanied the refugee trains across Iowa to Winter Quarters, and there remained treating the sick until July, 1848. Then, as the emigrant trains left Winter Quarters for the Salt Lake Valley, Levi and his wife turned East. Upon Brigham Young's advice they were leaving their son with his aunt Rhoda and uncle Willard to be taken to Utah while they filled a calling to the presidency of the British Mission. Levi served as counselor in the presidency of the mission for five years, until 1853, when they returned to the United States and finally made their way to Utah to see their son. But Levi's health was broken and he did not return to medical practice.[43] Early the next spring, he watched as his beloved brother, with whom he had finally been reunited, passed away.

Levi lived on until 18 June 1876, dying while his cousin Brigham was away from Salt Lake City in Utah's Dixie. He had been ordained a patriarch two years before.

The thirteen doctors discussed in this chapter were just a few of the doctors that had an impact upon the life of Joseph Smith. They were perhaps the most important, but there were many others.

One of the others was Doctor Philastus Hurlburt. His name "Doctor" may have been part of his given name rather than a title, but he may also have purchased a Thomsonian patent. This man joined the Church in its very early days and was one of the first to be excommunicated for adultery. In wrath, he turned against the Church and fabricated affidavits disparaging the character of the Smith family. These were published in the first anti-Mormon book, *Mormonism Unvailed* [sic].

As with the case of Hurlburt, most of the doctors were against the Church. There were doctors participating in nearly every mob action against the Church and its members during Joseph Smith's lifetime. There were doctors in the mobs that drove the saints from Jackson County. There were doctors in the mob militias that drove them from Missouri. And finally, there were three doctors, in addition to Doctor Foster, in the mob action in Carthage that culminated in the assassination of Joseph and Hyrum Smith.

There were also faithful doctors who were members of the Church that had less of an impact upon Joseph Smith, such as Dr. Calvin Pendleton, who introduced Sappington's Pills to Nauvoo, and Dr. Priddy Meeks.

Truly, doctors had a major impact upon the life of the Prophet Joseph Smith, both for good and for evil.

Chapter Eight

Health And The Exodus

When the saints fled West from Nauvoo, they did not leave behind totally the health problems that had faced them in Nauvoo and other parts of the Middle West.

In the fall of 1845, when Brigham Young gave instructions as to what each outfit of five people should have as necessities for the Rocky Mountain journey, he specified relatively little in the way of what could be considered to be medical supplies. He asked each to have:

> One good strong wagon well covered with a light box; two or three good yoke of oxen between the age of four and ten years; two or more milch cows; one or more good beefs; three sheep if they can be obtained; one thousand pounds of flour or other bread stuffs in good sacks; one good musket or rifle to each male over the age of twelve years; one pound of powder; four pounds of lead; one pound of *tea;* five pounds of *coffee;* one hundred pounds sugar; one pound *cayenne pepper;* two pounds black pepper; one-half pound *mustard;* ten pounds of rice for each family; one pound of cinnamon; one-half pound cloves; one dozen nutmegs; twenty-five pounds salt; five pounds *saleratus;* ten pounds dried apples; one bushel of beans; a few pound of dried beef or bacon; five pounds dried peaches; twenty pounds dried pumpkin; twenty-five pounds of seed grain; one gallon *alcohol;* twenty pounds of *soap* for each family; four or five fish hooks and lines; fifteen pounds of iron and steel; a few pounds of wrought nails; one or more sets of saws or grist mill irons to a company of one hundred families; one good seine and hook for each company; two sets of pulley blocks and ropes to each company for crossing rivers; from twenty-five to one hundred pounds of farming and mechanical tools; cooking utensiles to consist of bake kettle, frying pan . . . plates, knives, forks, spoons and pans as [few as] will do; a good tent and furniture to each two families; clothing and bedding to each family, not to exceed five hundred pounds; ten extra teams for each company of one hundred families. [Italics added to indicate medical items.][1]

The items in the list that could be used for medicinal purposes would make a few botanic remedies. Notably absent from the list were such things as Sappington's Anti-Fever Pills, which he may have considered to be not needed any longer after leaving Nauvoo.

The plans were to leave Nauvoo in early April, but vexatious law suits and threats of federal military intervention to stop the exodus caused the early beginning of the abandonment of Nauvoo. Unfortunately, only a few families had been able to equip themselves with the outfits prescribed by their leaders by the time that the wagons of Charles Shumway started the great exodus across the Mississippi River on 4 February 1846.[2]

Each family was to have eighteen months of supplies on hand, but when loyal Church members saw their leaders leaving, many of them did not wait until they could comply with this requirement. Instead they hurried on to be with the heads of the Church. As a result, within a few weeks all the supplies of the leaders and those who had made the provisions as requested were used up to take care of those who did not. Thus all came under privation.

As the majority of the Church members moved out from Nauvoo, those who were left behind because of lack of funds to acquire outfits to move, or because of sickness, were harrassed by mob action of their Illinois neighbors. The last of the thousands to flee Nauvoo under the guns of mob troops left in September.

A compasionate visitor happened upon the camp of the 600 to 800 refugees that had been thrown out of Nauvoo. Colonel Thomas L. Kane's description of them was:

> It was after nightfall when I was ready to cross the river on my return . . . I headed higher up the stream than the point I had left in the morning, and landed where a faint glimmering light invited me to steer. Here among the dock and rushes, sheltered only by the darkness, without roof between them and the sky, I came upon a crowd of several hundred creatures, whom my movements roused from uneasy slumber on the ground. Passing these on my way to the light I found it came from a tallow candle in a paper funnel shade such as is used by street vendors of apples and peanuts, and which flaring and fluttering away in the bleak air off the water, shone flickeringly on the emaciated features of a man in the last stage of a bilious, remittent fever. [Malaria] They had done their best for him. Over his head was something like a tent made of a sheet or two, and he rested on a but partially ripped open old straw mattress, with a hair sofa cushion under his head for a pillow. His gaping jaw and glazing eye told how short a time he would enjoy these luxuries, though a seemingly bewildered and excited person, who might have been his wife, seemed to find hope in occasionally forcing him to swallow awkwardly a measured sip of the tepid river water from a

burned and battered bitter smelling tin coffee pot. Those who knew better had furnished the apothecary he needed, a toothless old bald head, whose manner had the repulsive dullness of a man familiar with death-scenes. He, so long as I remained, mumbled in his patient's ear a monotonous and melancholy prayer, between the pauses of which I heard the hiccup and sobbing of two little girls who were sitting upon a piece of driftwood outside. Dreadful indeed were the sufferings of those forsaken beings, bowed and cramped by cold and sun burn, alternating as each weary day and night dragged on. They were almost all of them, the crippled victims of disease. They were there because they had no homes, nor hospitals, nor poor house, nor friends to offer them any. They could not satisfy the feeble cravings of their sick. They had not bread to quiet the fractious hunger cries of their children. Mothers and babies, daughters and grandparents, all of them alike, were bivouacked in tatters, wanting even covering to comfort those whom the sick shiver of fever was searching to the marrow.[3]

Colonel Kane had come upon what were probably the worst conditions that faced a group of the Mormon exiles. Hearing of the conditions of those who had been forcibly expelled from Nauvoo, Brigham Young immediately sent back help to them, but it took about three weeks for that help to arrive.

On 9 October, before starting the trek westward, these refugees were to witness what to many of them was just as much a gift from God as his feeding the Israelites in the wilderness: flocks of quail suddenly alighted in the camp, and the saints were able to capture many of them alive as well as to kill many more.[4]

But those who had left Nauvoo before these last refugees, had also had their hard times. Initially, record cold had frozen over the Mississippi River, and though this was by some looked upon as a blessing because it allowed many to leave by driving wagons across the frozen river rather than waiting for slower ferry transportation, the cold increased the discomfort and misery of those who were in camp at Sugar Creek in Iowa and moving West. When the thaw came they were plagued by muddy roads, often nearly impassable. Childbirth continued among the fleeing saints, and illness and sickness followed them, taking the lives of hundreds.

In his wisdom, Brigham Young ordered the establishment of more permanent camps at Garden Grove and Mount Pisgah, where gardens were planted to grow food for those who were to be the later companies to go West. The remaining cemeteries bear mute evidence of the deaths and illness of these camps.

It was at Mount Pisgah that Captain James Allen appeared, on 26 June 1846, with orders to recruit a battalion of men to serve in the Mexican War which had recently broken out. Although the enlistment of the battalion was a direct result of the efforts of the Church to secure assistance on their march West, the call came as a surprise, and opened up additional health problems for the saints.[5]

Allen had been instructed to recruit the battalion and then to march it to Santa Fe, where he was to receive further orders to march on to California. This meant that the battalion was to march on the Santa Fe Trail, and the Santa Fe Trail had health problems.

The frontier and long stretches of the Santa Fe Trail between the frontier, then on the Missouri-Kansas line and the Arkansas River, were badly infested by mosquitoes. The innumerable mosquitoes were considered terrible pests, but there was no inkling that they carried the dreaded ague. And protection against the mosquitoes was impossible, even though forewarned travelers on the trail carried cloth mosquito netting.[6]

Camping in low places along streams to secure water and wood, the Santa Fe traveler was attacked by myriads of mosquitoes. Smudges were raised, faces and beds veiled with mosquito netting, tobacco smoked, and exposed parts smeared with the crushed leaves and stems of pennyroyal, and even plastered with mud. In spite of all, numerous stings and the inevitable danger of being inoculated with the malaria parasite was an ever-present danger.

The Mormon Battalion's first goal was Fort Leavenworth, in what later would be Kansas. It was here that in 1827, when the Fort was under construction, the soldiers were severely stricken by malaria. At one time, 77 were down with malaria, 65 took care of the sick, leaving 32 for duty. Children and their mothers were sent away to Liberty, Missouri, but not before one six-year-old had died. By 1829, when Inspector George Croghan visited the Fort, he found much unfinished work because the garrison had been so reduced by sickness. Because of repeated epidemics of malaria at Fort Leavenworth, there was agitation in Washigton, D.C., to remove the Fort to another site. But where could it be moved to escape the deadly miasma?[7]

In 1827, the Kaw Indians came to the mouth of the Kansas River to receive their annuities from the federal government. Most of them fell ill, and 70 of them died of malaria.[8]

At Council Grove, the Santa Fe Trail crossed the Neosho River. Where this river, as the Grand, enters the Arkansas River, in 1824 was established Fort Gibson. From the first this Fort felt the heavy burden of malaria. In 1834, an expedition started from Fort Gibson under the command of General Henry Leavenworth, Colonel Henry Dodge, and Lieutenant Philip St. George Cooke (who was in 1846 to become commander of the Mormon Battalion). Malaria took a heavy toll of the expedition. Twenty-three men were soon pronounced unfit and sent back to Fort Gibson. Lieutenant Cooke held out for 100 miles before he returned to the Fort. Leavenworth died of "a bilious fever" 21 July 1834, at Cross Timbers where a "sick camp" had been established. Dodge pushed on, "his back trail being marked by a succession of pathetic brushwood huts occupied by sick and dying dragoons." This devastating campaign resulted in the loss of over 100 enlisted men, General Leavenworth, Lieutenant George McClure, and the Prussian botanist, Carl Beyrich.[9]

Those who regularly used the Santa Fe Trail knew that it was a deadly trail, infested with malaria of the worst kind. But those who used the trail had been introduced to Dr. Sappington's Anti-Fever Pills by the doctor, who resided at the eastern terminous. As a result, they used Sappington's Pills as a prophylactic and were able to traverse the trail without acquiring the deadly ague and fever.[10]

Thomas Lawson (1781-1861) was Surgeon General of the U.S. Army from 1836 until 1861, including the period of the Mexican War. His biographer, Colonel P. M. Ashburn has said, "He was a good doctor according to the standards of his day of bleeding, blisters, salivation and tartar emetic." In other words, he was one of the "good old school." His medical supply list as late as 1850 is heavily weighted with cathartics, emetics, blistering agents, knives for bleeding and cupping glasses.[11] One of his pet medications was Fowler's Solution, an "edema arsenicalis" containing arsenic and calomel (mercurous chloride).[12] He grudgingly allowed two ounces of quinine for 100 men for one year.

There had been some use of quinine by the army on the Santa Fe Trail. For example, in 1835, Colonel Henry Dodge commanded three companies of cavalry on a 1600-mile tour from Fort Leavenworth. Although it returned in the "sickly season" via the Santa Fe Trail, reaching Fort Leavenworth on 16 September 1835, it had had very little malaria because it had used quinine.[13] But if quinine was to be used by military groups, it had to be specially requisitioned by commanding officers, or purchased by individuals.

There was very little quinine available to the American troops during the Mexican War. The Missouri Volunteers, who also covered the trail during 1846, were forewarned by their commanding officers, and most volunteers brought with them their own Sappington's Pills. Unfortunately, the Mormon Battalion was largely unacquainted with the trail and its health problems, that knowledge being held largely by their enemies, the Missourians. So the battalion marched the trail having only the quinine-less medication of the army's medical list.

When the Mormon Battalion marched out of Council Bluffs for Fort Leavenworth, it had as assistant surgeon a botanic doctor, Dr. William McIntyre. Soon after its departure, Colonel Allen died in Fort Leavenworth, after he had sent the battalion on ahead. At Council Grove a young lieutenant of the regular army, Andrew Jackson Smith, claimed the command of the battalion and brought with him an old school doctor from Missouri, George B. Sanderson.[14] With malaria on the trail, no quinine, and an old school surgeon as Battalion surgeon, and a botanic assistant surgeon, the medical course of the Battalion was on colision course.

At the same time that Lieutenant Smith took command, a letter was received from the Church's leadership:

> To Captain Jefferson Hunt and the Officers, and Soldiers of the Mormon Battalion:—
>
> We have the opportunity of sending to Fort Leavenworth this morning, by Dr. Reed, a package of twenty-five letters, which we improve, with this word of counsel to you all: *If you are sick, live by faith, and let the surgeon's medicine alone if you want to live, using only such herbs and mild foods as are at your disposal.* If you give heed to this counsel, you will prosper; but if not, we cannot be responsible for the consequences. A hint to the wise is sufficient.
>
> In behalf of the Council,
Brigham Young, President
>
> W. Richards, Clerk. [Italics added][15]

Even though most of the Mormon Battalion soldiers had been in malarious Nauvoo, malaria nonetheless hit the battalion hard. Young Lieutenant Smith, urged on by Lieutenant Dyke, his Mormon adjutant, pushed the battalion on forced marches beyond the endurance of many battalion members. Soon men were clamoring to ride in the sick-wagon, and legitimately so, as malaria struck them. Dr. McIntyre began to administer his herbs to little avail, but Dr. Sanderson issued an order that no medication should be given to the men without his approval, especially the botanic medicines which he considered to be of no value, and possibly even dangerous.

Following Brigham Young's advice to let the surgeon's medicine alone, the battalion members refused to take his medication, but still clamored to ride in the sick-wagon. Dr. Sanderson allowed no one to ride in the wagon unless they reported to sick call and took his medication. As malaria hit harder, the battalion members' resolve began to weaken and more and more reported to sick call and took tablespoonful doses of Fowler's Solution (arsenic and calomel) in order to ride in the sick-wagon. But resentment was strong against the medication administered to each person in turn from an old rusty spoon, without benefit of a washing of the spoon in between patients.

It was about this time that a battalion member reported overhearing a conversation between Lieutenant Smith and Dr. Sanderson in which the good doctor said that he wished that he could "send as many as possible of those damned Mormons to hell."[16] Though he may have felt otherwise, he nevertheless treated the battalion members with the best medicine he had available, and according to the best tenets of the old school of medicine of

HEALTH AND THE EXODUS

which he was a member. But he was irked that the battalion members wanted botanic medicine, to which he was opposed.

As the battalion was about to leave the Arkansas River to pass over the Cimarron Cutoff to New Mexico, a trip which would be a long forced march with little water, Lieutenant Smith singled out a sick-detachment to march to Pueblo, now in Colorado, to winter there. Also sent along were most of the women and children that had heretofore accompanied the battalion. The men didn't like this action, done without any consideration of their desires, although it was undoubtedly in their best interests.

When the advanced detachment of the battalion arrived in Santa Fe, the general in command, a friend of the Mormons named Alexander Doniphan greeted them with a 100-gun salute, much to the chagrin of his fellow Missourians also in Santa Fe. Then he introduced the battalion's new commander, Lieutenant Colonel Philip St. George Cooke.

Colonel Cooke, in response to battalion members' desires, increased the responsibility of Dr. McIntyre, and largely curtailed Dr. Sanderson's responsibilities. When the next two sick detachments were selected to be sent to Pueblo because they couldn't continue the march to California, it was Dr. McIntyre who did the selection.[17] Medical peace was restored to the battalion with this action and as the battalion passed beyond malaria country.

The Mormon Battalion sick detachments were gathering at Pueblo, meeting with a company of saints who were on their way to Fort Laramie.

In April, 1847, the pioneer company rolled out of Winter Quarters (the temporary camp built upon the lands of the Omaha Indians across the river from Council Bluffs) and went West to Fort Laramie where it met the Mississippi Company and the combined sick detachment of the Mormon Battalion. The pioneer company proceeded West, leading the other two companies into the Salt Lake Valley.

In what is now western Wyoming, a disease broke out among the members of the pioneer company which made at least one-fourth of the company sick. The disease was short-lived in the case of most of its victims, but in the case of a few it caused up to a two-week-period of illness.

This disease was called Mountain Fever. The Mormons were not the first victims of Mountain Fever by a long ways. It had struck many of the companies on the Oregon Trail, and it had appeared with devastating effect at several of the rendezvous of the mountain trappers, and would plague many others who went West after the Mormon pioneers.

On the morning of 12 July 1847, Brigham Young became sick and by noon he was forced to stop his trek. By evening he was "very sick," "raving and insensible." Other reports indicate that he had excruciating headaches and high fever that day. His head felt "as if . . . [it] . . . were being mashed between rollers." He also had severe aches and pains in the back and joints.

The next day Brigham was "a little better," and was "considerably better" the following day. On the third day after the onset of his illness he felt well enough to rejoin the main body of the expedition. Within two days, however, he was again "very sick," and once again forced to stop his journey. Most of the camp activities were cancelled and a special prayer meeting held because Brigham appeared to his brethren to be "nigh unto death." The next afternoon he was again "sensibly better." By the twentieth his health had improved sufficiently to allow the expedition to proceed, but he still required transportation in a bed prepared in the back of Wilford Woodruff's carriage.[18] So it was that a sick Brigham Young rode as a patient into the Salt Lake Valley, and overlooking the valley from his sickbed declared, "This is the right place, drive on."

The etiology of Mountain Fever was—and still is—the source of considerable speculation.[19]

Although typhoid fever had been found, in 1838, to be a different disease than typhus, it took until about 1850 for this evidence to begin to be accepted by the medical world. Then American doctors began to have problems differentiating between typhoid and malaria. Since they had no idea that different germs might cause different diseases, they had to differentiate diseases by symptoms. Eventually they came to recognize most of the differences between the two diseases, but when they could not tell the difference they called the illness "typho-malarious." This supposed disease entity delayed the proper identification of differences between the two diseases for many years.

Dr. Thomas B. Hall, medical historian of the Santa Fe Trail, claims that Mountain Fever was nothing more than malaria, but located in the mountains instead of the plains where most malaria is found.[20] Other medical historians claim that it was actually typhoid fever.[21] They note that typhoid was later found to be rather common because of the polluted waters in the Rocky Mountains, especially along trail routes, and that Mountain Fever was no longer found in areas where it had been, when typhoid fever was found to be present in that area. If it was typhoid, it was the same disease that caused Joseph Smith's osteomyelitis when he was a child.

Dr. Lester Bush, Jr., has stated that the symptoms of Brigham Young's illness are strikingly similar to those of Colorado Tick Fever, which should not be confused with the much more serious Rocky Mountain Spotted Fever. He states that it appears most likely that Brigham Young and his brethren were victims of Colorado Tick Fever.[22]

Those saints who spent winters in Winter Quarters, both in 1846-47 and 1847-48, suffered from scurvy, which they called blackleg.[23] By 20 December 1846, almost one in ten people was sick with scurvy. On the 4,000 camped on the Missouri River during the winter of 1846-47, over 600 died.[24] The camps were extremely short of vegetables and fresh or dried fruits which might supply them Vitamin C. Fortunately, some potatoes had been planted and they contained enough Vitamin C to help in some cases. The other saving factor was that in the early spring of 1847 wild horseradish and Jerusalem artichokes were found on the bottomlands and were eaten to help ward off blackleg.[25] Scurvy also was to plague many of the companies of Mormons as they moved West. The Army of the West, of which the Mormon Battalion was a part, also suffered from scurvy, developing "Splint" which was a swelling and subcutaneous hemorrhage of the legs, in some cases so severe as to make soldiers unable to walk, with sore mouths, bleeding gums, and followed by lethargy.[26]

Another disease that took a great toll in Winter Quarters and on the Mormon Trail, as well as on the Santa Fe Trail, was typhoid fever, that which was differentiated from Mountain Fever. For those that were on the Trail, who took sick with typhoid, there was no medicine. They could only lie in the lumbering wagons until they died or recovered.[27]

Dysentery and diarrhea, now designated as bacillary or amoebic dysentery according to the causative organism, were frequent causes of illness in Winter Quarters and also on both the Mormon and Santa Fe Trails.[28]

In mid-February, 1847, Brigham Young was one of those sick with dysentery. He was "taken very unwell, being much distressed in the stomach and bowels. Fainted away, apparently dead for several moments, and it was with much ado that he could be kept from falling asleep to await the resurrection morn."[29] However, his recovery was rapid and he was soon about performing his responsibilities.

It is interesting to note that, on 11 August 1846, Philip St. George Cooke, on his way to Santa Fe, had suffered a very severe attack of acute diarrhea "due to turtle soup and goat cheese he had eaten the day before at San Miguel."[30] He was able to proceed to Santa Fe and participate in the takeover of New Mexico by the United States, but this illness may have been one of the reasons (to allow him time to recover) that General Kearny left him behind in Santa Fe, where he took over command of the Mormon Battalion.

It is also generally conceded that measles and diphtheria may also have been present at Winter Quarters, and it is certain that they appeared on the trails in the westward-moving companies.

But the most deadly disease of the trails did not appear until the third year of the Mormon migration. Some have said that cholera was in Winter Quarters and at Mount Pisgah and Garden Grove as early as 1846, but this is highly unlikely in view of the epidemic nature of the disease and the fact that the second great pandemic did not reach the United States until very late in 1848.

In December, 1848, a shipload of emigrants from Germany, where cholera was raging, arrived in New Orleans.[31] The disease quickly spread up the Mississippi River. Within one month St. Louis suffered its first casualty. Of the 100 or more cholera victims in St. Louis in January 1849, the majority were landed from river steamers from downstream. By April, 126 deaths were reported in St. Louis, including 9 Mormons from Europe who were headed west on a river steamer.[32]

The major immigration route of Mormon converts from Europe in 1849 was from Liverpool, England, to New Orleans, then up river by river steamers to St. Louis, then on up the Missouri River to Kanesville (Council Bluffs), which had by then succeeded Winter Quarters as the starting point of emigrant companies. This unfortunately exposed the Mormon immigrants to the major focal points of the 1849 pandemic of Asiatic Cholera.

By May, 1849, St. Louis was in panic. On 9 June, 26 died; 37 died on the following day; and 402 deaths occurred in the week ending 17 June. The next week 636 died, and 739 the following week; all this in a city of 63,471. At such a rate cholera would have killed every person in St. Louis within a few months.

Not only was St. Louis a key city on the Mormon immigration route, it was also a key city on the route of the hordes of people that were beginning to be drawn West by the California Gold Rush. Every person passing through St. Louis was potentially exposed to cholera—from the cholera-free East, or from the cholera pestholes on the lower Mississippi. Thus each person was a potential cholera carrier, even though he may not suffer from identifiable disease, and these carriers proceeded to contaminate every trail west—Mormon, Oregon, and Santa Fe.

In Kanesville the new Mormon paper, the *Frontier Guardian,* in 1849 made no mention of cholera cases in Kanesville. Instead, it exulted, "We have great reason to be thankful that we have escaped her as well as we have."[33] But saints were dying of cholera on the riverboats to Kanesville, and on the plains hundreds died. Nearly every journal or diary of the trip contains stories of these deaths.

On 21 August 1850, the *Frontier Guardian* acknowledged that cholera was present in Kanesville:

> There have been several cases of cholera in our town this season, but not enough to create the alarm which at present exists. There have been but twelve deaths since the commencement of the season.[34]

The article also condemned the "practice that is prevalent among the female portion of our community of going from one house to another mourning over the sick and diseased." The paper counseled, "If you feel like mourning, wait till the season is more healthy, and no cholera lurking in our midst."

The Mormons and the Forty-Niners were not the only victims of cholera on the plains—the poor Indians also suffered from it. George Bent, owner of Bent's Fort on the Arkansas River on the Santa Fe Trail, in what would later be Colorado, heard from his Cheyenne Indian mother's people that havoc was wrought among the Indians. Half of the Cheyenne perished, according to their tribal traditions. The Comanche and Kiowa were also hard hit.[35]

The American cholera epidemic of 1849 began to subside, but never completely ceased before a new pandemic struck in 1853 and 1854. In 1853, some 800 to 850 persons died in St. Louis, and in 1854 the city had the highest cholera death toll of any American city, with 3,547 deaths.[36] All of central Missouri along the Mississippi and Missouri Rivers was hard hit by the pandemic. A Scandinavian contingent of immigrating Mormons was especially hard hit, losing 150 out of a company of 700.[37] Cholera was prevalent in all the companies of immigrating Mormons who came up the Mississippi River and crossed the plains.

In 1849, the new apostle, Charles C. Rich, was sent to California with instructions to prepare an alternate route for immigrants via western California. A General Epistle of the Presidency announced this route that would "save three thousand miles of inland migration through a mostly sickly climate and country." But shortly afterward, cholera appeared in the California port cities of San Francisco, San Pedro, and San Diego—cities on Apostle Rich's new route. The new route idea was abandoned.[38] Sacramento was also devastated by cholera.

On 2 August, 1854, Brigham Young wrote to Elder Franklin D. Richards, who was in England supervising the shipping of immigrants to America. President Young ordered Richards to discontinue shipping the saints via New Orleans, and to instead ship them to Philadelphia, Boston, or New York, where they could travel by train most of the way to the trail embarkation points. This would also bypass the cholera centers at New Orleans and St. Louis. Those who had to sail to New Orleans were instructed to do so in time that they might get off the rivers before warm weather and the cholera season set in.

Certainly the exodus was not a movement free from health problems. It was instead frought with them. Hundreds of saints died on the trails West from accident, disease, and premature aging.

Chapter Nine

The Trouble With Doctors

The 15 September 1843 issue of the Church's newspaper, the *Times and Seasons* carried what would now be called a "letter to the editor" by an individual signed P-----S. The polemic was titled "Physician Heal Thyself." He stated "that [the common practice of] medicine destroys as many lives *prematurely,* as war." He continued with the statement, "What greater sign of death, and loss of faith, can be supposed, than to see *a physician's horse hitched before a sick ones door?"* He stated that it was evident that the Good Shepherd had no faith in doctors, nor lawyers, or hypocrites. He concluded, "O saints, saints! the just shall live by faith! No doubt but cases may occur, where medical operations may be requisite; but generally speaking 'herbs and mild food' with good nursing would be better for the patients person and pocket than all the nostrums of *materia medica."* [Italics in original.][1]

The editor of the *Times and Seasons,* John Taylor, appended a lengthy comment to the contribution, saying: "There is a good deal of sound common sense in the above remarks. We believe that if we only had faith, 'all things are possible to them that believe;' and we would not plead our want of faith. . . . But if we have not faith to be healed, as many of us have not, then we think our course is clearly defined . . ." He went on to quote from the *Doctrine and Covenants,* Section 42.

Elder Taylor then stated, "From these testimonies, it is very evident that the Lord expected that all men would not have faith to be healed; that if they had not faith to be healed, we must not condemn them; but 'bear with their infirmities,' inasmuch as they break not his laws."

Elder Taylor pointed out that those persons were to be nourished with all tenderness, with herbs and mild food. Then he asked, who is to administer those herbs? Partially answering his question, he pointed out that they are not to be administered by the hands of an enemy. Again asking who is to administer them, he asked if the heads of all families should do it, and pointed out that "We should presume that all are not competent." He then cited from the Word of Wisdom the statement, "And again, tobacco is not for the body, neither for the belly; and is not good for man; but is an herb for bruises and all sick cattle, to be used with judgement and skill.'' He said if judgement and skill is needed for treatment of cattle, how much more is it needed for treatment of men.

Elder Taylor then went on, "We should judge, then, . . . that a person who is acquainted with the physiology of the human system, and the nature and medicinal properties of herbs, is more competent to judge of those things, and to administer with judgement and skill, than the one who is ignorant, both of the organization of the human system, of the medicinal properties of herbs, and the nature and effects of disease. It is also evident that, if there is any danger, or wrong, in the administration of herbs, it is from their being in the hands of unskillful men, and particularly in the *hands of an enemy.*"

He then stated his regrets that as saints, "we have not all faith, either to be healed, or to cast ourselves into the hands of God . . ."

"We are aware that this community have been a good deal imposed upon by quacks; that nostrums of all kinds have been administered by injudicious hands, producing the most deleterious effects; and that many have slept in the dust, who, if they had been let alone, would still have been in the land of the living; but that is no reason why those who have not faith should not be aided by herbs, administered with care and skill by judicious hands."

John Taylor then concluded, "If the heads of families are themselves acquainted with the nature of diseases, the medicinal properties of herbs, and *the mode of compounding, preparing and applying them,* so much the better. If they are not, the advice and counsel of those better informed, we think, could not be injurious." [Italics added.][2]

As editor of the *Times and Seasons,* John Taylor, an apostle and member of the Quorum of the Twelve, worked under the direction of, and closely with, Joseph Smith. In view of Joseph Smith's own actions in use of medications, it is apparent that John Taylor's response to the communication reflected those of the prophet also.

The fact that a person in Nauvoo would write a letter to the editor of the Church's newspaper, however, indicates the growing anti-doctor feelings that were present in the community. These feelings would continue to grow as the exodus to the West proceeded and as the Intermountain community of Latter-day Saints began to grow.

Until the Nauvoo period, most of the converts to the Church were from the frontier regions of the American continent. The growth of botanic medicine on the frontier had far outpaced the "old school" of orthodox medicine in growth of adherents and practitioners among these people, and the majority on the frontier were followers of the botanic schools. As a result, the doctors who came to Nauvoo were for the most part botanic physicians, but a few from the orthodox school did come.

The first from the orthodox school had been Dr. John Cook Bennett, who had rapidly taken high places of responsibility in the community and Church, only to be excommunicated and to leave Nauvoo in disgrace, to become the bitterest enemy of the Church until that time.[3] But Dr. Bennett was not truly and old school doctor, so though the Church and its members suffered from his actions, his actions really did not impact too much on the old-school-botanic controversy.

The coming of Dr. John M. Bernhisel somewhat helped in causing the Church membership to be more receptive toward orthodox medicine, but since he really did not establish a practice, but became the prophet's aid, very few townspeople had an opportunity to weigh the efficacy of his medical care.[4]

Dr. Robert Foster, however, did make a major impact upon the attitudes of the Latter-day Saints toward medicine. Although it is impossible to tell for certain, he has generally been considered as, and in all probability was, a doctor of the old school. The fact that he was one of the anti-Joseph Smith leaders in the *Nauvoo Expositor* controversy, and was one whose actions caused the imprisonment and death of the prophet and patriarch, caused a very negative reaction among members of the Church to his type of medication.[5]

The practice of such botanic physicians as Dr. Levi Richards, the prophet's physician; Dr. Calvin Pendleton, who introduced Sappington's pills to Nauvoo; and Dr. Priddy Meeks, a pure Thomsonian physician who seemed to make miraculous cures; together with the support of botanic medicine by the Prophet Joseph Smith, and by apostles Brigham Young and Willard Richards, himself a botanic physician, helped to establish a favorable attitude toward botanic medicine among the Latter-day Saints as they left Nauvoo.

As the Mormon Battalion was recruited and sent off to the Pacific coast, Brigham Young had seen to it that a good botanic physician accompanied them, and he had cautioned both by personal counsel before they left, and by letter to them, to avoid the use of orthodox medicine. The ensuing conflict between the Battalion members and Dr. George Sanderson, the old school doctor named by the army to be Battalion surgeon, caused heated resentment.[6] Brigham Young had even included a negative comment on the Sanderson problem in his letter sent on 6 January 1847 to the three apostles then in England.[7]

The first year in the Great Salt Lake Valley was virtually a doctorless period, of either old school or botanic doctors. It remained for midwives like Patty Bartlett Sessions, who reached the valley in the fall of 1847, to take care of the medical problems beyond the capabilities of the family heads. Apparently only Priddy Meeks, a botanic physician who was a late-season arrival, spent the first winter in the valley.[8]

There were many botanic physicians that came into the valley in the first few years of settlement. But apparently only a very few old-school doctors came into the valley. Doctors Samuel L. Sprague and John M. Bernhisel came into the valley about the same time in 1848, but early in 1849 Bernhisel was dispatched to Washington, D.C., as the saints' representative, and except for occasional visits West he remained there for ten years. Dr. Sprague apparently never practiced medicine full-time after his arrival in the valley. Dr. William France also arrived in the early 1850s and likewise did not practice medicine full-time. It was not until the arrival of Dr. Washington F. Anderson, in 1857, that an old school doctor who practiced full-time arrived in the valley.[9]

In the early years of the valley, the policy of the Church leadership was to discourage full-time medical practitioners, either botanic or old school. The *Deseret News,* the official Church newspaper which was edited by Dr. Willard Richards, botanic physician and member of the First Presidency of the Church, editorialized on 18 September 1852, "Two physicians have removed to one of our more distant settlements and gone to farming; three more have taken to traveling and exploring the country; three have gone to California to dig gold, or for some other purpose; and one has gone to distilling; and we are beginning to get some alcohol, which is desirable for gentlemen's shoe-blacking, hatter's water-proofing, chemical analysis, washing the bodies of the well to prevent sickness and the sick that they may be made well when such there be. Those physicians who remained have very little practice and will soon have less (we hope).''[10]

In late 1851 and 1852, the *Deseret News* published part of a series of letters between Brigham Young and a Dr. David Adams, of Fairfield, Illinois. The doctor expressed a sympathetic attitude toward the doctrines of the Church and stated a desire to move to Utah, "with one hundred persons, good and true," provided he could make a living in the practice of medicine in Utah. He asked, "What are the most prevalent diseases in Utah? Do you think a physician, well qualified in his profession (regular graduate, and some twenty years experience) can support a family there?"[11]

President Young's answer was perhaps his best statement upon his attitude toward medicine in that period of his life. He told of the experience of the saints in recent years in Missouri and Illinois which had drained their finances to the very dregs. Yet they had left their families to serve their nation in war, and to go into foreign countries to carry their Gospel message. He then asked, "Shall we then offer inducements of earthly prosperity to any man to come and unite his destiny with ours?" He then advised the doctor, if he cared to come, taking his chances, and obeying the laws of the Gospel in sincerity, he would be welcomed. "The Church, however, does not beg anyone to come and join with them, but those who come, and are deserving, will be blessed."

It was then that he expounded upon his attitudes towards medicine, "People die in all countries, in this as well as all others, although there is a difference in all countries in relation to sickness and in the manner of their deaths. I do consider this a healthy country, as healthy as any in which I have ever lived or traveled; and yet when once a disease gets hold of a person, it is rather apt to terminate one way or the other sooner than in those low countries where a man may always be dying, until some friendly physician shall interpose and quietly put him away according to the most approved and scientific mode practiced by the most learned M.D.'s. The most prevalent diseases here are fevers, which are not very common and childbirths.

"These diseases are easily managed by intelligent physicians. As to supporting a family by medical practice, we have physicians who find considerable employment, yet it is no uncommon thing to see them at work in the canyons getting out wood, plowing, sowing, or harvesting their crops, which, I think betokens a healthy state. As an individual, I am free to confess that I would much prefer to die a natural death to being helped out of the world by the most intelligent graduate, new or old school, that ever scientifically flourished the wand of Esculapius or any of his followers.

"I have given you a sketch upon a few items contained in your letter, which, though hasty, may give you an idea or two of our notions of things, and whether it shall prove satisfactory or not, it makes no difference to me, inasmuch as truth will appear and triumph in the end . . . We have health and freedom, and as long as we have these blessings from God, we shall flourish in our enterprise. I do not wish to discourage you or your company of 'one hundred good and true,' of whom you speak, but largely to disabuse your minds of what may be a disappointment to you."

The attitudes of Church members towards doctors and medical practice were intertwined with attitudes relating to other current events affecting the community. When Utah was organized as a territory in 1850, the governor and other principal territorial officers were appointed by the President of the United States. The governor was Brigham Young, and one of the territorial Supreme Court justices was also a Church member, but most of the others were not Church members. Those who came from outside the ranks of Mormonism had many problems of adjustment, and some ran away to Washington in 1851 to complain of the wickedness of the Mormons.

Mrs. B. G. Ferris, wife of one of those territorial officals, wrote a book about the Mormons after she had left the territory, and in it she told of being accompanied as she left the territory by a medical doctor named Coward and a dentist vaguely known as Dr. H-----. Both were leaving Utah because of dissatisfaction of different kinds. She thought Dr. Coward's trouble was drink and said Dr. H----- was leaving because of poor collections on his bills for dental work. Mrs. Ferris admits that Dr. H----- previously had similarly failed to establish himself in the States.[12]

One of the charges that this group of disaffected territorial officials made against the Mormons was the murder of a Dr. John R. Vaughan, a citizen of Indiana, who was supposedly on his way to California in the spring of 1851.[13] Perhaps Dr. Vaughan was not just passing through, for the *Deseret News* of 1 July 1850 carried the following advertisement, "J. M. Vaughan, M.D., Physician and Occulist. Well known in the States as a successful physician and practitioner, having located in Salt Lake City for the practice of medicine in its various branches, will promptly attend any call with which he may be favored. Though a graduate of the old school, Dr. Vaughan is wedded to no sect or system of medicine, but is ever ready to avail himself of all lights that shine upon the healing art, in its present improved condition."[14] This incident is virtually ignored by the major historians who have written on Utah. Ann Eliza Young, the disbelieving wife of Brigham Young (she called herself his nineteenth), mentions this incident in one of her anti-Mormon diatribes, and in spite of her anti-Mormon feelings, she credits it to Dr. Vaughan's alleged intimacies with a plural wife of a friend he was visiting in Central Utah. The friend avenged his wife's honor.[15] The actions of such non-Mormon old school doctors passing through the territory increased the feelings of the saints against orthodox doctors.

Soon old school, or orthodox, doctors were being called "poison doctors." In his journal, Priddy Meeks, who was a Thomsonian physician, records: "Old Dr. Cannon, a 'poison' doctor, and poisoned against the Mormons too, could get but little to do among the sick; said if we would give him all the surgery to do he would quit doctoring; and so we did and he joined the Council of Health and proved a great benefit to us . . ."[16]

In 1856, another group of territorial officials left Utah and descended on Washington with cries that the Mormons were in revolt. Without checking on the accuracy of their charges, President Buchanan dispatched an army to Utah to put down the alleged rebellion. The army also had a secondary charge, to remove Brigham Young from the governorship, and install a new non-Mormon governor. The Mormons maintain that they were never in rebellion, but difficulty between Mormons and non-Mormon territorial officials and residents had caused a hue and cry to go up to that effect. Thus, in 1857, the Mormons found themselves facing a federal army. In the light of their past experiences, they felt that they were being unjustly persecuted, and prepared to resist.

One of the most effective of the agitators that instigated this Utah, or Echo Canyon, War was Dr. Garland Hurt, an orthodox doctor who had been appointed Indian Agent for Utah Territory.[17] His bitter accusations had helped bring down on the saints what they thought would be one of their most severe trials, and another step toward hostility to orthodox doctors had taken place. The fact that the anticipated severe trials did not actually take place did not lessen the negative feelings toward this doctor.

The actions of the Mormon militia, the new Nauvoo Legion, which destroyed much of the army's supplies, left the federal army stranded on the borders of the territory during a severe winter. Undoubtedly the army could have been resupplied the next spring, and marched into the valley supposedly in triumph, but the saints let it be known that they were prepared to destroy their homes and all crops, to literally scorch the earth, and to begin guerilla warfare.

Through the intercession of Colonel Thomas L. Kane, a non-Mormon friend of the Church from Pennsylvania, the Mormons agreed to let the army come into Utah provided that they camped at least forty miles from major centers of population. The saints also greed to accept the new governor, and sent a detachment to escort him into the valley. Governor Cummings was brought through Echo Canyon at night and treated to the impressive sight of many campfires along the overhanging cliffs and at bends of the canyon, each with a marching sentinel. (It was years later before he found that there had been only a few sentinels who had moved from one campfire to another, keeping pace with his travel.) When the army arrived in Salt Lake City, it found a deserted city, with houses prepared for burning and men standing by with torches. The army remained in Utah at Camp Floyd, forty miles southwest of Salt Lake, until the Civil War, when its commander, General Albert Sidney Johnston, left to fight for the South and the army was called East to help save the Union.

The old school doctors that accompanied the federal troops to Camp Floyd had little affect upon the practice of medicine and the attitudes of the saints towards orthodox medicine, but they were responsible for some lurid descriptions of the supposed physiological deterioration of the Mormons that were published in the national press.[18]

During the Civil War, after the abandonment of Camp Floyd, California Volunteers, under command of General Conner, took over the vacant lands that the territorial legislature had set apart as a campus for the University of Deseret (soon to be the University of Utah), and established Camp Douglas on those heights overlooking Salt Lake City. The doctors among the California troops, and doctors among the camp followers, began to have closer association with the people of Salt Lake. During the period from 1861 to 1865, thirty-four physicians arrived in the valley.[19] Although many left at the conclusion of the war, some stayed on.

General Conner, very bitterly anti-Mormon, encouraged his soldiers to prospect during their free time, and to establish a mining industry in Utah. This industry, which had been discouraged by the Mormon Church's leadership, began to build a larger non-Mormon population in the territory. The old antipathy between Mormons and non-Mormons began to grow until it was climaxed by the abandonment of plural marriage by the Mormons many years later. The fact that most of the old school doctors were non-Mormons increased the antipathy of the Mormons to orthodox medicine.

One of the weak chinks in the saint's armor was their tenuous claim to their lands and property. The Organic Act creating the Territory of Utah did not make provisions for recognizing the land claims of the early settlers, nor did it make provision for recognition of future claims. It left to future Federal Congresses the assignment of land after it had been surveyed by the territorial surveyor, and Congress delayed passing acts to help settle the problem, and also the surveying was done very slowly. The Homestead Act, which Congress did pass, only increased confusion.

The anti-Mormon part of the non-Mormon population soon found that this problem of land claims could be exploited to the discomfiture of the saints. Most of the members of the federally-appointed territorial Supreme Court were among the anti-Mormons. The saints feared that these judges might deprive them of their homes and property.[20]

In 1866, several non-Mormons decided to contest the Mormon's land claims. Three of them claimed sites west of town and were driven off by armed Mormons. Meanwhile, Dr. King Robinson, an old school doctor who had come with Connor's troops and had married an apostate from the Mormons, determined to seize a particularly choice bit of Salt Lake real estate. Early in the city's history the City Council had set aside the Warm Springs on the northern outskirts of the city as a park. Fifteen years earlier, the city had built a bathhouse on the site. Dr. Robinson planned to use the site for medicinal purposes and filed a claim on the land. Robinson went ahead and built his own bathhouses and Utah's first bowling alley on the property, but the city police evicted him, and shortly thereafter Ribinson's buildings burned.

Dr. Robinson filed suit against the city in the territorial courts. The fears of the Mormons were aroused. It was generally conceded that if the court was allowed to make a ruling, that it would be against the Mormon-controlled city government. It was further believed that if the city lost the decision, all property rights established by the early settlers would be placed in jeopardy, and that newcomers could dispossess the Mormons from their homes. Thus, Dr. King Robinson, husband of an apostate and first Sunday School superintendent of the Gentile Sunday School, became the most bitterly hated doctor ever to come into Utah.

At 11:30 on the evening of 22 October 1866, Dr. King Robinson was called to care for "John Jones," who supposedly had a mangled leg. He was accompanied by the "patient's brother." On Main Street, near Third South, seven armed men assaulted and shot him. The anti-Mormons claimed that one of the murderers was a Salt Lake City policeman, but apparently most of the police force were busy at a circus that evening. The police chief testified at the inquest that he was not notified of the death until the next morning. The murderers were never apprehended, and both the murder case and the law suit against the city were never concluded.

The murder of Dr. King Robinson seemed to be the climax of the anti-doctor feelings of the Mormons. From this point on, the feelings of the saints seemed to have softened toward the orthodox doctor; not immediately, but over a period of a few years.

The anti-doctor feelings of the Mormons were not unique to them. From the 1820s through the 1860s, many people feared orthodox doctors, feeling that they might take away more lives than to preserve them.[21] But among the Mormons, the feelings also became confused with the growing Mormon vs. anti-Mormon disputes, since orthodox doctors were perceived as being aligned with the anti-Mormons.

The feelings were not all one-sided, Mormons against anti-Mormons. The doctors likewise looked disdainfully at the Mormons. Particularly disliked by the doctors was the Mormon practice of first using faith healing, and only then, if it failed, looking for medical care. Surgeon E. P. Vollum, United States Army's report from Fort Douglas to the Surgeon General in 1875 is typical of this attitude:

> The great mortality in the children here is confined chiefly to the Mormon population, and it may be traced to the absence of medical aid, nursing, proper food for sick children, and neglect of all kinds. Among the many mottoes that decorated the Tabernacle on the last anniversary of the advent of the Mormons into Utah was, "Utah's Best Crop: Children." Abundance doubtless cheapens the value of anything, children as well, especially when the issue of several women are begotten in poverty, and all mingled together and contending like birds in a nest for the morsels within reach. The children of Salt Lake City may often be seen in groups insufficiently clad, the lower half of the body bare, playing about in cold water, that flows directly from the mountains, and down each side of the streets, in front of residences. The consequence is catarrhs, pneumonia, fevers, and bowel complaints. The nonsensical mummery of the "laying on of hands" is taught and practiced by the priesthood, as a cure for disease, and the faithful and more ignorant resort to it with confidence. Many marvelous cures are narrated as having been brought about by the sacred touch and incantations of the priests; this, with the tea of the sage-brush, and other old woman's slops, constitute the treatment of most of the sick Mormon children, with such consequences as might be expected.[22]

But Dr. Vollum did not understand that things were beginning to change in Utah, and that more acceptance of medical care by the Mormons was on its way.

Chapter Ten

Botanic Medicine In Zion

Within a few short years after the arrival of the Mormon Pioneers in the Salt Lake Valley in 1847, settlements of Mormons spread throughout the Great Basin. Although Salt Lake City remained the focal point of the settlements, the majority of the settlers were soon in outlying colonies.

The settlement pattern of these outlying communities was carefully orchestrated by Brigham Young. Each colony was sent out with a spiritual/temporal leader, who usually was soon designated as bishop over the colony. As nearly as possible, members of the Church with specialized training needed in the colony were called to serve "missions" in those colonies, to provide the colonies with the talents needed. Among those called on missions, in addition to the blacksmiths and school teachers, etc., needed by the colonies, were midwives and doctors.

Nearly every colony had a doctor sent to it. There was no shortage of those calling themselves doctors in the Intermountain colonies, but these doctors, in the majority of cases, were botanic practitioners who had little or no formal medical education. Dr. Ralph T. Richards and Dr. S. M. Budge have both claimed that, until 1871, there was not one graduate of a medical school in the outlying colonies; however, more recent studies have indicated that there were a few trained doctors in the colonies.[1]

It was not expected that the doctors would practice medicine full-time in the colonies. It was expected that they would become farmers and otherwise participate in the labors of colony growth and development. A person was to earn his bread by the sweat of his brow, and practicing medicine was not considered to be work requiring the sweat of the brow. He was needed there should medical emergencies arise, but it was thought that there would be little need for doctors because the colonies would be so healthy.

In actuality, the need for medical care in these colonies was very great. Utah had one of the highest mortality rates in all the United States and its possessions. The accident rate in the colonies was also very high.[2]

The early settlers in the colonies relied first upon priesthood blessings and faith healing. Scarcely a journal of the time fails to note at least one miraculous recovery.[3] If a person was not healed after a priesthood blessing, then home medications were applied. If these in turn were not sufficient, then the doctor or midwife (nurse) was called.

In 1857, Brigham Young had counseled the saints, "It is God's mind and will that every father and mother should know just what to do for their children when they are sick. Instead of calling for a doctor you should administer to them mild food, herbs, and medicine that you understand." Twelve years later he would reiterate, "Learn to take proper care of your children. If any of them are sick, the cry now, instead of 'Go and fetch the Elders to lay hands on my child,' is, 'Run for a doctor.' You should go to work to study and see what you can do for the recovery of your children. If a child is taken sick with fever, give it something to stay that fever or relieve the stomach and bowels, so that mortification may not set in. Treat the child with prudence and care, with faith and patience, and be careful in not overcharging it with medicine. If you take too much medicine into the system, it is worse than too much food . . . It is the privilege of a mother to have faith and to administer to her child; this she can do herself."[4]

Non-Mormons criticized the saints for inadequate medical care of their children. Dr. Vollum's observation of the Pioneer Day Tabernacle banner, "Utah's Best Crop: Children," and his statement that "abundance doubtless cheapens the value of anything, children as well" was reflected by other outside observers, and may well have had some truth in it.[5] The Mormon doctrine that all children who died under the age of accountability (eight years old) would be saved in the Celestial Kingdom (the highest eternal glory) could not help but have an impact upon the attitudes of the saints toward attempts to prolong children's lives.

The experiences of Dr. Priddy Meeks are typical of the doctors sent to the colonies. His experiences are better known than others because toward the end of his long life he took the time to fill several journals with his life story, and that life story, in turn was published in the *Utah Historical Quarterly* in 1942. Arriving in the Salt Lake Valley late in 1847, he was sent in 1851 to Parowan in Southern Utah, where he remained farming and practicing medicine until late in his life when he joined the United Order settlement of Orderville. A few years after his arrival in Parowan, Dr. Calvin Pendleton, another botanic physician, but of the Eclectic or Wooster Beech branch of botanic medicine, moved to the same community. Dr. Meeks, with his pure lobelia-based Thomsonian botanic medicine, clashed with Dr. Pendleton's more liberal botanic practice. In his journal Dr. Meeks recorded several case histories:

> **Case 1.** James McKann, teamster in General Johnston's army that came to kill off the Mormons, he was brought to my house for me to amputate both feet which was froze as high as 2 or 3 inches above

the ankles. I did not know what to do. It come into my mind as by inspiration to give him cayenne pepper inwardly, and nothing else. In 16 days he was well and walked 9 miles, and said he could of walked farther. He only lost 5 toenails from both feet.

Case 2. The worst case of inflammatory rheumatism I think I ever saw was cured in one week by taking a little chew of Indian root and half that amount of yellow dock three times a day, swallowing it down every time. Jennette Clark was the woman cured.

Case 3. Mary Smith, a young girl, had a bunch growing on her upper lip close to her nose protruding above her nose, which was entirely stopped. She could not breathe through it. All she took was equal quantities of burdock, yellow dock and dandelion in powders, and a snuff of yellow dock for her nose, and the tumor gradually vanished away and left her a smooth face. Some said it was a canker sore, while others said it was a cancer sore. Howbeit, it got well under the above treatment.

Case 4. While living at Parowan a man by the name of Bishop was brought to me from Buttermilk Fort, Millard County, Utah, in a bad fix with his back half bent; could not straighten up. His kidneys and urinary organs were all affected, so that he could not walk a step. I gave him nothing but burdock seeds and dandelion tea, and in twelve days he was well enough to go home rejoicing.

Case 5. While I lived in the city, Andrew Love had been under Dr. Bernhisel's treatment for a very bad case of kidney complaint and he was given up. I gave him nothing but burdock and dandelion, and he soon recovered to the joy of all.

Case 6. In the first settling of the Salt Lake Valley Lorenzo D. Young's wife had the phthisis [tuberculosis] for twelve or fifteen years. She could not live in a crowded fort and had a house built some rods outside on higher ground. I gave her nothing but bitter root or Italian hemp root, and it cured her entirely. I think she had it no more. Ten or twelve years afterwards she said she never had it any more after taking that medicine.[6]

The colonies' midwives were also kept very busy with a high birth rate. When midwives were not functioning as midwives, they also served as nurses for their communities.

Throughout the entire territorial period of Utah history, the saints, both male and female, felt that it was not proper for men to deliver children.[7] A male doctor would be called in for assistance only in the most serious cases. This had also been true in the Middle West when the saints had been settled there.

Very early in Church history, Joseph Smith had associated childbirth with the healing ordinances of the priesthood. During the Nauvoo period he blessed and "set apart" many women to be midwives. It was customary that a woman would not be set apart as a midwife until after she had been married and had born a child of her own. Some of the sisters set apart had been midwives even before joining the Church, as had been Patty Bartlett Sessions, probably the most famous of all Mormon midwives; but some were neophytes and had to learn on the job.

As Brigham Young organized the emigrant companies leaving for the Great Basin, he usually saw to it that one or more midwives accompanied each company. As the colonies were settled, he likewise saw that midwives accompanied the settlers into each colony. In each case, the midwife was set apart to heal and provide medical care and deliver children in the communities. At first, Brigham Young himself set most of the women apart, but later the task was delegated to other priesthood leaders.

In 1849, the botanic doctors in Salt Lake City had organized a "Council on Health" that endeavored to enlighten the community on health needs. One of its tasks was to help train midwives. By 1856, after the Council had ceased to function, others took up the task, in cooperation with women's groups in the Valley. With the reactivation of the Relief Societies, that organization took over the function of training midwives. Until the 1870s, the botanic school of medicine predominated in the education of midwives, and midwives were trained in botanic medicine in addition to midwifery.

The settlement of Cache Valley is typical of other colonies of early Utah. The first settlement of the valley took place in 1856, in the southern end of the valley at Wellsville. Settlement of Mendon took place in 1859, followed by settlements in Smithfield, Providence, Richmond, and Logan shortly afterward. The first doctors and midwives did not arrive until 1859, but within three years after that nearly every one of the settlements had their own botanic doctor and botanic midwife. It was to be another decade, until the arrival of the railroad in the valley, before medical-school-trained orthodox doctors arrived in Cache Valley.

During the early years of settlement in Cache Valley, tuberculosis was endemic and its communities were subjected to frequent epidemics. Mountain Fever was an early plague which died out after 1870, being replaced by waves of Typhoid-Fever epidemics. Smallpox epidemics hit the valley at least four times in ten years. Diphtheria was one of the most persistent and most prevalent diseases. Measles occurred in frequent periodic epidemics. Scarlet Fever and Mumps were prevalent much of the time.[8] One disease, more prevalent than any other, was pneumonia. For this disease, the most common treatment was the mustard plaster. Also used was a flaxseed-meal poultice placed on the chest.

Approximately 80% of all illnesses will eventually heal themselves regardless of treatment or lack of treatment (barring heroic medical treatment). Richard Daines, in writing of the early medicine of Cache Valley, has said, "The most striking feature of medicine during the pioneer period . . . is the futility of both the afflicted and the healer to affect the course of nature in any but insignificant or negative ways. At best the measures taken might have a palliative effect. At worst they aggravated the injury, prolonged the illness, or multiplied the suffering. In effect, all that stood between the pioneer and debilitating sickness was his own common sense, a few rudimentary public health measures, and a mix of ineffective and potentially harmful folk remedies."[9]

In the Mormon colonies, the people began to prepare their own medications. For the most part these medications were based upon botanic medical principles, since that is what they had been taught to accept. Thus, while across the nation botanic medicine was waning in popularity and useage, in the Mormon colonies botanic medicine continued to hold a firm grasp, and the treatments and medications thus practiced became a part of the growing folklore of the Mormon people.

There were certain medications that were present in nearly every home. First among these was olive oil, or sweet oil as it was often called. Though the *Salt Lake Sanitarian* would lament that it was often adulterated with cottonseed oil and/or other oils,[10] it was the major medication of the Mormon colonies. The Elders of the Church consecrated the oil to heal the sick, and used it in the ordinances of anointing and blessing the sick, but it was also used to rub the outside of the body and was given inwardly to cure ailments of many kinds, either by itself or compounded with other medications. It became usual for the midwives to wash the bodies of expectant mothers and to anoint the bodies with oil as a blessing was given.

Possibly the second-most-used medication was lobelia, the basic herb of Thomsonian botanic medicine. Priddy Meeks said of it, "Lobelia is the most powerful diffusive stimulant known in medicine. After taking a dose, it instantly permeates the whole system, removing obstructions wherever found, and restoring a healthy action wherever needed, and is one of the most powerful relaxants known in the science of medicine, and yet perfectly harmless with the laws of life and health, and a surer quicker and more powerful anti-poison (I think) is not known and probably never will be."[11] This emetic, which would rapidly empty a stomach, was the last of the great supposed panaceas.

Cayenne Pepper, or Red Pepper, was also very heavily used, and was supposed to heal by causing sweating. Sage, both tame sage and wild sage brush, was heavily used in teas. Another heavily used medication, mixed into many compounds for external and internal use, was turpentine.

One very potent drug was frequently used, and evidently was not recognized as a dangerous addictive drug. This was laudanum, a tincture of opium.

Various common household foods were also often used as medications, such as onion, which was used for poultices and warmed and placed in the ear to relieve earache, and garlic. Mustard was the main ingredient of the famous mustard plaster that was applied to burn out a cold or influenza. Ginger was also brewed into a tea to help fight colds and to warm the sick.

Other herbs were in quite common useage, including Golden Seal, Slippery Elm Bark, Sarsaparilla, Saffron, Pine Gum, Peppermint, Hops, Hoarhound, and Dandelion.

One remedy, that would now appear quite repulsive, was fresh cow or horse manure, mixed with lard and various other materials, and often used to fight burn injuries. Another common burn treatment was fresh potato pealings.

Following are some of the medications used by Patty Sessions, the well-known midwife:

Salve for old sores: Bark of indigo-weed root boiled bown, bees-wax, mutton tallow, a very little rosin.

Jaundice: Take one tablespoonful of castile soap shavings, mixed with sugar, for three mornings; then miss three until it has been taken nine mornings.

Bowel complaint: Take one teaspoonful rhubarb, one-forth carbonate of soda, one tablespoon brandy, one teaspoon peppermint essence, half-teacupful warm water; take tablespoonful once an hour until it operates.

Vomiting: Six drops laudanum, the size of a pea of soda, two teaspoons of peppermint essence, four cups water; take a tablespoon-ful at a time until it stops it; if the first does, don't repeat it.

Heart-burn: Laudanum, carbonate soda, ammonia, sweet oil, camphor. Also for *milk leg inflammation* or *sweating.*[12]

As communities became less isolated in the 1870s and 1880s, medical school-trained doctors of the orthodox type began to come into the larger communities, but they faced an uphill battle for acceptance by the local saints. Even in Salt Lake City, where nearly all the orthodox doctors had settled until that time, botanic medicine still held the position of the preferred medicine. Those communities that remained isolated until well into the twentieth century had botanic folk medicine even more firmly entrenched.

The concept of having lay medical practitioners—fathers or mothers—in each home was very acceptable to the thinking of many saints. If the priesthood was to be a lay priesthood, why not a lay corps of medical practitioners? Some, like Priddy Meeks, felt that botanic medicine was inspired of God and was the only medicine God wanted man to use.

On 3 January 1858, Joseph Young, Brigham's brother and senior president of all the Seventies in the Church, expressed his feelings about lay medical care. He said, "Let us look at this thing. There is a class of people who do not believe in sustaining professional doctors. I am one of them. There is a certain class of people again in the community, who, when they are sick, the very first motion they make is to call for a doctor. Which of these is right? Neither of them. I will not say that I would not send for a doctor in some instances, for example, to perform some difficult operation, if I knew he was a good surgeon; then there are some instances of sickness in which I would not send for a doctor, because I understand the nature of the disease, and know how to treat it as well, or better, perhaps, than any doctor, and aided by the blessings of the Lord, I can check it, and that is my duty."[13]

Later, other general authorities found it expedient to caution members of the Church that the first step in care of the sick was faith healing. Faith healing should be commensurate with home care.

Like Joseph Smith, Brigham Young had seen the dangers inherent in use of orthodox medicine in the early days of the Church and the first two decades in the Mountain West. Joseph Smith had used the best medicine he could obtain. In his later life he had primarily utilized the methods of botanic medicine and had had Levi Richards serve as his personal physician, but he had also utilized treatments from John C. Bennett and later from John M. Bernhisel, both doctors of the orthodox school. Brigham Young likewise primarily used botanic medicine but, as early as 1858, he had developed a friendship with Dr. Washington F. Anderson and had begun to utilize some of the orthodox medications prescribed by Doctor Anderson. Both Joseph Smith and Brigham Young could have been called eclectic, since they chose the best from what was offered by contemporary medical care. Brigham's statement, "It appears consistent to me to use every remedy that comes within the range of my knowledge, and to ask my Father in Heaven to sanctify that application to the healing of my body,"[14] was a guide he propounded to all the saints.

There was, however, a significant faction of Church members that could not accept the paths that their Church's leadership now began directing them toward. As medications increased in number and complexity, some saints began to take literally the instructions regarding use of herbs as found in Doctrine and Covenants 42:43, "And whosoever among you are sick, and have not faith to be healed, but believe, shall be nourished with all tenderness *with herbs and mild food* . . ." [Italics added.] To them to accept medical care beyond the use of herbs was a violation of God's commandments.

Though these people did not blanch at making their own extracts and combinations of medicines from herbs, it became unacceptable to them to use medications that had been extracted from herbs by commercial druggists and drug firms, even though more than 80% of all drugs then in the *U.S. Dispensatory* and the *National Formulary* were extracted from herbs and offered more uniform dosage.

These people continued to harbor the fear of orthodox medicine that had been so justifiable earlier in their Church's history. This feeling has become entrenched in some of the folklore of Mormonism, and has found resurgence in twentieth-century acceptance of non-orthodox, or quack, medications. To some individuals, it is perfectly all right to be under the care of a botanic or naturopathic doctor, or even a chiropractor, but they feel that it is a violation of their faith to be under the care of an orthodox medical doctor.

Recent sociological studies have indicated that because early leaders of the Mormon Church utilized and advocated botanic medicine and it became entrenched in the medical folklore of the saints, the saints are more likely to accept unproven medical remedies today.[15] This has caused enough concern among the present Church leadership that an editorial appeared in the *Church News* on 19 February 1977, from which the following is excerpted:

> The Church . . . deplores the patronage of health or medical practices which might be considered ethically or legally questionable.
>
> People with serious illness should consult competent physicians, licensed under the laws of the land to practice medicine.
>
> There are times when we should pray for the sick, and through the priesthood lay hands upon the head of the ill and bless them . . . Certainly, through divine intervention, the sick continue to be made well.
>
> But our belief in the divine power of healing should in no way preclude seeking competent medical assistance.

The February 1977 editorial was shortly followed by another, dated 18 June 1977. This statement was similar to the first, but much more detailed:

> From the beginning of time the prophets have taught us how best to live in this wicked and confusing world, and have assured us, as did Lehi of old, that "man is that he might have joy."
>
> They have likewise taught us to avoid extremes and "be temperate in all things" (D&C 6:19; Alma 38:10). This applies to our health habits as well.
>
> But sick people should be cautious about the kind of care they accept as treatment for their illnesses. Some unprincipled practitioners make extreme claims in offering cures to the sick. They take money from their patients, give them no help, and in some cases seriously harm them.
>
> Frequently, fads are advocated under the guise of the Word of Wisdom by unauthorized persons with unwarranted claims respecting

health. Some questionable practitioners use other phases of religion, too, like the raising of the right hand to the square as a part of a health ritual. At times, they assume to speak in the name of the Church and even give "official" interpretations related to health.

They have displayed pictures of presidents of the Church or of the Temple to give an "authoritative" backdrop to their teachings. Their exhibits of foods and remedies are enhanced by copies of the scriptures obviously placed there to give further appearance of credibility to their projects.

The Church officially disclaims all such pretensions. Also it completely disclaims any sponsorship or endorsement of such teachers, remedies, foods or fads. It does not and cannot promote remedies of any kind. It deplores the use of ritualistic practices in connection with supposed cures as bordering on the sacriligious.

The use of health practices which are questionable either legally or ethically is likewise deplored. People who have health problems are advised to counsel with competent professional practitioners who are properly licensed under the law of the land. . . .

Chapter Eleven

The Changing Medical World During The Utah Territorial Period

When the Mormons moved west into the Great Basin they no longer had intimate relationships with the practice of medical care as it was developing in the States. Particularly in the early period of their isolation, it took from months to years for information about medical changes to reach them in the Valley.

A person living in a community watches changes come and go in a natural pattern of progression, though he may be largely unaware of the extent to which changes are being made. But let a person leave a community for a time and then come back to it, and the extent of the changes will be readily apparent. In a sense, this is what happened to the Mormons in relationship to medicine in the United States. Although individual Church members and leaders made trips to the East and saw some of what was happening, it was not until the Civil War and the coming of the railroad to Utah that the Mormons became reimmersed into the ongoing development of America, and the Church leadership began to realize what had been taking place in the field of medicine.

Dr. Fielding H. Garrison, the great medical historian, recognized that in the nineteenth century there was a major revolution that took place in the field. He called it the modern scientific movement, and stated that it did not attain its full stride until well after the middle of the century.[1] It was just before the middle of that century that the main body of Mormons moved West, and the movement was going full speed as they were reimmersed into that ongoing development.

The progression of American medicine may be likened to a swampy valley with beaver dams that have been filled with growths that separate streams meandering across the swamp. Following the American Revolution, the main stream of American medicine followed a heroic path, and it was felt that heroic efforts must be taken to restore health to those who were sick. The result was the over-emphasis of phlebotomy (blood letting) and purging, usually by means of massive doses of calomel, and use of "mineral" medications such as arsenic and strichnine. These were methods that eased many a person to a premature death.

There were other streams of medicine, less heroic in practice. Perhaps the most important of these was the botanic medicine stream initiated by Samuel Thomson, and for a time it became the largest stream, even larger than orthodox medicine. It was this stream that sent a flow with the saints into the Rocky Mountains. But other streams had broken off Thomsonianism even before the death of the old doctor in 1843. Further fractioning took place very rapidly after the Mormons had moved West, and Thomsonianism was nearly unrecognizable by the time of the Civil War, with its main branch, Neo-Thomsonianism, disappearing in the early 1870s. One branch, eclectic medicine, which attempted to gather the good out of Thomsonianism, regular medicine, and all other branches, continued longer, but finally died out completely in post World War I and depression times. Another stream, homeopathy, came into the swamp from Germany and began to gain a firm American footing at about the time that the Mormons moved West. Many of the doctors who had been Thomsonians joined the homeopathic branch. This stream, which advocated miniscule doses of medications so that they would not damage the patient while trying to heal him, continued on as a small stream until it finally merged into the orthodox stream in the depression years just prior to World War II.

Two streams arose at a late period of the swampy morass and still exist parallel to orthodox medicine. Dr. Andrew Still founded Osteopathy, which is now gradually merging with orthodox medicine, but the merger is not yet complete. Last to come was chiropractic, which like osteopathy emphasized manipulation of the body, but decided that spinal manipulation was the panacea. Finally a branch called naturopathy, with hazy connections to the botanic medicine of Samuel Thomson, survives, in many cases melded with chiropractic, as the opposition to orthodox medicine.

The main stream of American medicine, which the other branches began to call allopathic medicine, slowly began to divorce itself from heroic practices. It began the revolution that finally made it acceptable to the Mormon hierarchy, and to gather in the other branches of medicine.

It was the infusion into allopathic, or old school medicine, of the main stream of worldwide medical practice that led to the major changes in medicine. These changes began in Europe.

In 1819, Rene T. H. Laennec developed a very simple diagnostic instrument. He found that by using a hollow wooden tube he could listen easier to sounds inside the body, like the beating of the heart. He went on to catalog those sounds, describing what a normal heart sounded like, and what a malfunctioning heart sounded like. But then it took almost half a century before the medical profession in general began to improve his instrument and to use the stethoscope as a major diagnostic tool.

Then in 1833, in Great Britain, J. J. Lister made an important improvement in the microscope, the achromatic microscope. This allowed scientists to more easily study the animalcules that had been described way back in the 1500s. This single discovery was one of the most important steps in the revolution of medicine. It opened the way for the development of microbiology, or bacteriology.

Meanwhile, the Americans had not completely missed out on the revolution. An army surgeon had had a French-Canadian patient with a shotgun wound in the stomach that would not heal up, and he began to experiment by dangling different types of food through the fistula in the stomach. In 1833, William Beaumont finally described for the world his experiments on digestion. But why should the Mormons who were having their troubles in Missouri worry about that crazy doctor in Wisconsin who was dangling pieces of string holding food into a man's stomach?

Then in 1843, less than a year before Joseph Smith's death, Oliver Wendell Holmes had published a scientific paper in a medical journal about the contagiousness of puerperal (or childbed) fever. No one, not even in the United States, paid much attention to this obscure paper until four years later a Hungarian named Ignaz Philipp Semmelweis discovered the same thing. Even then, no one would pay attention to their piece of advice—midwives and obstetricians should wash themselves carefully between each delivery to eliminate the contagion that would otherwise be carried from mother to mother as their children were born. Forty years later, puerperal fever was still a problem in the Mormon colonies because the midwives did not always follow this advice.

Meanwhile, back in France, another seemingly unimportant, but eventually drastic change was being created. Pierre-Charles Alexandre Louis, a French physician, had become frustrated with one method of healing. He was at one of the world's largest hospitals and was able to perform a test to see if blood letting helped or hindered in the treatment of influenza, one of the most trying diseases in the hospital. Half of the patients were bled, half were not. He found that blood-letting did not help, and in fact the patients that had been bled fared worse than those who had not. When the American translation of his work, *Researches on the Effects of Bloodletting in Some Inflammatory Diseases,* was published in 1836, heroic medicine was given a very great shock. Soon every use of blood-letting was challenged. While textbooks continued to recommend it, by the 1850s it was no longer commonly used. Only a few diehards, like Mormon John M. Bernhisel, would advocate it in the 1870s.

Back in America, another very important step in the revolution was taking place. In 1842, Dr. Crawford Long, in a small town in Georgia, used ether as an anesthetic in performing an operation. But word didn't get out from that small town about the innovation. Four years later, in 1846, while the Mormons were on the plains of Iowa, a dentist in Boston named William T. G. Morton tried ether anesthesia. And soon after that the Mormon's nemesis, John C. Bennett, was also performing dental surgery with ether, and had in fact cornered part of the ether supply and distribution business in Massachusetts. In England in 1847, Sir J. Y. Simpson used chloroform as an anesthetic in obstetrical cases, so the world had two anesthetics. Now a person could be operated upon without having great pain, and surgeons did not need to rush through surgery because of that pain and trauma. More meticulous surgery was possible.

About this time the use of Lister's microscope was beginning to make its impact. A young Frenchman was hired by some wine makers to find out why it was that occasionally a batch of wine would be sour and bitter instead of tasting as it would have been expected to. Using the microscope, this young man found that the sour wine contained a different bacteria than did the good wine. He came up with the idea that there may be good bacteria and bad bacteria.

In 1860, another Frenchman, Andre Alfred Lemaire, discovered that carbolic acid would kill most bacteria. The next year the first Frenchman, Louis Pasteur, discovered anaerobic bacteria. Now the theory that bacteria could cause diseases had solid ground. Although it took years to be accepted throughout the world, and was fought against strongly by many in the allopathic school of medicine, the theory ultimately became the basis for understanding of disease.

In 1867, a young British surgeon put two and two together and got twenty-two. Joseph Lister took Lemaire's discovery that carbolic acid killed bacteria, and Pasteur's discoveries of the pathogenicity of bacteria and put them together. He performed the first antiseptic surgery by sanitizing everything in the operating room with a spray of carbolic acid. And he had far less post-operative infections than other surgeons had.

During the Civil War, another event took place in America that was destined to change medicine dramatically. For many years there had been a minority of orthodox doctors that felt that the use of heroic doses of calomel (mercurous chloride) was detrimental to their patients. One of these had been Oliver Wendell Holmes. But the majority of medical practitioners, particularly those from the Middle West and South, advocated copius use of calomel. Because of the strong opposition of the unorthodox medical sects to calomel, and strong orthodox support, calomel had become the symbol of orthodox medicine. Any attacks upon the use of calomel were looked upon as attacks upon the whole profession of allopathic medicine.

Because of the large numbers of doctors serving in the Union Army during the Civil War, and variations in the quality of medical care given the troops, the Surgeon General instituted a corps of inspectors to visit the units and inspect the type of medical care being given, and to report on what they found. They were also authorized to perform autopsies on dead Union soldiers to verify the causes of death reported by the surgeons. It was soon apparent that far more Union troops were dying from diseases such as typhoid, cholera, and diphtheria, than were dying from battle wounds. The inspectors found, upon autopsy, that many of these non-battle deaths had gangrenous intestines filled with hardened impactions of calomel. (Remember Alvin Smith, brother of the prophet?) It was obvious that the gangrene was killing many soldiers instead of the diseases, and that the gangrene was caused by copius use of calomel.

Surgeon General William A. Hammond ordered the removal of calomel and emetic tartar from the supply tables of the army. The order whipped up a furious action on the part of organized medicine. The American Medical Association accused the Surgeon General of grossly insulting the medical profession and maligning two most valuable remedies. They demanded his removal as Surgeon General. Secretary of War Stanton acceded to their demands and sacked Dr. Hammond. But the evidence Hammond's inspectors had turned up was too damning to be buried. The use of calomel started dropping, and although it took some fifteen years for its use to be nearly completely stopped, most of its use had halted by the late 1860s.[2] Heroic medicine was no more.

Now it was time for the Mormons to be reimmersed into the mainstream of medical development. Until this time, Brigham Young had often expressed his concern about the imperfect science of medicine. As late as 1869, he had insisted that the initial step that should be taken by the saints in the case of illness was to rely first on priesthood faith healing, and then to carefully select reliable medical practitioners for care.[3] As early as 1857, he had started to accept personal medical care from an orthodox doctor, Dr. Washington F. Anderson, who had also become a close friend. Now he began to let other members of his household turn to orthodox medical practitioners. Within a short time he was sending L.D.S. youth on missions to the East to medical schools.

Brigham's faith in the future of medicine was not misplaced, because the pace of improvements in medicine accelerated through the end of the Utah territorial period, and beyond into the twentieth century.

In February, 1870, George Q. Cannon, editor of the *Deseret News,* wrote an editorial that was a serious discussion of the "germ theory" as it was being brought to the attention of the world. The discussion was based on an article by Professor John Tyndall of London. Tyndall had told of the deadly dust in the air which was being constantly breathed into the lungs. With the dust go countless germs which are implanted and grow within the body, thus producing disease.[4]

The works of Louis Pasteur had inspired many studies in bacteriology, and the Germans took up the gauntlet, the challenge of finding the bacteria that caused the deadly diseases. In 1874, Paul Ehrlic developed improved microscopic techniques, using dried blood smears and methods of staining bacteria, etc. One after another of the killer germs was isolated. In 1876, the young German, Robert Koch, grew anthrax bacilli on artificial media. The following year Pasteur found the cause of malignant edema. Then, in 1878, Koch found the cause of traumatic infection. In 1880, Pasteur isolated streptococcus and staphylococcus bacteria, and Carl Joseph Eberth isolated the typhoid bacillus. In 1882, Koch found the tubercle bacillus. The next year Edwin Klebs discovered the diphtheria bacillus. Finally, in 1884, Koch found the cholera bacillus.

Then the study of immunization (immunology) opened. Pasteur opened the field by developing a vaccine against anthrax in 1883. In 1889, Emil von Behring found that bodies developed antitoxins, and the next year he developed a method of treating diphtheria with antitoxin.

Meanwhile, in 1886, Franz von Soxhlet developed a method of sterilization of milk so that it could be used for infant feeding and eliminate the cause of the Mountain West's greatest child killer, cholera infantum, or epidemic diarrhea.

Two great developments in surgery took place in 1886. The first was the introduction of steam sterilization in surgery. No longer did the operating theater have to be bathed in a spray of carbolic acid. Then an Irish doctor in Massachusetts, Reginald H. Fitz, described and named appendicitis, nine years too late to help Brigham Young.

Then, in 1895, another great diagnostic tool was discovered. Wilhelm Konrad Roentgen discovered the x-ray that could see into bodies and take pictures, and which could be used to help heal tissues deep in the body.

And an army doctor, John Shaw Billings, who spent part of his time as a pathologist, and the rest as a collector of medical literature, who dreamed of building a great medical library for the world, and then proceeded to do it, found a solution on how to keep up with all the changes that were taking place in medicine. In 1879 and 1880 he launched the *Index Medicus,* which indexed all medical periodicals he could acquire from throughout the world, and the *Index-Catalogue of the Surgeon General's Library.*

The modern scientific movement in medicine would accelerate into the twentieth century, with Mormondom accepting its improving medical care.

Chapter Twelve

Brigham Young And Medicine

As the attitudes of Church members towards medicine were largely reflections of Joseph Smith's during the first fourteen years of the Church's history, so the attitudes of his successor, Brigham Young, were reflected in the attitudes of the saints for the next thirty-three years, as Brigham led the Church.

Brigham Young was the ninth of eleven children in his family, and he grew up in an environment very similar to that of Joseph Smith's youth. It may be safely assumed that he grew up and was exposed to similar epidemics and diseases as was Joseph Smith.

Certainly it may be safely assumed that his family did not escape the ravages of tuberculosis in its various forms. His mother probably was a victim of the disease, undoubtedly the reason for her early death. If he was not exposed to tuberculosis in his youth, he certainly was exposed in young adulthood. His wife of young adulthood, Miriam Works, died of consumption. He had married in 1824 at age 23, and his wife died, after giving him two children, in 1832.[1] Brigham, however, did not appear to have been personally afflicted with the disease.

As he grew up, he undoubtedly was exposed to the so-called childhood diseases, which were very dangerous in those days. However, the earliest bit of information about his health in childhood is a report that he had mumps "on one side" when he was fourteen years old.[2] Otherwise, there is no record of his medical history. It has also been said that he was "tortured" on occasion "from his youth" with an intermittent rheumatism.

After his mother's death he was apprenticed to learn the trade of carpenter, painter, and glazier. In this occupation he was exposed to lead poisoning, but there is no indication of after effects. He may have been saved from these by joining the Church and abandoning the trade in order to serve the Church.[3]

As a convert to the Church, Brigham Young did not appear to have formed any allegiance with a school of medical thought. However, it was soon apparent that he had espoused the botanic beliefs of his leader, Joseph Smith.

The first serious adult illness of Brigham Young was his "seasoning" to malaria, or ague and fever, as he joined the Church membership in the vicinity of Nauvoo. He had temporarily settled in the ruins of old Fort Des Moines in Montrose, across the Mississippi River from Nauvoo, when he was stricken. Brigham was only one of hundreds of saints to be stricken with this disease. He was then thirty-eight, remarried and the father of three more children (including twins). He and other apostles had gone about blessing the sick and attending to the needs of his fellow saints, but soon he himself was stricken and bedridden.[4]

This epidemic of malaria was the occasion when Joseph Smith, himself also stricken with malaria, rose from his sick bed and went about Nauvoo and Montrose, healing the sick in his massive charismatic healing. Brigham was one of those called forth from the sick bed to accompany the prophet. He "arose and was healed." His recovery, however, seems not to have been altogether complete. Eight weeks later, his health was still "so poor I was unable to go thirty rods to the river without assistance." He nevertheless departed on a mission to England in mid-September, being conveyed initially on horseback or in a bed "fitted up" in a wagon. A month later he wrote that he was "unable to sit up," and after yet another month—in mid-November—that among himself and his companions "there was not a healthy man." When he reached England he was so emaciated that his cousin, Willard Richards, did not recognize him. Brigham and the rest of the apostles had apparently recovered their health by the time they finished their missions in England. Their return to Nauvoo did not require another period of "seasoning" to ague and chills.

On 1 February 1840, on his way to England, Brigham fell while jumping onto a New York ferryboat, "putting my shoulder out of joint." His account of the episode suggests that this might have been a recurrent orthopedic problem. He reports:

> I asked brother Hedlock to roll me over on my back, which he did; I directed brothers Kimball and Hedlock to lay hold on my body, and brother Pratt to take hold of my hand and pull, putting his foot against my side, while I guided the bone with my right hand back to its place. The brethren wound my handkerchief round my shoulder and helped me up. When I came to a fire I fainted, and was not able to dress myself for several days.[5]

After Brigham's return from England, until he was forty-two (in November 1842) he remained well. Then he was "suddenly attacked with a slight fit of apoplexy [a loss of consciousness]." The next morning he "felt quite comfortable," but that night he was "attacked with the most violent fever I ever experienced." Thirty hours after the onset of the fever, "the skin began to peel from my body, and I was skinned all over." He remained sick abed for a total of eighteen days. Dr. Lester Bush has conjectured that the most likely cause of this illness was scarlet fever with a secondary infection.[6]

But Brigham's problems were not over when the fever broke. That day, according to his journal account:

> I was bolstered up in my chair, but was so near gone that I could not close my eyes, which were set in my head—my chin dropped down and my breath stopped. My wife, seeing my situation, threw some cold water in my face; that having no effect, she dashed a handful of strong camphor into my face and eyes, which I did not feel in the least, neither did I move a muscle. She then held my nostrils between her thumb and forefinger, and placing her mouth directly over mine, blew into my lungs until she filled them with air. This set my lungs in motion, and I again began to breathe. While this was going on I was perfectly conscious of all that was pressing around me; my spirit was as vivid as it ever was in my life, but I had no feeling in my body.[7]

Brigham's wife clearly anticipated our modern mouth-to-mouth resuscitation, but she was doing much as many of her contemporaries would have done had they the presence of mind to act. Mouth-to-mouth resuscitation had been a technique in use since Bible times and was still popular among society at large in the first half of the nineteenth century.[8] It lost vogue in the last half of that century, only to be reintroduced a century later.

It took until mid-January 1843, nearly eight weeks after the first fit of apoplexy, before Brigham Young was able to leave home and resume his normal functions. He felt, however, even as late as the next August, that he had not wholly recovered from the illness.

After Brigham assumed the leadership of the Church following Joseph Smith's martyrdom in 1844, and as he led the saints west, he suffered disease and affliction right along with his fellow saints. Although he apparently escaped scurvy, he did have diarrhea and other diseases that struck the camp. Perhaps the most dramatic episode of his Winter Quarters illness took place in mid-February 1847 when he was "taken very unwell, being much distressed in the stomach and bowels. Fainted away, apparently dead for several moments, and it was with much ado that he could be kept from falling asleep to await the resurrection morn." His recovery was rapid. Three hours later Brigham informed a visitor that "I have frequently [fainted] away but never died before."[9]

Perhaps the most celebrated illness Brigham Young had was his Mountain Fever attack on the pioneer trip to the Salt Lake Valley. (See Chapter Eight.) It was severe enough that the camp suspended operations to have a special prayer meeting, pleading for the sparing of the life of their leader. It was while still recuperating from this illness that Brigham Young entered the Valley riding on a bed in the back of Wilford Woodruff's carriage, and acknowledged, after overlooking the Valley, "This is the right place, drive on."

Although Brigham Young and Willard Richards were first cousins, it is not known how well acquainted they were prior to Willard's joining the Church. It is obvious, however, that they became well acquainted and remained as close associates and friends after their mission together in England. As Frederick G. Williams was instrumental in acquainting Joseph Smith with Thomsonian medicine, so undoubtedly Willard Richards acquainted Brigham Young with Thomsonianism. Brigham gave every evidence in later life of being well acquainted with this practice of medicine, and he regularly attended, in the 1850s, the meetings of the Council on Health founded by them in Salt Lake City.

One concept of medicine propounded by Samuel Thomson reoccurs in Brigham Young's addresses in the Mountain West time after time. Rarely does Brigham bring up the concept of faith healing or medicine in his discourses without that concept being included in his address.[10] Thomson had taught that each parent—father or mother—should be the doctor for that home, that there was no need for a professional body of doctors.

Brigham Young accepted this Thomsonian concept, but melded it with the concept of priesthood healing. Thomson's concept dovetailed with the concept of the Gospel of a lay priesthood with that authority in each home. Then Brigham Young added that the woman had the right to give healing blessings in her home, in addition to, or in lieu of, the priesthood member's blessings.

From Brigham Young's 1856 discourse, which advised the sick to do all in their power to heal themselves before calling for a priesthood blessing,[11] to his last discourse on health before the Weber Stake Relief Societies on 19 July 1877, just a few weeks before his death,[12] he emphasized preventive medicine by utilizing the Word of Wisdom, and the necessity of home health care.

Through the first twenty years of his leadership of the Church, he was a very strong advocate of botanic medicine. In 1846, he wrote to the soldiers of the Mormon Battalion: "If you are sick, live by faith, and let the surgeon's medicine alone if you want to live, using only such herbs and mild food as are at your disposal."[13] It was unfortunate that the Battalion members were not able to keep his instructions because of the actions of orthodox doctor, George B. Sanderson.

Shortly after Brigham Young began his tenure as governor of the territory of Utah, the legislature passed, in 1851, its first health law. It is probable that one or both of two Thomsonian doctors that were members of the legislature, Willard Richards and his brother Phineas Richards, drafted the law. It provided stiff penalties (not less than $1,000 and not less than one year at hard labor) to anyone giving any deadly poison under pretence of curing disease without first explaining its nature and effects in plain English, and procuring the "unequivocal approval" of the patient.[14]

The following year the Seventh General Epistle of the First Presidency (18 April 1852) advised the Church: "When you are sick, call for the Elders, who will pray for you, anointing with oil and the laying on of hands; and nurse each other with herbs, and mild food, and if you do these things, in faith, and quit taking poisons, and poisonous medicines, which God never ordained for the use of men, you shall be blessed."[15]

Brigham told the Board of Health, "If the people want to eat calomel, let them do it and be damned. But don't feed it to any of my family. If any doctor does and I know it I would kill him as quick as I would for feeding arsenic."[16] He did, however, reluctantly concede that in rare instances calomel might be beneficial:

> But there is constitutions, and situations in life, wherein you may administer calomel to persons, and it will do them good when nothing else will. But is it good in every case? No. Not one in fifty thousand, but we will reduce that and say one to five thousand. It will produce death in five thousand where it will do good only to one person.[17]

Brigham's prejudices against doctors were quite pronounced in the first few years after the saints' arrival in the Valley. He declared, "A worse set of ignoramuses do not walk the earth."[18] Then he fulminated against them, that they put the ability to heal into the hands of a few and keep the rest ignorant. Useful medical knowledge should be imparted to all; those unwilling to share their knowledge were "corrupt."[19] Even as late as 1869, *Harpers Weekly* reported Brigham's claim that "at Salt Lake they had no sickness till the doctors came. Then they, being too lazy to delve and hoe like others, made people ill, in order to get a living by doctoring them![20]

In 1862, Brigham created an analogy, comparing the saving of souls by missionaries to the saving of bodies by physicians. In it he coincidentally shows his philosophy toward medicine:

> We are to be like good physicians; and if we see the sick—those afflicted with pain and distress in the head, eyes, teeth, or in any of the limbs or other portion of the body, it is our duty to have the medicine— the remedy to administer to that pain, to heal, to cure, to rebuke the disease and save the sick like a good physician, and not to kill them by dosing down the medicine as do some of our doctors. Administer the medicine in all mildness, and with good judgement and discretion. Seek until you learn the medicine to administer to each patient, and how much to give to each.... You may go to a man taken with a fever, and if you treat hom as you did a similar case last week, you may consign him to the grave. You ought to know better.[21]

The coming of the railroad to Utah in 1869 created a revolution in the thinking of the saints. True, for some time there had been a growing body of non-Mormons in Utah, but the railroad opened the way for a much larger influx of non-Mormons. In fact, it had been hoped by some that the railroad would be the death knell for Mormonism. It was not the death knell, but it did create changes in Mormon thinking. One evidence of this impact was the fact that within a five-month period, three discourses by Brigham Young on spiritual healing, health, or medicine, were recorded for the *Journal of Discourses* (which carried important talks by Church leaders).[22]

In each of these talks Brigham emphasized the first place of faith healing. If there was sufficient faith, doctors would not be needed. Brigham was happy to say that he "had never been under the necessity of calling a doctor to [his] family for forty years." He had had them in, but not from necessity. He liked them when they were gentlemen. However, he maintained that the Latter-day Saints had proven that communities without doctors were healthier than communities with doctors, and wagered that a study of the next thirty years would show that the community without doctors would far excel the community with doctors.[23] Another theme in the talks was his charge that parents should learn sufficient medicine to be able to care for their children without need for calling in doctors.

Long before this, Brigham Young had become a close friend of Washington F. Anderson. He had even accepted Anderson's medications upon occasion, and Brigham was undoubtedly aware of what was happening to the field of medicine. Then, in 1867, he called Willard Richard's son, Heber John Richards, to a mission in the East to learn medicine in a medical school in New York City. He later called another of Willard's sons, Joseph S. Richards, to the same mission. By 1871, Heber was back in Salt Lake in practice with Dr. Anderson, who apparently was not a Mormon, but very likely was a secret member of the Church.[24] In 1872, Brigham also called his nephew, Seymour B. Young, to attend medical school.

In effect, Brigham had established a priority for medical care: first, home care, which should simultaneously provide faith healing through parental and priesthood blessings and home medication with medicines which the parents understood; second, care by well-qualified and judicious doctors.

In 1875, Brigham still emphasized the importance of the parents in medical care:

> And it is the duty of every father and mother to live so that they may have the mind and will of the Lord concerning their duties to their families. If they are not called to exercise the priesthood which they hold, more than to administer to their children, it is their duty to live so as to know how to teach, leave and advise their children; and if they

are disposed they have the privilege for it is God's mind and will that they should know just what to do for them when they are sick. Instead of calling for a doctor you should administer to them by the laying on of hands and anointing with oil, and give them mild food, and herbs, and medicine you understand; and if you want the mind and will of God at such a time, get it, it is just as much your privilege as of any other member of the Church and kingdom of God. It is your privilege and duty to live so that you know when the word of the Lord is spoken to you and when the mind of the Lord is revealed to you.[25]

Brigham was worried about some of the trends that he saw developing in medicine. He spoke of "a growing evil in our midst. It will be so in a little time that not a woman in all Israel will dare to have a baby unless she can have a doctor by her."[26]

He defined a good doctor in an 1873 conference address: "It is that man or woman who, by revelation, or we may call it intuitive inspiration, is capable of administering medicine to assist the human system when it is besieged by the enemy called Disease; but if they have not that manifestation, they had better let the sick person alone." He continued, "I say that unless a man or woman who administers medicine to assist the human system to overcome disease, understands, and had that intuitive knowledge, by the Spirit, that such an article is good for that individual at that very time, they had better let him alone."[27]

After Brigham Young entered the Salt Lake Valley for the second time, in 1848, he never again returned to the East. But he did travel extensively in the West among the Mormon colonies. He maintained a youthful appearance and vigorous schedule for many years. He did, however, succumb to several lengthy illnesses which, although not as severe as those experienced earlier, came more frequently.

He had quite a bit of respiratory difficulty during this period, and one wonders if it was a manifestation of the tuberculosis which he had been exposed to long ago. In April, 1851, he had a "cold" which was sufficiently debilitating to keep him from attending the important semi-annual general conference of the Church. That fall, he returned from a trip with another "severe cold," and "immediately" taking to his bed, "was hardly out of his house" during the entire month of November. A year later he was again down with a "high fever." While Brigham felt well enough two or three *weeks* later to go to his office, he thereupon suffered a relapse and it was another three weeks before he had "recuperated sufficiently to resume his work." He was sick in March, 1854, and unable to officiate at the funeral of Willard Richards. Then in the winter of 1857-58, more serious problems returned and he recorded that his "bodily afflictions would not permit me to walk much" for nearly two months, at the end of which he wrote that they "still hinder my efforts in speaking or exercising." Following the Utah War, Brigham again fell ill in October and missed general conference.[28]

In the 1860s, Brigham's rheumatism began to be a more regular plague to him. He was confined to his home both by the rheumatism and by respiratory ailments for most of the winter of 1865, and was also frequently troubled by rheumatism in 1867 and 1870. In 1865, he had a respiratory ailment he called "lung fever." In the winter of 1869-70, he suffered a "little with the mumps." This time "on both sides." In view of the reported youthful case, was this or that case correctly diagnosed?[29]

During the 1870s, Brigham Young had many more cases of "colds" and other respiratory illnesses. He reported "severe" colds and fever in the summer of 1872 (at age seventy-one), and again that winter. The following fall, he recorded that he "contracted a severe cold which brought on a chill followed by fever from which I have been confined to my room for several days." This convalescence lasted several weeks. In 1874, he had a severe case of "influenza" and was incapacitated for several weeks, but this was complicated by a serious problem.[30]

In 1874, Dr. Seymour B. Young, Brigham's nephew (the one that he had sent to school in New York), discovered that Brigham had a "Stopage" of the urine through enlargement of the prostate gland." Seymour turned to the accepted treatment and while attending Brigham for "20 days and nights," he "drew off his water [with a catheter]" until he finally "got him educated . . . to draw off his own water." Brigham was regularly catheterized during the last years of his life. In October, 1875, the trauma of self-catheterization led to a local spasm and hemorrhage which required two weeks of treatment.[31]

Brigham's health continued to degenerate, though he remained active in his functions as Church leader, until 1877. On Thursday afternoon, 23 August, Brigham fell ill, experiencing primarily "an inclination to vomit," but was not sick enough to curtail his activities. About 11 p.m. that evening he was suddenly "seized with a violent vomiting, purging and cramping" which lasted almost continuously for the next six hours. The next morning, Brigham asked for a "mild opiate" which was injected into each foot. Brigham continued to receive small doses of opium for the next several days. On Monday morning "increasing symptoms of nervous prostration" were evident. Tuesday morning "warm stimulating injections [enemas]" were given. By Wednesday morning, August 29, it was apparent that the end was rapidly approaching. At 2 p.m., several brethren administered to him, and he roused briefly to respond "in a clear and distinct voice, 'Amen.' " He died soon after.[32]

There has been much controversy over the cause of Brigham Young's death. Among the causes conjectured have been pyelonephritis, arsenic poisoning, typhoid fever, paratyphoid, bacillary dysentery, and mesenteric thrombosis or diverticulitis.³³ In later years Seymour B. Young, the principle attending physician, concluded that it must have been appendicitis. Unfortunately this clinical entity was unknown in 1877. Dr. Young often lamented the fact that appendicitis had not been discovered just a few years earlier, for had it been, he felt, Brigham's life could have been saved.³⁴

After Seymour B. Young returned from medical school, Brigham Young began to use his medical services. As Brigham aged, those services were needed more and more as Brigham's attempts at self-medication became less and less efficacious. He was administered to by the priesthood many times, but medical help was needed, and in his final illness his doctor nephew called in the aid of Brigham's old friend, Dr. Washington F. Anderson, and the two of them in turn called in two more doctors who were not Mormons as consultants. They were the attending doctors of Holy Cross Hospital, Drs. Joseph Mott Benedict and Francis Denton Benedict, his brother. By these actions preceding his death, Brigham Young opened the door to acceptance of medicine by the saints.

Chapter Thirteen

Hospitals And Public Health In Utah, 1850 to 1910

To the saints arriving in the Mountain West From Nauvoo and other parts of the world, hospitals were places for people to go to die. People who went to hospitals, to their way of thinking, usually came out in a casket. It was better for a person to be cared for by his loved ones in his home. In spite of the high amount of illness present in Nauvoo, there had been no plans for hospitals in the community. Hospitals were only found in the largest cities, and then they were largely for the care of indigents who had no family or friends to care for them.

With this attitude, it is no wonder that their community would survive for a quarter of a century before hospitals would be organized among them for care of the sick of their community. Only once, for a period of two years, in that intervening time, did a hospital appear in the land of Zion, and then that hospital drew its patients from transients who were on their way through, on the way to gold fields.

Irwin Pizer, in his discussion of the medical aspects of the westward migration, noted that as the emigrants went through Salt Lake City they found that there were physicians who might be sought out for medical aid. He noted Dr. Priddy Meeks' method of treatment of "Mountain Fever": "tell them to jump all over in the City Creek, and crawl back into their tent and cover up warm and they seemed to recover under that treatment as fast as any other." Pizer remarked that the Mormons were not above treating the emigrants to a little humbug when he pointed out Meeks' cure, not realizing that this was the same type of treatment that Meeks would have given the saints as his best method of treatment.[1] Although there were physicians in Salt Lake City at the time, most of them were botanic practitioners.

It was this demand for patient care by transients that caused a botanic doctor, Dr. Ezra Williams, to turn his new home into a hospital for two years.[2] Williams had migrated to Deseret in 1849, and began to practice medicine. Shortly after his arrival in Salt Lake, he built a log cabin on Main Street, across from the temple site. This cabin was not large enough for his rapidly growing family, so in 1851, he erected a seven-room adobe house where the west wing of the Church Office Building now stands on North Temple Street. The family occupied it for a few months and then moved back to the old log cabin.

Dr. Williams' wife recorded in her journal: "We gave up our new home for a hospital when the gold rush of '52 was on. Many of the emigrants contracted mountain fever and the doctor took them in and cared for them until they recovered. One man remained all winter and we put him to work turning legs for furniture."

The hospital was kept open through 1853, and then Dr. Williams' family reoccupied the building as a dwelling. The house stood until 1918, when it was torn down to make room for the Joseph Smith Memorial Building, which housed for many years the Genealogical Society of Utah. That building in turn was torn down to make way for the skyscraper Church Office Building.

At this late date, it is impossible to measure the volume of Dr. Williams' business in the hospital. Dr. Ralph Richards, who counted the number of deaths appearing opposite his name in the City Cemetery books, has said, "He must have been pretty busy as he had 60 per cent more deaths to his credit than the nearest competitor from 1851 to 1859." [3] So came, and so went, Deseret's first hospital, unused by the local populace, but a godsend to the transients passing through. It was to be nearly twenty years before what would now be called a hospital was to be built in Zion.

As time went on, it was found that Zion was not a utopia. Hard work had always been viewed as a benefit, and it was felt that this would bring good health to Zion's inhabitants. To a large extent this was true, but it became more and more apparent that Zion had citizens who were mentally disturbed. Thus, at much the same time as "insane asylums" were being built across the United States, one was built in the Salt Lake Valley. The city chose as the site of its insane asylum a hundred-and-sixty-acre tract with independent water rights far east of the outskirts of the city, south of the entrance to Emigration Canyon, overlooking the Valley. It was built about 1870. Little is known about its first few years of existence.

In 1874, Dr. Seymour B. Young, Brigham's nephew, returned to Salt Lake City from medical school and began practice. About two years later he was appointed to the part-time position of City Physician, and as such found himself in charge of the institution. About 1878, Dr. Young purchased the property from the city and conducted a hospital for the insane, and the institution became known as Dr. Young's Insane Asylum. The house's outside was of plaster and cement and was kept immaculately clean and white. Because the building stood out on the hills above the city, it soon came to be frequently called "The White House on the Hill."

It was enveloped in a mass of locust trees and green lawns and flower gardens. Under Dr. Young's direction, the grounds were beautifully laid out in flowers and shrubs. Many acres were brought under cultivation. Wheat, garden vegetables, and fruit were raised on the place. A herd of cows were kept for milk and butter; hogs and chickens were also kept.[4]

Dr. Young espoused the theory of work therapy, and many of his patients assisted in the cultivation of the land and care of the animals. Although many of the apartments had iron bars at the windows and doors, yet in the main all of the inmates had liberal privileges of playing in the large shady yard. Many of the feeble minded were taken to the home of Dr. Young in the city, and there received intensive treatment and were sent home later well and strong. A resident superintendent and matron lived at the institution all the time.

The patient load for the hospital came not only from Salt Lake City but from the entire territory and from surrounding states and territories. When the Territorial Insane Asylum was opened in Provo in 1885, the demand for Dr. Young's Asylum dropped and it soon closed. It had been Utah's second hospital, and the first in which the majority of patients were Mormons.

During the Civil War, when General Patrick Connor brought his California Volunteers to Utah, he brought a large contingent of non-Mormons who would remain in Zion. This non-Mormon populace felt a stronger need for medical care and hospitals than did the local Mormons. A Post Dispensary staffed by orthodox doctors was indispensable to the soldiery. General Connor had urged the development of mining by his troops during their free time, and valuable mining properties were discovered as a result. (Brigham Young had urged the Mormons to not develop mining because he felt that they needed a solid base of agriculture first.)

As the soldiers were discharged and became civilian miners and businessmen, the pressure for hospital medical care grew, but until 1869 and the coming of the railroads, mining was on a precarious level because many of the minerals were of low concentration in the ores, and shipment or effective smelting was difficult. With the railroads it became possible to both smelt economically and to ship ores, and mining boomed. And with the boom in mining came an increased demand for hospitals.

On 30 April 1872, Major Edmund Wilkes, a vestryman of St. Marks (Episcopal) Cathedral in Salt Lake City, and mining and smelting tycoon, led out in the founding of the first allopathic general medicine hospital in Utah. A month later, the hospital was placed under the permanent control of the Episcopal Church. Dr. John F. Hamilton was made the medical director of the hospital and was the only doctor to serve in the hospital for twenty years.[5]

On 13 May 1872, St. Marks Hospital opened in a rented adobe house on the corner of 4th South and 5th East. In 1876, a larger house one block north was purchased. Though the hospital was organized solely for the accommodation of industrial casualties from the mines and smelters, the policy was soon liberalized to permit the treatment of private citizens who needed hospitalization—principally surgery. The miners and smelter workers had $1 per month deducted from their pay checks, and for that they were eligible for complete medical care in the hospital.

In 1874, two years after Salt Lake's first allopathic hospital was opened, Dr. H. J. Powers opened a hospital in Ogden, at Grant Avenue and 25th Street.[6] It survived through 1882 and was succeeded by the Union Pacific Hospital in 1883. Ogden was the terminal point of the Central (later Southern) Pacific and Union Pacific Railroads and had a large gentile population.

In 1875, the Catholic miners and smelter workers in the intermountain area requested that the Reverend Lawrence Scanlan, who afterwards became the first Bishop of Salt Lake, organize a hospital for them. He petitioned the Sisters of the Holy Cross to open a hospital, and Sisters M. Holy Cross and Bartholomew were sent to undertake the work.[7] The medical staff at first consisted of Dr. Allen Fowler and the two brothers, Doctors D. and J. M. Benedict. This hospital, too, was opened in quarters on 5th East Street, this time in a converted barn. In 1882, Bishop Scanlon purchased an entire city block of ten acres, at 10th East and 1st South, and began construction of a one hundred twenty-five-bed hospital.

In 1880, another hospital, the Keely Institute, was opened in a mansion near the Union Pacific Depot on West South Temple Street.[8] This hospital specialized in the treatment of "drunkenness as a disease."

With the influx of allopathic doctors of the Mormon faith into the Salt Lake community in the 1870s, largely under the auspices of Brigham Young or the Female Relief Society, many of them took advantage of the facilities of St. Mary's Hospital (as Holy Cross Hospital was known for a period of time). Brigham Young even had the two Drs. Benedict from that hospital's staff as consultants during his final illness, though he had not been a patient in the hospital.

Though Brigham Young had counseled against the saints participating in the mining industry, many of them did become employed in the mines as they were opened by the gentiles (non-Mormons). A Welsh or Cornish miner convert to the Church found it convenient to gain employment in Utah in his trade rather than to take up a new trade. Since they had paid for medical treatment by reason of their monthly payroll deductions, they felt entitled to use those hospital services, and did use them.

The women doctors returning from Eastern training had, in many cases, received training in hospitals in Philadelphia, Boston, or Baltimore, and desired that kind of facility in Salt Lake City. They also found in Salt Lake City the same prejudice against women doctors found elsewhere in the medical profession. Since many of them had been sponsored by the Relief Society in their training, it was natural that they would turn to that organization to fill the need. So it was that on 17 July 1882, in the old Twelfth Ward, in a small building on 5th East Street between South Temple and First South Streets, the Deseret Hospital opened its doors. John Taylor, who had succeeded Brigham Young as president of the Church, dedicated the hospital.[9]

Eliza R. Snow, widow of both Joseph Smith and Brigham Young, president of the Church-wide Relief Society organization, was chosen president of the hospital, with her Relief Society counselor and co-Brigham Young-widow, Zina D. H. Young, as vice-president. Emmeline B. Wells, who held a like position in the Relief Society was secretary; with Matilda M. Barrett, treasurer. The medical staff of the hospital, with the exception of Dr. Washington F. Anderson and Dr. Seymour B. Young, was all female. Dr. Ellen R. Ferguson was named Resident Physician, with Drs. Romania B. Pratt, Ellis R. Shipp, and Elvira S. Barney as visiting physicians and surgeons. Later Dr. Martha Paul Hughes succeeded Dr. Ferguson, and still later Dr. Pratt stepped into the position. President Angus M. Cannon, of the Salt Lake Stake of the Church, became priesthood adviser, and soon married as a plural wife Dr. Martha Hughes Paul, who was then Resident Physician.

The facilities on 5th East were soon overcrowded, and the hospital moved into a building recently vacated by the University of Deseret (Utah) at 1st North (now 200 North) and 2nd West (now 300 West). The hospital was soon the center of the Relief Society's efforts to train nurses and midwives, and to teach health and hygiene to Mormon women. It had only one major problem: many Church members assumed that it was a charity hospital and should take care of them gratis. They balked at paying its fees, originally three dollars a week, later raised to six dollars a week. In 1890, the hospital closed because of insufficient finances.

The year the Deseret Hospital closed, 1890, Ogden city opened a hospital which it operated for a short time.[10] In 1897, the city leased the vacant building to a group of doctors and it was reopened as the Ogden General Hospital.

In 1877, Charles T. Jackson, who maintained a commercial chemical laboratory in Boston, visited Salt Lake City and analyzed the waters of the Warm Springs on the city's northern outskirts (the ones that had been the center of the Dr. Robinson incident). Jackson, who had demonstrated to Dr. W. T. G. Morton the anesthetic properties of ether before Dr. Morton introduced it to the world, claimed that the Warm Springs waters had valuable therapeutic properties.[11]

The city was feeling the impact of the closing of the Deseret Hospital, and the hospital board of St. Marks Hospital chose a new site for their hospital on property adjacent to the Warm Sprints. By 1893, the first building of the new hospital was finished, and three years later the capacity was doubled to about sixty patients. By the time the wing was finished, the hospital had a capacity of 125 beds. Dr. Hamilton retired as medical director of St. Mark's Hospital with the opening of the new hospital in 1893, and the medical staff was immediately increased. The number of non-industrial or private patients increased markedly.

Utah had many dentists during its territorial period, and many were Mormons. The feeling of antipathy which had grown up against physicians apparently did not affect them. One of the most colorful dentists was Dr. William H. Groves. In 1862, Dr. Groves joined the Mormon Church and moved from California to Utah. Although he had been a fancy dresser and socialite in his early days in Utah, toward the end of his life he drastically changed his patterns of living and became a bachelor recluse in a poorly furnished room over an undertaking parlor.[12]

In April, 1895, Dr. Groves had a heart attack, and Dr. Joseph S. Richards was called in. The patient was taken to the new St. Mark's Hospital, the staff of which Dr. Richards had just been admitted to, for treatment. On the way to the hospital, Dr. Richards was told by Dr. Groves that the reason Dr. Groves had been miserly of late was so that when he died he could endow a library. Dr. Richards replied to Dr. Groves, "After you have been in the hospital a few days and realize what wonderful service and fine care is given to sick people by the nurses, you will come to the conclusion that there is more need for a hospital than a library." The pessimistic critic of modern hospitals may feel that there was a conspiracy afoot, because Dr. Groves received such good treatment that he was convinced of the truth of Dr. Richard's remarks. He rallied from his heart attack long enough to have his will rewritten in order to bequeath his estate to the LDS Church to establish the Dr. William H. Groves Latter-day Saints Hospital.

The hospital record of St. Marks Hospital for Dr. Groves reads as follows: "W. H. Groves, American; received April 8, 1895; Mormon; Physician [should have been Dentist]; private patient Dr. Richards [Joseph S.]; Angina Pectoris; tumor under clavicle; hospital number 7458." This was the first time the term "Angina Pectoris" appeared in the records of Salt Lake hospitals.[13]

The gift was the catalyst which renewed Mormon interest in having their own hospital. Even with the gift, it took some time to generate enough support to build a hospital.[14] During the eight years from the death of Dr.

Groves, in April, 1895, until the hospital building was started in July, 1903, the trustees named in the will showed only occasional signs of interest in the project. In the meantime, the endowment was diminishing in value because of declining real estate prices. Most of Dr. Groves' property was located on the west side of Salt Lake where values were dropping fastest.

Finally, in 1900, the Board of Trustees commissioned an architect to draw plans for a hospital to face north on the corner of 1st South and 1st West (an area now part of the Salt Palace Convention Center complex). But the trustees decided that there was not enough growth room on that site and they started a search for a larger site, finally choosing a site at C Street and Eighth Avenue in the Avenues section of Salt Lake, looking down over the city. When the building was built, it used the plans originally drafted for the downtown building.

When the Groves properties were sold it was found that the properties, originally estimated as being worth between $75,000 and $85,000 when given, only brought $50,000, far short of the $180,000 the building would cost to build. A gift from the Church's Fifteenth Ward of $10,000 helped. They had just sold their ward house to the Oregon Short Line Railway as a depot site. The Church itself provided $120,000 of the building costs. Additional miscellaneous gifts totalling more than $6,000 provided for furnishings for the hospital.

The hospital was dedicated 3 January 1905, by President Joseph F. Smith, who was then President of the Church. Also present were the Quorum of the Twelve, the Presiding Bishopric, the bishops of wards in the city, and the medical staff. The next day the *Deseret News* carried a small blurb on an inside page announcing the dedication. On 6 January, the newspaper carried a lengthy editorial commenting on the fact that the hospital had been dedicated three days earlier.

The editor of the paper, a Church leader who in spite of his plural marriage to a brilliant woman physician had opposed vaccination and other health measures, reflected the trauma that Church leaders were having reconciling themselves to the fact that the Church was now to operate its own hospital, while agonizing over the place of faith healing in the changing world situation.

Charles W. Penrose first exulted, "It gives evidence that 'Mormon' enterprise is abreast of the time, and that the Latter-day Saints are ready to avail themselves of scientific knowledge and progress, and are not slow to move with the march of modern thought and learning."[15] Then he entered into the subject of his concern regarding the place of faith healing. "The hospital is to be conducted along the lines of 'Mormon' regulations. These include faith as well as works, temperance, morality, cleanliness, order, and strict discipline without bondage and without bigotry. The afflicted of all shades of belief will be welcome there. The skill of the best physicians and surgeons and nurses will be utilized. While the ordinance of the Church for the benefit of the sick will be freely administered to those members who desire it, no one who objects or disbelieves in it will be under the least obligation or necessity to receive it.

"The prayer of faith is efficacious in all forms of affliction. But all people have not faith to be healed nor do all who have the faith possess it in the same degree. Remedies are provided by the Great Physician, or by Nature as some prefer to view them, and we should not close our eyes to their virtues nor ignore the skill and learning of the trained doctor. Surgery, with its wonderful advances, ought to be recognized and utilized to the utmost extent. That which we can do for ourselves we ought not to expect the Creator to do for us. Yet his blessings may be rationally as well as religiously invoked upon all human efforts for the relief of the suffering. It is the combination of that faith which gives hope and confidence, with every available material means that will render this institution peculiar in some respects, while the great adaptability for hospital purposes, the result of care, experience, research, and wise expenditure commend it as a rare and splendid establishment worthy of all that has been said of it in praise."

According to the provisions of Dr. Groves' will, Dr. Joseph S. Richards was to be medical director of LDS Hospital for life. He immediately recruited Dr. Samuel Clifton Baldwin as his right-hand man, and as the first orthopaedic surgeon on the staff. Dr. Baldwin was not a Mormon, as was the case with many of the doctors that Dr. Richards recruited for the staff. One Mormon that he did recruit was his son, Dr. Ralph T. Richards, who was fresh out of medical school. Only one woman doctor was on the early hospital staff, Dr. Jane Skolfield, a recent medical school graduate. Other women doctors had attending privileges.

It proved to be very difficult to recruit a nursing staff for the hospital. They finally recruited a Miss Waltz from the Wyoming State Insane Hospital as head nurse, but she left after a short time. She was assisted in the floor work by six practical nurses, nurses largely trained by the Relief Society. When Miss Waltz left, Dr. Baldwin telephoned Miss Liela Hard, a 1900 graduate of St. Mark's Hospital's school of nursing. She was nursing a patient in Rock Springs, Wyoming, when he asked her if she would like the job of operating-room supervisor. To tempt her, he had been authorized to offer her sixty dollars a month! She accepted and was head nurse from February, 1905, until April, 1908. In September, 1905, a nurse training school was opened in hopes of "growing their own" nurses.

The administration of the hospital was placed under the direction of the Presiding Bishopric of the Church. An employee of the Presiding Bishopric, John Wells, was given the part-time job of Superintendent of the hospital. Fortunately he was both conscientious and efficient. His typical work day began at 7 a.m. at the hospital. At 10 a.m. he went to the Presiding

Bishop's office, returned to the hospital at noon, and stayed until 2 p.m., then went downtown until 5 p.m. or 6 p.m., home to supper, and back to the hospital until 8 p.m. or 9 p.m. He was able to keep up this fantastic pace until 1908, when Bishop David A. Smith, a member of the Board of Trustees, succeeded him.[16]

With the opening of the hospital doors for the reception of patients on Monday, 9 January 1905, the Latter-day Saints had entered a new medical era.

Although the Latter-day Saints have always felt that faith healing takes first place when it comes to health practices, they have usually been rather pragmatic in their outlook to what is now known as public health.

In the early 1800s, nearly all the major cities on the East Coast had boards of health, but their acceptance by the populaces of their cities was often not very great.[17] For example, when cholera invaded New York City, the mayor disregarded the efforts of his board of health, fearing that they would hinder rather than help the city's health problems. Even years before when Samuel Latham Mitchill had organized the board, it had been largely ineffectual. Thus, when John Cook Bennett urged a Board of Health for the city of Nauvoo, it was looked upon by the Church leaders and citizens with mixed emotions. After he was excommunicated, it finally came to fruition because the Thomsonian physicians of the city saw an opportunity to create a large "Society of Health" out of the board.

In 1849, the botanic physicians in Salt Lake City organized a new Council of Health there.[18] Priddy Meeks claimed that he was responsible for it, but the meetings, at least initially, were held at Willard Richards' home. Willard, then a member of the First Presidency, appeared to lend the sanction of the Church to the project. As with other Thomsonian societies of health, they shared healing experiences and testimonies (in this case mixed with religious testimonies) and endeavored to teach the rudiments of botanic medicine to others.

One of the major teachings that found its place in their meetings was the concept that the Lord provided healing herbs to guard against and treat the illnesses found in the region. Thus Priddy Meeks and others were dispatched to the mountains to find herbs and to decide if they were helpful in treating local illnesses. This also helped the community to identify poisonous weeds which, in times of famine and limited crops, as they were then experiencing, were being eaten as food. Unfortunately, several persons died during this time from eating poisonous plants such as wild parsnips.

The Territory of Utah and City of Salt Lake soon passed several laws relating to health, the first of which was an endeavor to keep orthodox doctors from prescribing medications which botanics thought were poisonous, without fully justifying to their patients the use of each of them. The city later created a Board of Examiners, organized to weigh the qualifications of doctors before they were allowed to practice as residents of the city. Wilford Woodruff was to head this board for some time.

In the early days in the Salt Lake Valley, there was much exultation over the healthfulness of the valley, but by 17 April 1851, the First Presidency admitted in its Fifth General Epistle, "There has been more sickness in the valley this spring than usual, and several deaths, though the people in the other vallies [sic] have been well generally. We know of no reason why this valley is not as healthy in its location and character as any other, but as this is the place for the first arrival of the Saints, a greater proportion of the infirm stop here, where they can more readily procure the comforts of life, while the hardier portion go forward to newer settlements; and a great portion of the sickness in our midst arises from the seeds of disease and death sown in the system while tarrying and passing through the agueish regions of the western States. Sickness here is generally of short duration, and ends speedily in health or death. The families of the elders who are on foreign missions are in usual health at this time."[19]

The Church leadership tried to screen out diseases known to be dangerous to the community. One was small pox, but it got into the Valley in spite of their efforts. The *Deseret News,* on 13 August 1856, carried a letter of the First Presidency castigating a brother Benjamin Matthews for leading a company which, "contrary to all rules of propriety, fellow feeling, or even common decency, most carefully kept to themselves the knowledge of their having imported a disease so contagious and dreaded" as small pox. "Through such an unwarrantable course many lives have been wickedly jeopardized, without a word of warning, to an extent impossible to determine at present." It was announced that the Matthews company was camped on Big Cottonwood, and they were advised to move from the road into some "uninhabited and unfrequented stop, and to cease traveling or mingling with those who have not had the small pox; and all inhabitants liable to be infected are cautioned to keep entirely aloof from that company." In case any of the inhabitants should be seized by the disease, they were advised to use every precaution to prevent the spread of the disease.[20]

On 3 September, a follow-up letter on the subject was printed, reporting that fourteen persons in the Matthews camp had had the small pox, and that thirty persons outside the camp had also acquired the disease.[21]

Four years later, a city ordinance was passed appointing one or two physicians to see that no immigrants entered the city until they had been found to be healthy. Failure to comply with the ordinance meant a fine of $5 to $100 and imprisonment up to six months.

Though their knowledge of how to control diseases and epidemics may have been faulty and incomplete, and was strongly influenced by botanic medicine, the Latter-day Saints and the Church were interested in prevention of illness and in health care throughout the Utah territorial period. But like all other aspects of church growth and development, public health became subordinated to the very necessary demands placed upon the Church to even survive, that arose from the anti-polygamy drives and anti-Church drives that began in the 1860s and gradually grew in intensity until the issuance of the Manifesto of Wilford Woodruff in 1890.

But even as the Church leaders took to the "underground" to escape arrest and imprisonment, President John Taylor, on 8 April 1887, addressed an "Epistle of the First Presidency" for the guidance of the Church. In the epistle he addressed the problem of sanitation:

> Among the pressing requirements of the summer months is a special attention to sanitary measures. The Saints ought always to be cleanly in their habits, persons and surroundings. But during the heat of the summer this becomes particularly needful. Much disease can be avoided by frequent ablutions, simple diet and the destruction or removal of all refuse. Cleanliness is part of godliness. Filth is obnoxious to the spirit of the Gospel. It is the breeding place for epidemics. Our bodies, our houses, our gardens and outhouses should all be kept free from uncleanly accumulations. Individual effort in this direction is a necessity, and this should be supplemented by organized regulations in the various wards so that the atmosphere may not become charged with the germs of disease and death, arising from decaying vegetable and other matter festering in the sun, and from unwholesome vapors arising from dirt and neglected refuse. Let pure air and bright sunshine have free circulation in every apartment; remove everything in the house or around it that sends forth sickening odors; avoid the use of much animal food and of stimulants; preserve a cheerful spirit and a serene mind, and under the blessings of our Heavenly Father health and peace will abound and joy will dwell in the habitations of the Saints.[22]

The first state health department (board of health) came into existence in Massachusetts in 1869. With the success of the Massachusetts program, other eastern states established health departments. In the West, California also had one, and most of the states and territories surrounding Utah had been thinking about forming departments, but had not acted. In 1888, Dr. M. H. Hardy, of Provo, wrote an article that appeared in *Parry's Monthly Magazine* of Salt Lake City. It urgently presented the need for a Board of Health and health department for Utah. This was apparently the first effort in writing to organize a health department for Utah.[23]

In April of that same year, 1888, a new publication appeared in Salt Lake City. It was called the *Salt Lake Sanitarian* and was published and edited by "the Doctors Shipp." The Doctors Shipp were three persons from one polygamous family, M. Bard Shipp and two of his wives, Ellis R. Shipp and Margaret C. Shipp. Margaret had been one of the first women to go

East to medical school, but had returned shortly after because of homesickness for her children. Then Ellis had gone East to take her place and had been the second Latter-day Saint woman sent from Utah who graduated from medical school. Afterward Margaret completed her medical education. Bard claimed to have graduated from Jefferson Medical School after his wives had obtained their degrees.[24] Margaret divorced Bard and married B. H. Roberts, of the First Council of the Seventy, soon after the *Sanitarian* began publication, but she continued to write for the journal.

The *Salt Lake Sanitarian* was published only until 1890. It probably suspended operations because of lack of encouragement and appreciation, and only three or four sets of original issues are still in existence.[25] The *Sanitarian* was designed primarily for public use, although subscriptions by doctors were probably much appreciated. It reprinted articles from standard medical journals, usually American journals, and produced some local articles. Articles lifted from other medical journals included items by Theobald Smith, W. A. Vaughan, Cyrus Edson, and William H. Welch—all very respected doctors. If the materials published in the *Sanitarian* were read by many people they could not help but make a major impact on the health of the Latter-day Saints, who knew and highly respected the two women doctors of the publishing triumvirate. These women doctors were up to their necks in training midwives and practical nurses throughout Mormondom.

About this time, a young non-Mormon doctor named Theodore B. Beatty came to Utah to practice medicine.[26] He had been trained in the performance of the new surgical procedure called the appendectomy by Dr. Charles McBurney, who had identified McBurney's Point where abdominal surgery could safely be done by slitting between tendons, and then closed with minimal complications. Dr. Beatty soon performed what were probably the first successful appendectomies in Utah. But he left Salt Lake soon after to pursue advanced studies.

When Dr. Beatty returned to Salt Lake after his advanced training, he accepted the part-time appointment as Commissioner of Health for Salt Lake City for the term of 1893-1894. He immediately began an attack upon the causes of typhoid fever, which was taking a frightful toll in the city, primarily among children, but also among adults. With the City Physician he also began an exhaustive study of local health conditions, calling attention to the appalling death rate from "cholera infantum" (infant diarrhea) and the need for typhoid fever control.

When Utah obtained statehood in 1896, the proposed government was to include a State Health Commissioner, but no Health Department. Governor Heber M. Wells tendered the appointment to Dr. Beatty on a part-time basis, and he accepted at once. The salary was fixed at $1,000 a year. Very soon Dr. Beatty's flourishing medical practice dwindled to almost nothing as he spent more and more time trying to improve the health of Utah's citizens.

When Dr. Martha Hughes Paul Cannon (America's first woman state senator) was able to shepherd a law creating the State Board of Health through the legislature in 1898, Dr. Beatty was retained as Health Commissioner, still on a part-time basis. But the law allowed the Board of Health to pass regulations that had the effect of law unless vetoed by the legislature. Dr. Beatty proposed health ordinances, and the Board passed them, often to the chagrin of both the lay public and the practicing medical profession. Vital statistics of births and deaths and illnesses were required, and often opposed by the doctors, but if they were not sent in completely and correctly, Dr. Beatty would hammer away at the doctors until they completed them properly. Finally, Utah had the best vital statistical record of all the Mountain States.

Under Dr. Beatty quarantine laws were given teeth, and many an unhappy Utahn, both Mormon and non-Mormon, found himself under quarantine until the danger of transmission of a communicable disease had passed, despite what might have been an immediate detriment to his business. A major campaign spread statewide to eliminate typhoid fever. It took many years to get water supplies purified, but gradually they were. Laws requiring pasturization of milk were enforced. Food workers were required to have periodic health exams. When a town was unwilling to expend funds necessary to overhaul and make healthy its town water supply, Dr. Beatty threatened to quarantine the entire town until it agreed to do so. The town soon decided that it could find the funds to rebuild its water supplies. Typhoid fever finally came under control after killing hundreds, and perhaps thousands of Latter-day Saints.

When Edward Jenner introduced a successful vaccine for small pox in 1798, it was theoretically possible to eliminate small pox as a disease, but it took a century and three-quarters for that to take place. Intentional vaccination by autoinnoculation from small pox victims had taken place for many years before Jenner's discovery, but there had been severe negative effects from those vaccinations. First, many of the vaccinated patients had severe cases of small pox and some even died. Second, often the vaccinated patients became foci of infection from which epidemics spread. As a result, people were very suspicious of any attempts at vaccination, even Jenner's vaccination, not only in England, but also in the United States. Waterhouse had introduced Jenner's vaccination into the United States, and Dr. Nathan Smith (who was later to save Joseph Smith's life and leg) soon followed in use of vaccination. Catholic priests introduced vaccination at about the same time in New Mexico and California. But use of small pox vaccination remained controversial in much of the United States until the last quarter of the nineteenth century.

In 1870, when George Q. Cannon editorialized in the *Deseret News* about the germ theory of disease, one of the diseases discussed was small pox. Small pox had been a plague since it was first brought into the Valley. President Cannon had been in favor of vaccination.[27]

In 1888, the *Woman's Exponent,* the organ of the Relief Society, had also spoken out in favor of vaccination: "This is a subject which, by us as a people, is much neglected, and there is a great deal of prejudice against it, perhaps not without some cause. But if someone who understands would take the interest in it, and attend to it in the proper way, there need be no fear of transmitting disease from one to another."[28] The women doctors of Utah who were members of the Relief Society and were teaching their practical nursing and midwifery courses tried to instill confidence in vaccination against small pox in their students and other Church members. One of these doctors was Romania Bunnell Pratt Penrose, a plural wife of Charles W. Penrose.

One of Doctor Beatty's first efforts as Health Commissioner was an attempt to stimulate a wider acceptance of vaccination, and thus to eradicate small pox from the state. The years of 1896 to 1900, the first four years of Dr. Beatty's term as Health Commissioner, saw the plague of small pox everywhere in the state. Finally, the Board of Health passed an ordinance requiring compulsory vaccination of every child of school age before admission to school in 1900 and thereafter. But the eradication of small pox in Utah was not to come to pass, at least as a result of this regulation.

Charles W. Penrose had been appointed by the Church to be editor of its newspaper, the *Deseret News.*[29] In spite of his wife's attempts to get vaccination accepted, Elder Penrose began a rabid editorial campaign against vaccination. Elder Penrose had grown up in England where a compulsory vaccination law had been in force for many years. The law had aroused intense hatred as a violation of human rights, and Elder Penrose shared those feelings. As early as 1869, when he had been an editor of the *Millenial Star,* the Church's British organ, he had written an editorial against vaccination. Now as editor of the *Deseret News,* he wrote editorial after editorial against the state's new compulsory vaccination regulation.

On 17 May 1900, the First Presidency of the Church, President Lorenzo Snow and his counselor George Q. Cannon, had the following statement published in the *News:* "We are aware that there is a difference of opinion regarding the merits of vaccination, and while we regard it as a matter of individual preference, we have been reluctant to express ourselves publicly. Now, however, we feel to support the measure, and recommend that the people generally avail themselves of the opportunity to become vaccinated, using the utmost care to secure the services of those who are competent, and who will use care in supplying only the purest virus that can be obtained."[30]

In spite of this statement by the First Presidency of his Church, whose paper he was editing—a statement published in his own paper—Elder Penrose continued his campaign against compulsory vaccination for small pox. A bill, called the McMillan Bill, was introduced into the State Legislature that would veto the Board of Health's ordinance requiring compulsory vaccination. The sessions of the legislature were stormy, but finally the bill was passed. Governor Heber M. Wells vetoed the bill, but the legislature again passed it over his veto. Elder Penrose had been successful. Utah continued to have the highest rate of small pox in the United States, and other states were trying to find ways of circumventing the federal constitution so that travel of Utahns who might have been exposed to small pox could be halted or curtailed in their states. Finally, thirty years later, federal laws forced mandatory vaccination upon Utah.

The residual feelings against vaccination have persisted in parts of Utah to the present, feelings held for the most part by Latter-day Saints. The impact of one man was very potent. As late as 1979, the First Presidency of the Church found it necessary to issue another statement urging immunization of children.

Elder Penrose was ordained an apostle in the Church in 1904, still retaining his position as editor of the *Deseret News*. In January, 1905, it was an agonizing editor who acknowledged editorially that the Church had entered into the hospital business and that medical treatment should be accepted by Latter-day Saints along with priesthood faith healing.

Chapter Fourteen

Education Of Mormon Health Professionals

A revelation received by Joseph Smith in May, 1833, pronounced the aphorism that has since been a major guide to Latter-day Saints: "The glory of God is intelligence, or, in other words, light and truth." (D&C 93:36.) Nearly ten years later, as he instructed Church members regarding the Gospel, in Ramus, Illinois, he made another revelatory pronouncement upon the subject: "Whatever principle of intelligence we attain unto in this life, it will rise with us in the resurrection. And if a person gains more knowledge and intelligence in this life through his diligence and obedience than another, he will have so much the advantage in the world to come." (D&C 130:18-19.) These two revelations have become the basis upon which internal drives for better education have been imbued in Latter-day Saints.

In the early days of the Church, though education would be sought for and demanded in other areas, medicine and its related fields were not among the desired subjects. This undoubtedly was because of the antipathy toward orthodox medicine, and the simplicity of the Thomsonian teachings that were acceptable to those early saints.

Most of the health practitioners of the early Church, doctors of different schools of persuasion, midwives, or nurses, brought their knowledge of those practices with them into the Church. And these bits of knowledge seemed adequate as long as they were not separated by great distances from the major populated areas of the nation, and as long as faith healing seemed to be the only really effective way of treating illnesses anyway. It was when they were separated from the populated areas of the nation, and when it became only too apparent that many did not have the faith to be healed, that education of the populace in medicine became desirable.

The First Presidency arrived in the Salt Lake Valley to stay in 1848. Soon after Brigham Young asked his counselor in the presidency, Willard Richards, and Willard's wife, Hannah, to begin to teach the care of the sick among the residents of the Valley.[1] This Willard and Hannah began to do as a part of their Church callings.

In 1849, when Priddy Meeks and other botanic doctors presented to Willard the idea of forming a Council on Health, this appeared to be a good tool to fulfill President Young's charge to educate the people on health practices. Willard volunteered his home and thereafter, for several years, monthly meetings were held, with attendance up to 300 persons per session. Some of the sessions were divided into three groups—physicians in one group, midwives in another group, and lay attendants in still a third.

Until the Council fizzled out about 1856, after Willard's death and the moving of Priddy Meeks to the Southern colonies, it was the chief mechanism for educating newly-called midwives who were going out into the colonies to provide much of the medical help available in those communities.

Dr. William France was probably a British surgeon before his move to America, where he became a physician and surgeon and was considered to be an M.D. In 1855, he advertised in the *Deseret News* that he was soon to teach a course on obstetrics.[2] The first class session was well attended, with even Brigham Young present. How many continued the course is not known, nor is it known if he offered other classes between then and when he was called as a missionary to the Sandwich Islands (Hawaii) in 1860. He died soon after.

The Relief Society, which had been organized by Joseph Smith in Nauvoo, ceased holding meetings after his assassination in 1844. It did not meet again until several years after the saints were in the Valley. Then various bishops began to organize "Indian Relief Societies" in their wards (the first in 1851), and these gradually expanded from the Indian work. Among the tasks that they accepted was the teaching of health care.

There was no coordination of work between Relief Societies in the different wards until the last half of the 1860s; then Brigham Young assigned two of his plural wives to guide the program throughout the whole Church. As head of the program he chose Eliza R. Snow, who had also been a plural wife of Joseph Smith, and had been the secretary of the original Relief Society. To assist her he chose Zina D. H. Young, who was not only one of his wives, but the midwife for his family. She had many years of experience as a midwife and, though not formally trained, was probably one of the most knowledgeable midwives in the Church. Among the tasks assigned to them was the promotion of health care education among the saints and the training of midwives.

By 1869, Brigham Young had decided that it was advisable that the saints gain some first-hand knowledge of the new developments in orthodox medicine, and that they should gain that knowledge through Church members. That year he called Heber John Richards, oldest son of Willard Richards and just returned from a proselyting mission, to go to New York City and to enroll in Bellevue Medical College.[3] This was to be a special mission for Heber, and he would have to attend medical school for the two years of the college's curriculum. In 1871, Heber John graduated as the first Mormon from the Mountain West sent East to study medicine under Church sponsorship. He came back to Utah, attempted to establish a practice in Logan, and finally began practice in Salt Lake City.

In 1872, Brigham decided that another mission call to practice medicine should be given. He again called a recently returned missionary, this time his nephew, Seymour B. Young.[4] Seymour was also to go to New York City, but he went to the College of Physicians and Surgeons (now Columbia University's school of medicine). Two years later, Seymour graduated among the top students in his class, and returned to Salt Lake to establish a practice that included his esteemed uncle.

In 1873, even before Seymour had returned, Brigham Young called his third missionary to study medicine.[5] Again he chose a missionary just returning from a proselyting mission. He chose a younger son of Willard Richards, Joseph S. Richards, and sent him off to the same school where his brother had gone. Joseph S. Richards graduated in 1875, and returned to Utah where he was to become perhaps the most important doctor, medically speaking, in the Church. If he had a rival it was his second cousin, Seymour B. Young, who graduated one year before him.

As early as 1867, Brigham Young, in speaking of the place of the woman in the home and in the Church, had said that medicine was a suitable field for them to enter because it dovetailed with motherly responsibilities. In the fall of 1872, Eliza R. Snow addressed a Relief Society meeting in Ogden and told them that President Young wanted young women to become doctors.[6] But Eliza's message fell on deaf ears and there were no volunteers forthcoming. In conference in 1873, Brigham himself made a major point of calling upon sisters to become doctors.[7]

The Relief Society, under Eliza R. Snow, had been trying to prepare women for this calling. In 1872 through 1873, Sarah Kimball had been teaching a class in physiology.[8] Brigham's friend, Dr. Washington F. Anderson, had been teaching co-educational classes in nursing and premedical subjects. In 1874, Dr. Mary Barker taught medical and surgical classes under Relief Society sponsorship.[9]

One of those that heard Brigham Young's plea for women doctors was Romania Bunnell Pratt. She was the wife of Parley P. Pratt, Jr. (son of the famed apostle) and mother of five living children. Romania went to Eliza R. Snow and, in December 1873, received a call from Brigham Young to attend the Women's Medical College in Philadelphia.[10] Her husband was determined to publish his father's autobiography, so they sold their home in Salt Lake City and Romania's treasured piano to raise money for these purposes. Together they set off for New York, and Romania helped edit the autobiography and then moved on to Philadelphia to school as her husband returned home.

Romania returned to Salt Lake City after the first year, having run out of funds. In conference with Eliza R. Snow, it was agreed that the Relief Society would finance the last year of her education if she would agree to provide some services to the Relief Society after she returned to the Valley. Romania finally graduated from Women's Medical College in 1877, and returned to the Valley. The next year she taught Relief Society-sponsored classes in obstetrics, but Romania decided that she wanted to be more than a glorified midwife, as she felt obstetricians were. She returned to the East and took a residency in ophthalmology and otolaryngology, returning to Salt Lake as one of the first, if not the first, medical specialists in Utah. When she returned, her husband had taken plural wives and she felt unwanted, and she applied for and eventually was granted a divorce from him. After raising her children by herself, she married Charles W. Penrose in 1885 as a plural wife.

In 1875, Eliza R. Snow made a dramatic proposal that the legislature of Utah establish a medical school.[11] Only this medical school was to be for women only. She already had a dean in mind for the school, and announced her proposed dean as Romania B. Pratt, who would soon graduate from the Women's Medical College in Philadelphia. But Eliza's proposal never came about.

Soon after this Margaret Curtis Shipp, one of the wives of M. Bard Shipp, was given a mission call to attend Women's Medical College, but as a mother with a nine-month-old baby, she was extremely homesick and returned to Salt Lake after spending only four months in Philadelphia. The Relief Society had agreed to pay her expenses if she would return services upon graduation.[12]

Margaret's sister-wife, Ellis Reynolds Shipp, M. Bard Shipp's senior wife, also wanted to attend medical school. She was soon given a mission call to medical school, but the Relief Society did not feel that it could pay her way. In November 1875, she left for medical school.[13] At the end of the first year, her husband went to Philadelphia to see her and insisted that she go home to Utah during the summer. This she reluctantly agreed to do, and she also agreed to teach during the summer for the Relief Society. She taught classes for those who were anxious to learn what she had been studying. She returned to school in the fall in a pregnant condition, and gave birth to a child the next spring. She worked part-time to get herself through medical school, not borrowing any money from the Relief Society. Finally, on 14 March 1878, Ellis R. Shipp graduated from the Women's Medical College and soon returned to Salt Lake City to establish a practice.

Brigham Young had called six persons on missions to go to medical school, three men and three women. Of these people Seymour B. Young was to become a president in the First Council of the Seventy, Joseph S. Richards was to become long-time medical director of LDS Hospital,

Romania B. Pratt was to become Utah's first medical specialist and to marry a man who became counselor in the First Presidency, Margaret C. Shipp (who eventually did get her M.D.) was to teach many courses and to marry another of the presidents in the First Council of the Seventy, and Ellis R. Shipp was to gain the reputation as the outstanding woman doctor in the West, and to train hundreds of nurses and midwives. Together these six doctors revolutionized medicine in the Church.

But it didn't end with these six. On 13 August 1878, President John Taylor and George Q. Cannon set apart four women for the practice of medicine among the saints; the three called by Brigham Young, and Martha Hughes Paul, whom they called to attend the University of Michigan School of Medicine.[14] Martha Hughes Paul left for Michigan within a few days. She worked her way through school without Relief Society help, but with a little help from her step-father. When she graduated with her M.D. degree in 1880, she decided not to return home immediately, but to move to Philadelphia and study to obtain a bachelor's degree and a degree in elocution. She felt that the ability to speak would be vital to her new life-long calling as a doctor. She returned in 1882, in time to be medical resident at the new Deseret Hospital. Not too long after she became a plural wife of Angus Munn Cannon, president of the Salt Lake Stake and hospital advisor. A few years later she became the first woman state senator in the United States by defeating her husband in the election.

During the period from 1880 to 1884, two other women who had received missionary calls to attend medical school completed their medical degrees. In 1882, Margaret C. Shipp finally completed her degree at Women's Medical College.[15] In 1882, Elvira S. Barney completed medical school at Michigan, and in 1884, Emily Atkins completed hers. In 1880, Dr. Ellen Ferguson completed two years of post-graduate training and returned to the Valley. She had long since been recognized as a doctor, having completed British training before coming to Utah.

In 1880, Utah got a medical school, but hardly knew it. Again, it was a product of Latter-day Saint activity, but this time with the help of a Presbyterian doctor.[16]

In 1879, Dr. Frederick S. Kohler, a graduate of both the Eclectic Medical College of Pennsylvania at Philadelphia (a botanic type of school) and the Medical College of Ohio at Cincinnati (an orthodox medical school), moved to Morgan, Utah, in the Weber River Valley southeast of Ogden. He had previously been a Civil War military surgeon and had practiced in Pennsylvania, Ohio, and Indiana before moving to Morgan.

Dr. Kohler, a graduate of a school whose graduates had founded many medical schools, expressed his desires to found a medical school to the Church's local authorities, and on 31 January 1880, the Medical College of Utah was legally incorporated in Morgan. Bishop W. M. Parker of the

Morgan Ward was elected president and Anthony Peterson, vice president, and James M. Mason was elected secretary. Dr. Kohler was chosen as Dean of the Faculty. The school planned a three year course at a time when most medical schools in the United States, including all of those the called missionaries went to, required only two years. The students were also required to take bedside training, accompanying Dr. Kohler on his rounds throughout the town, another advanced concept in use in only one or two other schools at that time. The textbooks were all standard accepted texts used in other contemporary medical schools. The only irregularity the school allowed was to enable students with extraordinary talents or previous experience to test out of courses and take early graduation. It showed signs of being one of the most progressive and competent schools of its time.

But the school had a problem—lack of students. Most of the matriculants it had during its existence were from Morgan and its vicinity. It failed to draw from outside the community, and Morgan had only 333 residents in 1890 and probably had fewer in 1880-1882. Approximately six students attended the first session of the school in 1880. At the conclusion of that session it awarded an M.D. degree to one outstanding student who had been a midwife for many years, Mrs. Emeline Grover Rich, fifth of six wives of Apostle Charles C. Rich. It awarded a degree to one other student, probably at the end of its second term in the fall of 1881, to Benjamin Rush Kohler, the dean's son who had accompanied the dean on his rounds since early childhood and had assisted him much of the time. In this case young Rush had the equivalent of training that most other medical schools were requiring. There is one puzzle, however, that may never be resolved. The 1882 announcement lists four graduates of the school, two in addition to the two above, J. F. Costello of Pennsylvania, and D. J. McCauley of Iowa. Local residents claimed they had never seen the two, and a search of medical directories of the time fails to give any further enlightenment.

The third session of the medical college was scheduled to begin 2 August 1882. It was to have a faculty of four, which compared favorably with faculties of contemporary medical schools. The faculty was to consist of both Doctors Kohler, father and son, and Dr. Emeline Grover Rich, plus a Dr. Howard, who apparently never arrived at Morgan. In July one of the announcements of the college fell into the hands of the *Salt Lake Herald*. The paper began an editorial campaign against the school, intimating that it had investigated the college with the help of local practitioners of medicine in Salt Lake City. The school, already on a precarious base, evidently was not able to muster enough students to offer the session, much to the delight of the *Salt Lake Herald*. Thus Utah's first medical school was dead thanks to poor finances, lack of students, and a vicious editorial campaign by the *Salt Lake Herald*.

There were three significant aftermaths to the demise of the college. First, Benjamin Rush Kohler went East and obtained another medical degree from Western Reserve University in Cleveland, Ohio. He finally returned to Pennsylvania to practice medicine until his death in 1932.

Second, Bishop W. B. Parkinson, of the North Morgan Ward, who had been a student at the college, resigned as bishop and went East to study medicine. He graduated from Rush Medical College the next year, an indication that Rush had accepted his Medical College of Utah credits. He went on to additional medical study at the University of Louisville School of Medicine before he returned to Utah. He then settled in Logan and practiced there until his death.

Third, Dr. Kohler, the dean of the college, remained in Morgan for another five years, until 1887. During this time he continued to teach, but changed his teaching to preparation of midwives. Several of the most prominent midwives of Utah, two of whom have even been called doctors (Cordelia T. Smith and Helen Condie Thackeray) by students of early Utah medical practice, were his students. The Morgan school only had two legitimate medical degree graduates, but it trained more than twenty midwives after it ceased teaching medical students.

On 17 July 1882, the first hospital to be operated by the Church opened, the Deseret Hospital. Very soon after it opened, it began to informally train practical nurses and midwives, utilizing the talents of the corps of women doctors previously generated under the auspices and urging of the Relief Society. In June, 1887, it opened a School of Obstetrics and Nursing to formalize its training programs.[17] Hundreds of students completed these courses before they were finally dropped by the Relief Society. The courses lasted long after the hospital closed in 1890 for lack of sufficient funds.

In 1893, the territorial legislature passed a law requiring registration of all midwives as obstetricians.[18] There was a grandmother clause that let in all those who could prove that they had been practicing midwives, but from then on until 1932, when registration of obstetricians ended, strict training requirements, endorsed by Church leaders, were in effect for new registrants.

While the Relief Society was still training only practical nurses, the need for registered nurses with better training was seriously felt. Besides, most Latter-day Saint nurses were going out into the Mormon colonies. The non-Mormon hospitals in Salt Lake in particular were having trouble getting nursing staff. In 1894, St. Mark's Hospital, Utah's oldest allopathic general hospital, opened a School of Nursing to train registered nurses.[19] Seven years later, in 1901, Holy Cross Hospital opened another School of Nursing to train registered nurses. The Relief Society nurse training programs, producing practical nurses, continued on (from 1902 until 1916) under the direction of Dr. Margaret Shipp Roberts.

Once again the agitation for a local medical school was growing. In 1901, Brigham Young University proposed to its trustees that a medical school (and a law school) be organized at that institution.[20] But before action could be taken on the matter, a major dispute broke out among the faculty and local Church members about some of the liberal teachings of some faculty members. As a result, several of the faculty resigned. In 1904, one of them, Ralph V. Chamberlin, joined the faculty of the University of Utah.

During the 1904-1905 school year, Dr. Chamberlin began teaching histology and embryology in his classes in the Biology Department of the University of Utah. The classes were enthusiastically accepted, and in April 1905, a two-year medical school at the University of Utah was announced. The full two-year program of classes began in the fall-1905 quarter, and in April, 1906, a Medical Department was formally organized to meet state licensure laws of Utah.[21]

In 1904, a new hospital had opened in Salt Lake City, a gift of a widow of a rich Park City miner. But the Judge Memorial Hospital soon closed its doors for lack of patients and continuing funding. The faculty of the new medical school looked with covetous eyes at the vacant hospital, seeing in it the opportunity to expand their two-year program to a four-year program. Negotiations were about successfully completed for the hospital and expansion to a four-year program when opposition arose in other schools on the University campus. As a result of this opposition, and campus, politics, the school remained a two-year school for nearly half a century.

Although the University of Utah School of Medicine was not an operation of the Church, its first dean and many of its faculty were Latter-day Saints, and a large share of its students were Mormons. As many other secular activities of Utah cannot be logically divided from the Church, so too the medical school cannot be divided from the Church.

Meantime, a Church-sponsored and controlled health program was starting concurrently. In January, 1905, the Dr. W. H. Groves LDS Hospital opened its doors. It immediately had the same problems staffing itself with nurses as the two major non-Mormon hospitals in the city had experienced. As a result of this need, the hospital opened a School of Nursing to train registered nurses in 1906.[22] Meanwhile, the practical nurse program of the Relief Society was to continue for another decade. In 1920, the Relief Society also established a training program for nurses aids at LDS Hospital. The first class graduated on 1 August 1921.

Following World War I, the University of Utah began a nurse training program supported from federal funds, but when the funds dried up in 1921, the program ceased.[23] The University's next efforts in nurse training directly involved the Church's LDS Hospital School of Nursing. The University proposed a cooperative program whereby student nurses at that hospital, and also at the Salt Lake County General Hospital, could earn not only their RN diploma from the hospital, but by attending courses at the University could earn a bachelor's degree from the University. The program was begun in 1934, and continued until the hospital broke it off in 1952.[24] In 1941, the University began a Department of Nursing Education in the College of Education and with federal funding began a Cadet Nurse Corps, which lasted through World War II. In 1948, the nursing programs became a separate School of Nursing with its own dean, taking over the Salt Lake County General Hospital program.[25]

The agitation to expand the medical school curriculum from two years to four years never completely halted from the early 1900s. This was egged on by intermittent threats by the American Medical Association to cease accreditation of two-year schools, and by difficulty in placing two-year graduates in upper classes in other medical schools. World War II made these problems still more serious, with accelerated programs, etc., demanded by the federal government. As a result, in March, 1943, the first third-year medical class was entered, with approval for the school to become a full four-year medical school. In September, 1944, the first class graduated from the University of Utah with the degree of Doctor of Medicine.[26]

The school has since continued to grow and progress, first using the facilities of the Salt Lake County General Hospital as its teaching hospital, and finally, after much agonizing, being able to build its own hospital and medical complex. It has drawn national attention because of its cardiovascular research programs, using computers to aid diagnosis, and development of an artificial heart.

During the time that it appeared that the Utah State Legislature might not fund the new hospital and medical center, in the late 1950s, rumors were rampant on the University of Utah campus and in halls of the legislature. The rumors were that Brigham Young University was once again considering the possibility of founding a medical school and had even hired a probable dean, a renowned cancer specialist. These rumors stirred the interschool rivalry, and alumni in the legislature were able to pass the legislation needed for the center. After the legislative enactment, nothing further developed at Brigham Young University. Since that time the medical center has been added to frequently, with a new complex for the School of Nursing, one for the School of Pharmacy, and a large health sciences library building.

In the late 1940s, the staff of the LDS Hospital School of Nursing became increasingly more dissatisfied with the arrangement it had with the University of Utah, especially since the University had begun its own bachelor's degree nursing program. It was apparent that the bachelor's degree programs throughout the country were slowly taking over the RN programs. Did LDS want to be taken over by the University of Utah? In 1949, Clarence Wonnacott, the hospital's director, began holding sessions to discuss the possibility of Brigham Young University taking over the LDS Hospital School of Nursing. In 1952, the Church decided to open a School of Nursing at Brigham Young University offering a bachelor's degree program, and to have it take over the LDS Hospital's nurses training programs.[27] That fall the school opened, utilizing primarily the hospitals of the LDS Hospital system.

Meanwhile, an alternate nursing training system was developing across the country, and instead of all the RN schools being absorbed by universities offering bachelor's degree programs, many of them began to join with community colleges and smaller colleges in order to award associate (two-year) degrees to the registered nurses. After two years of training, instead of the three years formerly required by registered nurse programs, diplomas could be earned.

The Brigham Young University training programs in nursing were still new enough that this trend caused agonizing about the direction their programs should go. The problem was ultimately settled in a unique manner. They became one of the few institutions that went both ways, offering both an associate degree program and a bachelor's degree program. The associate degree program was begun in 1963.

In the early 1970s, the school also followed another national trend. The national programs of the National League for Nursing were recommending a plan whereby a nurse's aid with a one-half-year training school certificate could progress up the professional ladder as far as desired and capable of. The next step was the year-long program of training, producing a Licensed Practical Nurse certificate. Then came the registered nurse program in a college requiring two years of study and awarding an associate degree. Then came the four-year registered nurse college program awarding a bachelor's degree, followed in turn by master's degree and doctor's degree programs. Each step required only the additional training, and previous study could be applied to the study for the next step program. Brigham Young University agreed to enter the program and award the steps of associate degree and bachelor's degree.

From informal instruction to instruction under the canopy of the women's organizations, to the canopy of its formal educational institutions, the Mormons had come full round to acceptance of total modern programs. It was committed to offering a major segment of health science training in its educational institutions, and was supporting fully programs of other institutions that could provide the training the Church did not undertake itself.

Chapter Fifteen

The Growth Of The LDS Hospital System

With the acceptance of the fact that the Church was in the hospital business, and that medical treatment should be accepted by Latter-day Saints along with priesthood faith healing, the Church entered a new medical era. The opening of the Deseret Hospital in 1882 by the Relief Society had caused a stir in some of the more conservative Mormons, but when the Dr. Groves Latter-day Saints Hospital was opened on 9 January 1905, and it was being operated directly by the priesthood of the Church, the message of the acceptability of orthodox medicine finally hit home to members of the Church, ranging from the Apostle in the Quorum of the Twelve to the youngest deacon in the most remote town in the intermountain area, and from the Presidency of the Relief Society to the most humble mother in that remote town.

Dr. Groves' will had specified that the Presiding Bishopric of the Church should operate the hospital.[1] His decision was logical, since that administrative body was supposed to be in charge of all the temporal affairs of the Church while the First Presidency and the Quorum of the Twelve were especially responsible for the spiritual affairs of the Church, while also supervising the Presiding Bishopric and its programs. Certainly the operation of a hospital was a temporal affair, even though the spiritual blessings of faith healing could take place therein. But this was an indication of full acceptance of the importance of medical care by the Prophet of the Lord, then Joseph F. Smith.

During the next few years, the Church struggled to learn how to operate a hospital. It became necessary to employ a superintendent who would handle the management problems of the hospital. John Wells, who was also head clerk of the Presiding Bishopric's Office, was assigned the task. Fortunately he was quite effective, even though he faced many unknown problems.

As the Church was struggling to learn how to operate LDS Hospital, Ogden, the next largest community in Utah, was struggling to provide medical care in an overcrowded converted home. When a wealthy Ogden businessman and judge, Thomas D. Dee, died, his family chose to honor him by building a modern hospital as his memorial. But the hospital soon became more of an expense than the family had anticipated. When the hospital was built, it became necessary to borrow money to equip it. Financial problems multiplied and the trustees that had been appointed by the family were unable to pay off the original debt. It was feared that the hospital would have to close.

At this time there were three stakes (equivalent to dioceses) of the Church in the Ogden area. The stake presidents proposed that the Church take over control of the hospital.[2] They met with the First Presidency of the Church and the Presidency agreed to the plan for the Church to take control of the hospital, make it available for public use, and attempt to pay off the hospital's debts. The Thomas D. Dee family also accepted the plan. The board of trustees was changed to include only seven members—the three stake presidents, plus Judge Henry H. Rolapp, Dr. R. S. Joyce, Wm. H. Wattis, and Mrs. Maud Dee Porter.

The Church took over operation of the hospital in 1913, but it was not until 1 April 1915 that it came under the legal ownership of the Church. Thus the Church had a second hospital. A significant precedent, that the Church must own the hospital if it was to operate it, was established. Also, the precedent by Dr. Groves' will was also followed in the case of the Dee Hospital, it was run under the direction of the Presiding Bishopric of the Church.

Soon the Church found itself under the necessity of enlarging both hospitals in order to provide sufficient space.

Back in 1880, a Church-wide organization charged with programs for the children of the Church had been organized. In 1911, the president of that organization and her first counselor were walking in downtown Salt Lake City when they saw a crippled child. Until then there were no programs especially for crippled children, and the women felt that the Primary should provide some type of care for them. They made arrangements with the Dr. Groves LDS Hospital to care for a limited number of crippled children. As the years went by, however, it became more and more apparent that LDS Hospital was not properly equipped to care for long-term patients with crippling diseases. In 1922, President Felt and Sister Anderson met with President Heber J. Grant (by then President of the Church) and presented a plan for a children's hospital. As a result, the Church provided an old mansion at 40 West North Temple Street (across from Temple Square) and remodeled and equipped it for a hospital.[3] It was opened to receive patients in May of 1922. The hospital operated at its original location for thirty years. During that time it treated 5,907 resident patients and 3,498 out-patients.

As the Primary Children's Hospital accepted patients from all over the world, the need for more and more space arose. An adjacent mansion was also remodeled and connected to the original building, but still the demand grew. The operation of the hospital was funded largely from "birthday pennies" from the children of the Church. The week a child celebrated his birthday, he was honored in his local primary meeting and was given the opportunity of donating a penny for each year of his age. Other gifts in kind, of food, clothing, furnishings, etc., also helped with the operational costs. When it became absolutely necessary for a new building, all members of the Church were invited to contribute birthday pennies, not only on their birthdays, but also to an annual financial drive. In 1952, a new modern hospital building was completed at 12th Avenue and D Street, above LDS Hospital on the heights of northeast Salt Lake City. The hospital later expanded to general pediatric care from its initial crippled children's program.

In the 1880s and 1890s, a large number of Latter-day Saints moved onto the rich lands of the Upper Snake River Basin of Eastern Idaho. By 1920, these saints had convinced the Church that it should build a hospital at Idaho Falls.[4] There were six stakes in that area by that time. The saints had long felt a want for a hospital since they were so far from the Church's hospitals in Utah. When opened in 1924, the hospital had a capacity of sixty-five patients.

The same year that the Idaho Falls Hospital was opened, the president of the Cottonwood Stake Relief Society, Amanda S. Bagley, approached her stake president with a request for permission to open, and for assistance in opening, a maternity hospital.[5] At that time the stake covered a large portion of the southern part of Salt Lake County. Many of the women were still having their babies delivered in their homes, and some occasionally in doctors' or midwives' offices. It was felt by the Relief Society that a safe maternity service at reasonable cost was needed by the women in the south half of the Salt Lake Valley.

The stake presidency agreed to the project and a home in the southeast part of the business district of the city of Murray was purchased and remodeled for maternity hospital purposes. It opened with 10 beds as a maternity home. In its first ten months of operation it had a total of 101 patients, with a peak load of 11. It soon expanded to 23 beds.

The recession of the 1920s, which largely struck the farming communities, and the depression of the 1930s, which struck all, put a halt during those periods to expansion of the number of hospitals operated by the Church. Of the five hospitals, three were under the direction of the Presiding Bishopric, one was operated by the Primary Association of the Church, and the maternity hospital was operated by a local stake Relief Society, the second hospital operated by the Relief Societies.

In 1878, the Star Valley in Wyoming, just east of the Idaho border, was settled by the Mormons, and remained a stronghold of the Church. A Dr. S. H. Worthen began to build a small hospital in Afton, the Valley's largest town, just before World War II.⁶ But Dr. Worthen was called into military service and left the hospital uncompleted. The isolation of the Valley during war years made imperative the completion and opening of the hospital. Dr. Worthen sold the building to the Church and it was completed by them in October, 1943. It had 16 beds.

During the same period the community of Roosevelt, in the Uinta Basin of northeastern Utah, felt the same isolation and need for a hospital. The Church opened a small hospital in the community in 1943 also. The hospital was turned over to Duchesne County in 1967.⁷

At the conclusion of World War II, several hospitals joined what was becoming a system of hospitals. The first of these was a small hospital in Fillmore, Utah (the town Brigham Young had planned as the capitol of the territory). A 25-bed hospital which had been financed jointly by the Millard Stake and the Church was completed in 1948.⁸

In 1914, a hospital, which had antecedents back to near the turn of the century, called the Utah-Idaho Hospital, was opened in Logan, Utah, the largest community in Cache Valley.⁹ The Valley, which extended into southern Idaho was the service area for the hospital. The hospital later was renamed in honor of William Budge, one of the pioneer doctors of Cache Valley. There were several Doctors Budge practicing in the community, and they were directors of the hospital at various times. In 1947, the controlling interest in the hospital was purchased by the Church for $125,000. The seven LDS stakes in Cache County raised half the price while the general Church funds paid the rest. The hospital was remodeled in 1948, and reopened as the Logan LDS Hospital.

In 1949, a hospital, Sanpete LDS Hospital, was opened at Mt. Pleasant, in central Utah's Sanpete Valley.¹⁰ It was the result of the promotional activity of the three LDS stakes in the Valley, and the mayors and city councils of the towns to be served. Again the local members raised half of the $200,000 construction costs while the balance was made up from general Church funds.

In 1939, the community of Provo, then Utah's third largest city, was able to build its first general hospital.¹¹ (It had had for many years the Utah State Mental Hospital, but no general hospital.) It was assisted in the construction of the hospital by a grant from the Commonwealth Fund, a national eleemosynary foundation interested in improvement of health care. By 1952, the growth of Provo and its neighbor, Orem, had crowded the hospital to a critical stage. The community was desperately searching for funds to enlarge the hospital and to purchase newer equipment.

The Church was approached as a possible source of funding, but the Church was not willing to fund the hospital in its precarious financial state, with its questionable operational qualtiy standards. The Church was also concerned about the quality of the training that could be given in that hospital to the Brigham Young University School of Nursing students that were then beginning to use the hospital for a portion of their training. The Church finally agreed that if the hospital were to be given to the Church that they would run it for the community and eventually increase its size to meet community needs. Both the Commonwealth Fund and the community organization agreed, and in 1953 the Church took over operation and ownership of Utah Valley Hospital. Three years later the Church began a major enlargement of the hospital.

Up to this time, the policy adopted when the Dee Hospital was acquired had been the guide in the acquisition or building of new hospitals. But now communities and local government units were eligible for Hill-Burton Funds from the federal government. Although any non-profit corporation could apply for these funds, the Church had not yet incorporated its hospitals, and the federal government also gave preference to local governmental units.

The Mormon community of St. Anthony, in eastern Idaho, was able to get Hill-Burton funds to build the Fremont General Hospital.[12] But then the town faced a dilemma—how to operate the hospital. Since the town populace was largely Mormon, it was natural that they would look to their Church for an answer to the problem. Because of strictures inherent in the federal funding apparatus, it was deemed to be all but impossible to give the hospital to the Church as the Dee policy required. Finally, the Church agreed, because it felt a need to serve its membership, which were the majority of the community, to operate the hospital for the community under a contractual basis.

This decision opened Pandora's Box. Other Idaho communities were at that time also building hospitals with Hill-Burton funds. And they felt the need for expert help also in operation of their hospitals. Two of these towns were on opposite sides of the Snake River in southern Idaho. One town, Burley, the county seat of Cassia County, had a populace approximately 40% Mormon, while the other town, Rupert, the county seat of Minidoka County, had a smaller percentage of Mormon population. Both of these counties approached the Church as to whether it would assume operation of their hospitals on the same basis as the Fremont General Hospital was operated by the Church.[13] The Church agreed to operate these two hospitals. The Cassia Memorial Hospital opened first and then the Minidoka Memorial Hospital, both in 1960. In 1969, the hospital in Rupert, which had a smaller Mormon population, terminated its operational agreement with the Church. These hospitals were considered to be self sustaining and would not be a cost to the Church.

Shortly after this, the Church opened a small hospital in Panguitch, near Bryce Canyon in southern Utah. This was a 15-bed hospital.[14]

A community hospital had existed in Richfield, in central Utah, since the 1930s, but early in the 1960s the largely Mormon populace awoke to find that the Sisters of St. Benedict, a Catholic nursing order of nuns, had purchased their hospital. This displeased the populace, and the local Church leadership began an extended negotiation with the Sisters in hopes that the Mormons could acquire the hospital. Soon the Church decided to build its own hospital and rest home.[15] Facing this fact, the Benedictines eventually gave up their hospital.

Over the years, the Dee Hospital in Ogden was added to many times by the Church, but by the 1960s it was apparent that the aging building was in need of extensive renovation in order to continue to serve as an effective hospital. The leadership of the Church decided that it would be less costly to find a new site and build an entirely new hospital rather than try to make those renovations. It was decided to build a new hospital on Harrison Boulevard opposite the new Weber State College campus. The 1962 decision called for the old hospital to become a long-term care hospital.

By 1963, it had been decided to name the new hospital after the beloved president of the Church, a Weber County native, David O. McKay.[16] The hospital was to be completed by 1966, but construction did not get underway until that year. The hospital was finally completed and opened on 9 July 1969. But even before the McKay Hospital was completed, the Church had decided that the old Dee Hospital was not renovatable for long-term care and announced that a new Dee Hospital would be built adjacent to the McKay Hospital. It was scheduled for completion in 1970.

The last hospital added to the LDS Hospital System was added in the early 1970s. It was a small hospital in Tremonton, Utah, called the Bear River Valley Hospital. The hospital had existed since 1928.[17] Like the Fremont General and the Cassia Memorial Hospitals in Idaho, this hospital was not acquired by the Church, but was operated under contract with the owners.

Perhaps another hospital should be added to the roster, but it is really only a replacement for the old Cottonwood Maternity Hospital. As the southern part of Salt Lake Valley increased in population, demand for hospital services grew. In 1959, preliminary plans were approved for construction of a $1½ million hospital to replace the maternity hospital.[18] On 30 May 1961, ground was broken for the new building, which now was to cost $2 million and have a capacity of 120 beds. The new hospital was completed and dedicated by President Henry D. Moyle, counselor in the First Presidency, on 4 May 1963.

By the time of World War II, the area from Brigham City on the north to Payson on the south, along the Wasatch Front (the western slope of the Wasatch range of mountains) was beginning to show signs of becoming one large megalopolis. That area, plus Cache Valley, had become the major populated area of Utah. The valleys south of Payson and north of Brigham City still tended to be communicatively and culturally remote from the Wasatch Front. With the exception of the Idaho Falls Hospital, all the Latter-day Saint hospitals up until the beginning of World War II were in the Wasatch Front area where Mormon population was greatest.

Following World War II, the Church hospital development expanded into Cache Valley, to provide services for that more heavily populated area, moved into the Utah Valley part of the Wasatch Front, and expanded coverage in the Salt Lake Valley and in the Ogden area. Thus the entire heavily populated part of Utah was provided with Latter-day Saint hospital services. But a really significant area of growth was into the valleys of Utah, western Wyoming, and Idaho with smaller populations, remote from larger cities and medical services. The new hospitals meant that, for the first time, local doctors had proper facilities to do a service in keeping with modern medicine, and that deliveries, operations, and other medical services could be performed under proper conditions with proper facilities, in local communities.[19] Thus the Church was able to provide medical services for about half of its Church membership which was clustered in this mountainous region.

Up through the early 1960s, the governance of each hospital was under a board made up mostly of local Church leaders, local doctors, plus a member of the Presiding Bishopric of the Church.[20] With the exception of the Cottonwood Maternity Hospital and the Primary Children's Hospital, all were under the direction of the Presiding Bishopric. The general organization of the hospitals as a group was relatively informal and decentralized. Shortly after the end of the war, the central control of the Church hospitals was reorganized, and the Cottonwood Hospital was placed under the Presiding Bishopric. The Primary Children's Hospital was the only hospital which was not placed under their direct supervision, and in that case the Presiding Bishopric was to play an advisory role in its management.

In June, 1946, E. Howard Jenkins, who had been administrator of Salt Lake's LDS Hospital, was appointed the first coordinator of all the Church hospitals.[21] He was succeeded as administrator of LDS Hospital by Clarence E. Wonnacott, who prior to World War II had been a hotel administrator. Mr. Wonnacott served in that position, and was chairman of an informal advisory council of hospital administrators until 1962, when he was appointed as the executive director of all the hospitals that were operated by the Church.[22] With his new title of "executive director," he was to assist the Presiding Bishopric in long-range planning, policy making, and recruitment of administrative and supervisory personnel. He was to supervise 15 hospitals operated by the Church, which had a total capacity of 1,584 beds. By the end of 1963, the capacity had increased to 1,823 beds.

On 18 July 1970, it was announced that all of the Church hospitals would be consolidated under one board of trustees, and that Dr. James O. Mason had been appointed as Church Commissioner of Health Services.[23] Mr. Wonnacott was to remain as one of his top assistants. At this time the Church also incorporated a non-profit organization, the Health Services Corporation of The Church of Jesus Christ of Latter-day Saints, to own and operate the hospitals under the administration of Dr. Mason.

The Health Services Corporation had a Board of Trustees which consisted of the Presiding Bishop as chairman with his two counselors as vice chairmen, the commissioner, a secretary, a treasurer, and members appointed representing the localities where hospitals were operated, the Primary Association, and others as the Church desired.

By 1974, the Health Services Corporation was operating 15 hospital centers with a total of more than 2,000 beds. The Church was one of the major hospital operators in the United States.[24]

Chapter Sixteen

New Directions Of The 1970s and 1980s

On 6 September 1974, the *Deseret News* headline read "LDS Give Up Hospitals." The lead paragraph of the news article proclaimed, "Fifteen hospitals operated by The Church of Jesus Christ of Latter-day Saints in three states will be turned over to a new non-church, non-profit organization, the First Presidency announced today."[1]

After nearly a century of gradually moving into the business of operating more and more hospitals, suddenly (or so it seemed) the Church was divesting itself of all its hospitals and was to no longer operate any hospitals. What caused this sudden turn in events?

The roots of this decision by the Church were the changing nature of the Church itself. When the Relief Society had begun the Deseret Hospital in 1882, the Church was small and most of its membership was located within the Mormon colonies established under Brigham Young's direction. Over the years, as the hospitals had proliferated, they had come into existence in the heart-land of Mormondom. But suddenly that heart-land had become just that, the heart of an internationally spread, worldwide Church.

The Church has always been a missionary Church, sending missionaries to the ends of the earth to obtain converts. But in the 1880s, the missionaries were teaching the dogma of the gathering to Zion, and new converts were urged to migrate to the Zion in the tops of the mountains. Then the apparent capacity of Zion in the mountains to support its population was reached. In the second quarter of the twentieth century, Zion became a net exporter of population as the young of Zion moved to other parts of the United States for better professional opportunities and growth. The dogma of the gathering to Zion became an appeal to gather to stakes of Zion located throughout the world.

By the 1970s, there were stakes of Zion in every state of the United States, and stakes on nearly every continent of the world, plus many "islands of the sea." With the development of these non-heartland stakes, the success of missionary efforts at conversion leapt forward, and soon projections were being made such as that within a few years there would be more Spanish language speaking Latter-day Saints than English language speaking Latter-day Saints. The Church was faced with the facts that it could no longer be an insular body oriented to a Rocky Mountain culture.

The problem of getting adequate medical care to the Mountain West communities, which had seemed so important, began to seem minor when compared to the health problems that were being encountered in less affluent parts of the world. Now the mountain states populace began to appear affluent. Could a worldwide Church be justified in providing hospital care to just that affluent area? Did the Church need to expand its hospitals worldwide? For a while that appeared to be the answer, but soon it was apparent that such an expansion was beyond the Church's financial abilities. If it could not be expanded to the whole Church membership, was it justified in continuing to serve only this small region?

The rapid increase in Church membership also caused growing pains in other administrative areas within the Church. Internal studies were launched to develop means of coping with this growth,[2] and consulting groups, expert in administration of large organizations and businesses, were called in. Among those called in was a consultant group to study the Church's health programs.

Another factor had begun to impact upon the Church during the Great Depression of the 1930s. The Church fiercely valued its independence, but the United States federal government proferred financial assistance to the Church and its members in various ways. The Church found strings that soon became entangling and restrictive attached to those profers of funds. The Church soon deemed it wise to steer clear of those federal funds. This was particularly true as related to the Church's educational institutions, but it was also felt to be advisable in other areas. To accept federal funds meant acceptance of federal regulations and rulings. But as federal funds for hospital construction became available, the Church system was placed at a disadvantage to other hospital organizations that could and did accept those funds. In at least one case, for an expansion of the Idaho Falls LDS Hospital in the 1960s, federal funds were accepted by the Church.

After receiving the recommendations of the consultants, the First Presidency and the Quorum of the Twelve continued to study the problem, and ultimately the September 1974 decision to give up the hospitals was made.[3]

As the proselyting missions of the Church expanded in post-World War II years to less affluent parts of the world, they found poor health standards among the converts and those who were being taught the Gospel. Other world churches that had attempted to Christianize black Africa and other poverty areas of the world had long ago found it advisable to send medical missionaries with their proselyting missionaries. Now the LDS Church found it advisable to follow their lead.

When the Health Services Corporation of the Church was organized in 1970 under Dr. James O. Mason, a former associate director of the U.S. Center for Disease Control, one of its charges was to organize a health missionary corps. By early 1974, more than 100 full-time health missionaries were serving in 24 missions worldwide, in 17 different countries.

Thus, in September 1974, the First Presidency would announce, "After a thorough study and consideration, the Council of the First Presidency and Quorum of the Twelve has decided to divert the full efforts of the Health Services of the Church to the health needs of the worldwide church membership."[4]

The First Presidency affirmed that the decision "in no way signified loss of interest or concern on the part of the church for the sick and afflicted. To the contrary, it provides greater flexibility as the church assists members and others everywhere with their temporal needs. Worldwide Health Services, which emphasizes disease prevention and assists people in various parts of the world to appropriately use local health facilities and personnel, is being expanded to a major degree. This will require a substantial increase in the number of Health Services missionaries." The goal became to bring the health standards of members of the Church throughout the world up to those enjoyed by members in the heart-land.

On 1 April 1975, the Church completed the legal transfer of the 15 hospitals to Intermountain Health Care, Inc., the non-profit independent corporation it had established to own and operate its hospitals. The board of directors of the new corporation consisted of businessmen, educators, and health practitioners, both Mormon and non-Mormon. Thus the Church goes forward in new health directions.

In the 1970s, a series of revelations about the quality of Mormon health were made in the professional and public press of the world.[5] As early as the 1920s, Dr. John A. Widtsoe had produced gross statistics that seemed to indicate that Latter-day Saints as a people had better health than other people. In the 1960s, researchers studying cancer and heart disease noted that there were differences in the incidence of these diseases in people of different religious affiliation. Jewish people, for example, had low risk for cervical cancer, and Seventh-Day Adventists had low risk for cancer of the lung, colon, and other sites. In the 1970s, particularly the studies of Dr. Joseph L. Lyons, indicated health advantages for Latter-day Saints. They were using modern epidemiological methods and statistical techniques, so designed that they were accepted by the medical profession as unquestionably valid.

In early 1976, Dr. Lyons and his associates published a study in the *New England Journal of Medicine* on cancer incidence in Mormons and non-Mormons in Utah.[6] By taking all incidences of reportable cancer in the state from 1966 to 1970, and carefully comparing them with Church and public records, he was able to separate the nearly 11,000 cases by religion, and was able to correct his data for age distribution and other potentially confounding factors. The results showed very significantly lower rates of cancer among Mormon residents of Utah than among non-Mormon Utah residents. The study also showed that Utah as a whole had lower cancer incidence than the rest of the United States.

As the decade continued, Dr. Lyons was able to establish that the Mormons had significantly lower death rates and incidence of all but one of the three major killing diseases of the decade—heart disease, cancer, and stroke. Only in the case of stroke was the Mormon population not at a significant advantage. Although Dr. Lyons was not able to absolutely identify the reasons for this advantage, he felt assured in his own mind that the four prohibitions of the Word of Widsom—no tea, no coffee, no alcohol, and no tobacco—were factors in this avoidance of disease by Latter-day Saints. Thus the Word of Wisdom appears to be good preventive medicine.

By 1979, the vestigal antipathy to vaccination, which was enhanced by Elder Penrose's attacks against it early in the century, called forth an updated policy statement on the subject by the First Presidency: "We urge members of the Church . . . to protect their own children through immunization. Then they may wish to join other public-spirited citizens in efforts to eradicate ignorance and apathy that have caused the disturbingly low levels of childhood immunization."[7] Once again the First Presidency had spoken out affirmatively on a health matter.

Today's Latter-day Saint accepts modern medicine. But the discussion in the *Deseret News* of 20 November 1900 still is reflected in the attitudes of some Church members to doctors.[8] Dr. Charles L. Olsen, a Mormon Physician from Brigham City, had written wanting to know the real attitude of the Church toward those who choose as a calling one of the so-called learned professions, say law or medicine. In reply Elder Penrose said that the Church had never opposed learning, but encouraged it. "The Church has ever been a friend of education in the fullest sense." He told of the belief of the Church in healing by faith, "but all have not faith," and therefore there is need for other help. "But there is another side to the question." Hostility is sometimes aroused "by the airs of superiority assumed by the 'professionals.' . . . Their alleged opportunities, instead of opening their eyes to their own imperfections inflates their self-importance and leads them to look down upon their neighbors who have not received similar training with a lofty air of condescension and arrogance, and this is quite as offensive as the conduct complained of in their friends. This naturally provokes hostility." Elder Penrose had accurately described a feeling that is still prevalent in much of the world toward medicine and doctors, and also among many Mormons. The "professional attitude," intentionally engendered in some medical schools, is offensive to some who otherwise support and utilize modern medicine.

The First Presidency still urges the efficacy of faith healing. The Church's adult magazine, the *Ensign,* in August, 1977, carried a short incident narrated by the former Church Commissioner of Health, Dr. James O. Mason.[9] He recalled an incident when as a doctor he was called to the Primary Children's Medical Center to see a nine-year-old boy who, three days earlier, had complained to his parents of a headache and of not feeling well. The child had eventually been brought to the hospital with spinal meningitis, in serious condition. As he left the little boy in his room—unconscious, blood pressure falling, intravenous fluids with massive doses of penicillin started, he had serious doubts if the boy would survive, that he would ever be normal.

As Dr. Mason walked down the hall, he met the little boy's mother and father. The father asked Dr. Mason to assist in administering to the boy. So they returned to the room, where the father and Dr. Mason exercised their priesthood in behalf of the little fellow. The father anointed his son and then asked Dr. Mason if he would seal the anointing and give a blessing.

Dr. Mason said, "As we laid our hands upon that little boy, the Spirit whispered to me, 'Promise him he will recover. Promise him he'll have no after-effects from this infection.' And so, in the name of Jesus Christ and by the power of the holy Melchizedek Priesthood that I hold, I promised the boy that he would be healed and that he would have no after effects.

"As I left the room the second time that evening (even though earlier I had had grave doubts), after that manifestation of the Spirit I had an assurance that was much stronger than that of medical science or previous experience. I knew that he would live. And indeed he did. His recovery was uneventful and complete."

Today's Latter-day Saint accepts the ministrations provided by health care practitioners, but the guidance given more than a century ago by the prophet, Brigham Young, that no health care should be given by any practitioner unless that person has the promptings of the Holy Spirit, is inherent in the thinking of all devout Mormons.

So the Latter-day Saints go on, as individuals under patient care, accepting medical care and praying for the Lord to sanctify it to his well being. The devout Latter-day Saint as a health professional prays for guidance, inspiration, and even revelation, that his health care will suit the needs of his or her patients, and for the advancement and improvement of the ability to prolong life and improve the quality of that life.

Notes

Introduction

1. *History of the Church of Jesus Christ of Latter-day Saints,* edited by B. H. Roberts. Hereafter cited as DHC. Volume 2, p. 147.
2. Young, Brigham, Discourse Delivered in the Bowery 17 August 1856, *Journal of Discourses,* 4:24, 1857.

Chapter One

1. Kluger, Matthew J., "The History of Bloodletting," *Natural History,* 87(9): 78-83, November, 1978, p. 78.
2. *Ibid.,* p. 79.
3. Shryock, Richard Harrison, *Medicine and Society in America 1660-1860,* p. 68.
4. *Ibid.,* p. 69.
5. *Ibid.,* p. 69.
6. *Ibid.,* pp. 69-70.
7. *Ibid.,* p. 71.
8. *Ibid.,* p. 70.
9. Kluger, *op. cit.,* p. 79.
10. Risse, Guenter B., "Calomel and the American Medical Sects During the Nineteenth Century," *Mayo Clinic Proceedings,* 48:57-64, 1973, p. 57.
11. *Ibid.,* p. 58.
12. Holmes, Oliver Wendell, *Currents and Countercurrents in Medical Science, With Other Addresses and Essays,* p. 39.
13. George Washington's health and final illness have been the subject of much controversy and many articles. There are two basic sources of information on his death, the personal diary of his secretary, Colonel Tobias Lear, and a current newspaper account in the *Alexandria Times* written by two of his three attending physicians. An article by Wells, W. A., "Last Illness and Death of George Washington," *Virginia Medical Monthly,* 53:629-642, 1927, and a series of three articles by Willius, F. A. and Keys, T. E., "The Medical History of George Washington (1732-1799)," *Proceedings of the Staff Meetings of the Mayo Clinic,* 17:92-96, 107-112, 116-121, 1942, are generally considered the most scholarly Washington studies. A recent article by an otolaryngologist is of great interest, Scheidemandel, Heinz H. E., "Did George Washington Die of Quinsy?" *Archives of Otolaryngology,* 102(9):519-21, September, 1976.
14. Vogel, Virgil J., *American Indian Medicine,* pp. 3-4.
15. *Ibid.,* p. 6.
16. The articles generally considered as most complete on Samuel Thomson and his movement are extracted from a dissertation by Alex Berman, they are: Berman, Alex, "The Thomsonian Movement and its Relation to American Pharmacy and Medicine," *Bulletin of the History of Medicine,* 25:405-428, 519-538, 1951. Extensive discussion of Thomson is also included in Kett, Joseph F., *The Formation of the American Medical Profession,* pp. 20-21, 97-131, 138-140.
17. Waite, Frederick C., "Thomsonianism in Ohio," *Ohio Archeological and Historical Quarterly,* 49:322-31, 1940, p. 324.
18. *Ibid.,* p. 324.
19. Kett, *op. cit.,* p. 106.

Chapter Two

1. DHC 4:189-190. In editing Joseph Smith's manuscript for publication, B. H. Roberts added the word "raising" to the obituary, making it appear that Joseph Smith, Sr., was raising ginseng to send to China. Since successful cultivation of North American ginseng did not take place for another 80 years, it is obvious that B. H. Roberts erred in his editing. Further evidence is occasioned by the fact that a minimum of five years is needed, and six years is preferable, for raising marketable ginseng root. Father Smith was not in the business long enough to have grown even one crop. The first year ginseng grows three leaves and it strongly resembles the wild strawberry leaf. The second year it grows four leaves, and the third year it grows its full compliment of five leaves and reaches a height of 8 to 10 inches. The mature plant sometimes reaches the height of two feet, but usually is only 18 inches high; and it often has multiple leaf clusters and pods containing usually two seeds each.

2. Smith, Lucy, *Biographical Sketches of Joseph Smith, the Prophet, and his Progenitors for Many Generations,* pp. 49-50.

3. Heffern, Richard, *The Complete Book of Ginseng,* p. 45.

4. *Ibid.,* pp. 42-43.

5. Goldstein, Beth, "Ginseng: Its History, Dispersion, and Folk Tradition," *American Journal of Chinese Medicine,* 3(3):223-34, July, 1975.

6. Heffern, *op. cit.,* pp. 113-114.

7. Smith, *op. cit.,* p. 49.

8. Rosenberg, Charles E., *The Cholera Years: The United States in 1832, 1849, and 1866,* pp. 40-41.

9. Mack, Solomon, *A Narrative of the Life of Solomon Mack,* as cited in Anderson, Richard Lloyd *Joseph Smith's New England Heritage,* p. 164.

10. Smith, *op. cit.*

11. *Ibid.,* pp. 23-29.

12. *Ibid.,* p. 36.

13. *Ibid.,* pp. 46-47.

14. Smith, Joseph, "Manuscript History of the Church," Book A-1, Note C, p. 131, Church Historian's Office, Salt Lake City. It has been printed in several publications including Durham, Reed C., "Joseph Smith's Own Story of a Serious Childhood Illness," *BYU Studies,* 10:480-482, Summer, 1970; Bachman, Milton V., Jr., *Joseph Smith's First Vision,* 2nd ed., pp. 165-66; Wirthlin, LeRoy S., "Nathan Smith (1762-1828) Surgical Consultant to Joseph Smith," *BYU Studies,* 17(3):319-337, Spring, 1977, p. 320.

15. Donaldson, Gordon A., "The First All-New England Surgeon," *American Journal of Surgery,* 135(4):470-79, April, 1978, p. 473.

16. *Ibid.,* p. 474.

17. Dennis, Frederic S., "Smith, Nathan (1762-1829)" in Kelly, Howard A. and Burrage, Walter L., *American Medical Biographies,* pp. 1073-1076.

18. Wirthlin, *op. cit.,* pp. 326-327.

19. *Ibid.,* p. 329.

20. *Ibid.,* p. 329.

21. *Ibid.,* pp. 325-326.

22. Smith, Lucy, *op. cit.,* pp. 60-61.

23. *Ibid.,* pp. 62-65.

24. Smith, Nathan, *Medical and Surgical Memoirs,* pp. 97-121. This book, edited by his son Nathan Ryno Smith, reprinted Smith's earlier book and articles.

25. Smith, Lucy, *op. cit.,* p. 62.

26. Wirthlin, *op. cit.,* p. 334.

27. Smith, Lucy, *op. cit.,* p. 65.
28. Wirthlin, *op. cit.,* p. 335.
29. Donaldson, *op. cit.*
30. Dennis, *op. cit.*
31. *Ibid.,* p. 1076.
32. Francis, Samuel W., "Mitchill, Samuel Latham (1764-1831)," in Kelly, Howard A. and Burrage, Walter L. *American Medical Biographies,* pp. 806-807.
33. Aberbach, Alan D., "Samuel Latham Mitchill: A Physician in the Early Days of the Republic," *Bulletin of the New York Academy of Medicine,* 40:501-510, 1964.
34. Francis, *op. cit.*
35. Backman, *op. cit.,* p. 187.
36. See the unpublished Emerson Crosby Kelly manuscript of biographical information on early American doctors in the History of Medicine Division, National Library of Medicine, Bethesda, Maryland; also see the *Transactions of the Medical Society of the State of New York* for 1828, 1829, and 1830 in the Library of the New York Academy of Medicine, New York, New York. Further information is found in "Gain C. Robinson Day Book, 21 July 1823 to 2 June 1826" located in the King's Daughters' Library, Inc., Palmyra, New York, and cited in Porter, Larry C., "Alvin Smith: Reminder of the Fairness of God," *Ensign,* 8(9): 68-69, September, 1978.
37. See comments on the death of Brigham Young in Bush, Lester E., Jr., "Brigham Young in Life and Death: A Medical Overview," *Journal of Mormon History,* 5:79-103, 1978.
38. Smith, Lucy, *op. cit.,* pp.87-88; Rich, Russell R., "Where Were the Moroni Visits," *BYU Studies,* 10:255-258, 1969-70.

Chapter Three

1. Robertson, David, "From Epidauros to Lourdes: A History of Healing by Faith," pp. 179-189, in Frazier, Claude A., comp., *Faith Healing: Finger of God? Or, Scientific Curiosity.*
2. *Ibid.*
3. *Ibid.*
4. Porter, Larry, "The Joseph Knight Family," *Ensign,* 8(10):39-46, October, 1978, p. 41; DHC 1:83-84, 86.
5. Porter, *Ibid.,* p. 42.
6. Perkins, Keith W., "A House Divided: The John Johnson Family," *Ensign,* 9:54-59, February, 1979, p. 56.
7. Smith, George A., "Historical Discourse, 20 June 1869, New Tabernacle," *Journal of Discourses,* 13:79, 1871.
8. Porter, *op. cit.,* p. 43.
9. John Whitmer's History. Original in the Library of the Reorganized Church of Jesus Christ of Latter Day Saints. Typescript photocopy from Modern Microfilm Co., Salt Lake City.
10. Letter of Heber C. Kimball, in *Elders Journal,* 1(1):4-5, October, 1837.
11. *Latter-day Prophets and the Doctrine and Covenants,* Doxey, Roy W., comp. Volume 2, pp. 29-30.
12. Kimball, Heber C., "Journal of Heber C. Kimball," extract in *Times and Seasons,* 6(5):838-840, March 15, 1845.
13. "An Epistle of the Twelve Regarding the Nauvoo Temple, dated 14 January 1845," in Clark, James R. *Messages of the First Presidency,* 1:247.

14. Acts 19:12.
15. Williams, Frederick G., "Frederick Granger Williams of the First Presidency of the Church," *BYU Studies,* 12:243-261, 1971-72.
16. Waite, Frederick C., "Thomsonianism in Ohio," *Ohio Archeological and Historical Quarterly,* 49:322-331, 1940, p. 324.
17. Shryock, Richard H., "Sylvester Graham and the Popular Health Movement, 1830-1870," *Mississippi Valley Historical Review,* 18:172-183, 1931.
18. Winkler, Allan M., "Drinking on the American Frontier," *Quarterly Journal of Studies on Alcohol,* 29:413-445, June, 1968.
19. Stewart, Grace G., "A History of the Medicinal Use of Tobacco 1492-1860," *Medical History,* 11:228-268, July, 1967.
20. Widtsoe, John A. and Widtsoe, Leah D., *The Word of Wisdom: A Modern Interpretation,* pp. 87-88; Brown, Kenneth J., "Early Nineteenth Century Health Views and The Word of Wisdom (Section 89)," in *Sidney B. Sperry Symposium on the Doctrine and Covenants, January 27, 1979,* Brigham Young University, pp. 255-273.
21. Brown, *ibid.,* pp. 264-265.
22. Widtsoe, *op. cit.,* pp. 87-88.
23. Brown, *op. cit.,* p. 266.
24. Young, Brigham, Discourse of February 8, 1868, *Journal of Discourses,* 12:158.
25. Widtsoe, *op. cit.,* p. 85.
26. *Ibid.,* p. 28.

Chapter Four

1. Pratt, Parley P., *Autobiography of Parley P. Pratt,* p. 114.
2. Stenn, Frederick, "The Pioneer History of Milk Sickness," *Annals of Medical History,* 9:23-29, 1937, pp. 24-25.
3. Snively, William Dr., Jr. and Furbee, Louanna, "Discovery of the Cause of Milk Sickness," *Journal of the American Medical Association,* 196:1055-60, June 20, 1966, pp. 1056-1057.
4. Snively, *ibid.,* p. 1056.
5. DHC 2:66-67.
6. Snively, *op. cit.,* pp. 1058-60.
7. Chambers, J. S., *The Conquest of Cholera: America's Greatest Scourge,* pp. 18-19.
8. *Ibid.,* p. 27-29.
9. Divett, Robert T., "His Chastening Rod: Cholera Epidemics and the Mormons," *Dialogue,* 12(3):6-16, Fall, 1979, p. 8.
10. *Ibid.,* pp. 9-10.
11. DHC 2:80.
12. Chambers, *op. cit.,* p. 136.
13. Jennings, Warren A., "The Army of Israel Marched Into Missouri," *Missouri Historical Quarterly,* 62(2):107-135, January, 1968, p. 133.
14. DHC 2:114.
15. DHC 2:115.
16. Divett, *op. cit.,* p. 12.

Chapter Five

1. Ackerknecht, Erwin H., "Malaria in the Upper Mississippi Valley, 1760-1900," *Bulletin of the History of Medicine,* Supplement No. 4, 1945.
2. Ackerknecht, Erwin H., "Diseases in the Middle West," Lecture Nine, 1952, in Illinois University. College of Medicine. *Essays in Honor of David J. Davis,* 1965, pp. 168-181.
3. Dark, Harris Edward, "Frontier Malaria Fighter," *Today's Health* 44(5): 28-29, 80-82, 85-86, May, 1966, p. 29.
4. Findley, Thomas, "Sappington's Anti-fever Pills and the Westward Migration," *Transactions of the American Clinical and Climatological Association,* 79:34-44, 1968.
5. *Ibid.,* p. 38.
6. *Ibid.,* p. 39.
7. Smith, Lucy, *Biographical Sketches of Joseph Smith, the Prophet, and his Progenitors for Many Generations,* p. 258.
8. Cook, Lyndon W., "Isaac Galland—Mormon Benefactor," *BYU Studies,* 19(3):261-284 Spring, 1979.
9. Flanders, Robert Bruce, *Nauvoo: Kingdom on the Mississippi,* p. 40.
10. *Ibid.,* p. 34.
11. DHC 3:375.
12. Flanders, *op. cit.,* p. 51.
13. DHC 4:189.
14. Ackerknecht, "Diseases," *op. cit.,* pp. 168-181.
15. Ackerknecht, "Malaria," *op. cit.*
16. Flanders, *op. cit.,* p. 54.

Chapter Six

1. DHC 5:80-81 footnote.
2. Bancroft, H. H., *History of Utah,* p. 150 footnote.
3. DHC 4:288-292; Bennett, J. C., *History of the Saints,* pp. 20-24.
4. Roberts, B. H., *Rise and Fall of Nauvoo,* p. 136.
5. DHC 4:339, 341.
6. Wilson, Jerry A., *John C. Bennett,* p. 1.
7. *Ibid.,* p. 1.
8. Waite, Frederick C., "An Attempt to Establish a Medical College in Wheeling in 1831," *West Virginia Medical Journal,* 42:316-319, December, 1946.
9. "Dr. T. V. Morrow vs. Dr. J. C. Bennett," *Botanico-Medical Recorder,* 13:553-4, 13 September 1845.
10. B. [Bennett, John C.], "Doctor in Medicine," *Botanico-Medical Recorder,* 13:339, 1844-45.
11. Quaife, Milo M., *The Kingdom of Saint James,* p. 138.
12. Tyler, James J., *John Cook Bennett, Colorful Freemason of the Early Nineteenth Century,* p. 3.
13. *Ibid.,* p. 4; Waite, *op. cit.,* p. 316; S.A.L., "Communication," *Western Medical Reformer,* 5:12-14, 1845, p. 13.
14. Tyler, *op. cit.,* p. 3.
15. Morcombe, Joseph E., *History of Grand Lodge of Iowa,* 1910, cited in Hogan, Mervin B., *The Eccentric and Erratic John Cook Bennett M.D.LL.D.,* p. 7.

16. Godfrey, Kenneth W., *Causes of Mormon, Non-Mormon Conflict in Hancock County, Illinois, 1839-1846,* (Doctoral Dissertation, BYU, 1967), p. 113, as cited in Monnett, John D., *John C. Bennett—Opportunist,* p. 4.
17. Tyler, *op. cit.,* p. 4; Waite, *op. cit.,* p. 316.
18. Waite, *ibid.,* pp. 316-317.
19. Tyler, *op. cit.,* p. 3.
20. *Ibid.,* pp. 3-4.
21. Waite, *op. cit.,* p. 317.
22. Waite, Frederick C., "The First Medical Diploma Mill in the United States," *Bulletin of the History of Medicine,* 20(4):495-504, November, 1946.
23. Walter, Adolph E., "A Fictitious Medical Degree of the 1830s," *Bulletin of the History of Medicine,* 20(4):505-512, November, 1946, p. 510.
24. *Ibid.* p. 510.
25. Waite, "Diploma Mill," p. 497.
26. B., *op. cit.,* p. 339.
27. *Ibid.*
28. Illinois State Board of Health, *Medical Education and the Regulation of Practice of Medicine in the United States and Canada,* pp. 99-100.
29. Waite, "Diploma Mill," p. 497.
30. "The Eclectics vs. Dr. Bennett," *Botanico-Medical Recorder,* 13:306-309, 19 July 1845, p. 308.
31. Waite, "Diploma Mill," p. 497.
32. Waite, Frederick C., *Western Reserve University Centennial History of the School of Medicine,* pp. 12-21.
33. Wilson, *op. cit.,* p. 1.
34. "Eclectics vs. Dr. Bennett," p. 308.
35. Bennett, *History of the Saints,* pp. 14-15.
36. Roberts, B. H., *A Comprehensive History of the Church of Jesus Christ of Latter-day Saints, Century I.,* vol. 2, p. 49.
37. DHC 4:169-72.
38. Bennett, *History of the Saints,* p. 43.
39. DHC 4:170.
40. DHC 5:36.
41. DHC 5:36.
42. DHC 5:36.
43. "Important," *Times and Seasons,* 2(13):404, May 1, 1841; reprinted in Bennett, *History of the Saints,* p. 31.
44. DHC 5:4.
45. DHC 5:11.
46. Bennett, *History of the Saints,* pp. 40-41.
47. DHC 5:13.
48. DHC 5:18.
49. DHC 5:18-19.
50. DHC 5:22.
51. Hogan, *op. cit.,* pp. 5-7.
52. Quaife, *op. cit.,* p. 138.
53. "Dr. T. V. Morrow vs. Dr. J. C. Bennett," p. 354.
54. "Eclectics vs. Dr. Bennett, p. 307.
55. Bennett, John C., letter to Alva Curtis, March 28, 1846, *Botanico-Medical Recorder,* 14:127, 1845-46.

56. The Beineke Library archives of Yale University contain a large part of the official correspondence and records of the Strang church. In the archives are housed twenty-nine items regarding John Cook Bennett and the Strang church.
57. Fitzpatrick, D. C., *The King Strang Story*, p. 151.
58. Wilson, *op. cit.*, p. 2.
59. Bennett, *The Poultry Book*, extracts cited in Hogan, *op. cit.*
60. Correspondence in the Beineke Library.
61. Anderson, Mary Audentia Smith, *Joseph Smith III and the Restoration*, pp. 60-61, as cited in Wilson, *op. cit.*, p. 3, and Monnett, *op. cit.*, p. 13.
62. Wilson, *ibid.*, p. 3.
63. *Juvenile Instructor*, 3:111, July 15, 1868, as cited in Wilson, *ibid.*, p. 3.
64. Monnett, *op. cit.*, p. 13.
65. Hogan, *op. cit.*, pp. 29-30.

Chapter Seven

1. Gentry, Leland H., "The Danite Band of 1838," *BYU Studies*, 14(4):421-450, Summer, 1974, p. 425.
2. *Ibid.*, p. 425, note 18.
3. *Ibid.*, pp. 425-426, note 19.
4. *Ibid.*, p. 426.
5. *Ibid.*, p. 450.
6. Cook, Lyndon W., "Isaac Galland—Mormon Benefactor," *BYU Studies*, 19(3):261-284, Spring, 1979, pp. 261-262.
7. *Ibid.*, p. 262.
8. Waite, Frederick C., "Thomsonianism in Ohio," *Ohio Archeological and Historical Quarterly*, 49:322-331, 1940, p. 324.
9. Cook, *op. cit.*, pp. 263-264.
10. *Ibid.*, p. 267.
11. Flanders, Robert Bruce, *Nauvoo: Kingdom on the Mississippi*, p. 134.
12. Cook, *op. cit.*, pp. 283-284.
13. Flanders, *op. cit.*, p. 44; DHC 4:13.
14. DHC 4:19-21.
15. DHC 4:89.
16. DHC 4:107.
17. DHC 4:239, 250; 5:14.
18. DHC 5:252, 287, 348; Flanders, *op. cit.*, p. 188.
19. DHC 6:332-333, 341; 7:57.
20. DHC 6:344-345, 347-348, 355, 362.
21. DHC 6:363.
22. DHC 6:429-430.
23. DHC 7:146.
24. DHC 7:486-487.
25. DHC 7:513.
26. Barrett, Gwynn W., *John M. Bernhisel: Mormon Elder in Congress*, pp. 9-10.
27. *Ibid.*, pp. 13-15.
28. *Ibid.*, pp. 15, 17.
29. *Ibid.*, p. 17.
30. *Ibid.*, pp. 19-21.
31. *Ibid.*, pp. 21-25.
32. *Ibid.*, p. 28.

33. Gardner, Helen Richards, comp., *Levi Richards 1799-1876—Some of His Ancestors and Descendants,* p. 111.
34. "History of Willard Richards," in series, "History of Brigham Young," *Millenial Star,* 27:118-120, 133-136, 150-152, 165-167, 1865, p. 118.
35. Whitney, Orson F., *History of Utah,* vol. 4, p. 21-25, 445-448.
36. Gardner, *op. cit.*
37. Jenson, Andrew, *Latter-day Saint Biographical Encyclopedia,* vol. 1, pp. 53-56.
38. Whitney, *op. cit.,* pp. 445-448.
39. Gardner, *op. cit.,* p. 114.
40. *Ibid.,* pp. 114-115.
41. *Ibid.,* p. 115.
42. Whitney, *op. cit.,* p. 24.
43. Gardner, *op. cit.,* pp. 115-116.

Chapter Eight

1. Rich, Russell R., *Ensign to the Nations,* p. 7; Roberts, B. H., *Comprehensive History of the Church of Jesus Christ of Latter-day Saints,* 2:539-540.
2. Rich, *ibid.,* p. 4.
3. Kane, Thomas L., *The Mormons,* 1850, quoted in various sources, including Rich, *ibid.,* pp. 616-617.
4. *Ibid.,* p. 46.
5. *Ibid.,* pp. 57-59.
6. Hall, Thomas B., *Medicine on the Santa Fe Trail,* pp. 81-82.
7. *Ibid.,* p. 83.
8. *Ibid.,* p. 83.
9. *Ibid.,* pp. 83-84.
10. *Ibid.,* pp. 1-6.
11. *Ibid.,* p. 7.
12. *Ibid.,* p. 89.
13. *Ibid.,* p. 85.
14. Rich, *op. cit.,* p. 67.
15. Clark, John R., *Messages of the First Presidency,* 1:302.
16. Roberts, B. H., *The Mormon Battalion,* p. 28-29.
17. Rich, *op. cit.,* p. 70.
18. Bush, Lester E., Jr., "Brigham Young in Life and Death: A Medical Overview," *Journal of Mormon History,* 5:79-103, 1978, p. 85.
19. *Ibid.,* p. 85.
20. Hall, *op. cit.,* pp. 87-88.
21. Richards, Ralph T., *Of Medicine, Hospitals, and Doctors,* p. 20.
22. Bush, *op. cit.,* p. 86.
23. *Ibid.,* p. 84.
24. Reals, William J., "Mormon Winter Quarters: A Medical Note," *Bulletin of the Creighton University School of Medicine,* 4(3):46, November, 1947.
25. Hall, *op. cit.,* p. 99; Noall, Claire, *Guardians of the Hearth,* p. 32.
26. Hall, *ibid.,* p. 99.
27. *Ibid.,* p. 91.
28. *Ibid.,* pp. 91-92.
29. Bush, *op. cit.,* p. 84.
30. Hall, *op. cit.,* p. 92.

31. Divett, Robert T., "His Chastening Rod: Cholera Epidemics and the Mormons," *Dialogue,* 12(3):6-14, Fall, 1979, p. 12.
32. Barrett, James T., "Cholera in Missouri," *Missouri Historical Quarterly,* 55(4):346-347, July 1961.
33. "Cholera," *Frontier Guardian,* 25 July 1849.
34. *Ibid.,* 21 August 1850.
35. Hall, *op. cit.,* pp. 97-98.
36. Barrett, *op. cit.,* pp. 348-349.
37. Roberts, CHC, 4:79.
38. Divett, *op. cit.,* p. 13.

Chapter Nine

1. P----S. "Physician Heal Thyself," *Times and Seasons,* 4(21):325-326, September 15, 1843.
2. *Ibid.*
3. See chapter 6.
4. See chapter 7.
5. See chapter 7.
6. See chapter 8.
7. Clark, James R., *Messages of the First Presidency,* 1:311.
8. Meeks, Priddy, "Journal of Priddy Meeks," *Utah Historical Quarterly,* 10:145-223, 1942, p. 163.
9. Rose, Blanche E., "Early Utah Medical Practice," *Utah Historical Quarterly,* 10:14-33, 1942.
10. *Deseret News,* 18 September 1852, as cited in Richards, Ralph T., *Of Medicine, Hospitals, and Doctors,* p. 16.
11. *Deseret News,* 13 December 1851, as cited in Morrell, Joseph R., *Utah's Health and You,* pp. 16-17.
12. Ferris, B. G., *The Mormons at Home,* pp. 211-213.
13. *Congressional Globe,* 32nd Congress, 1st Session 1852, Appendix pp. 89-90.
14. *Deseret News,* 1 July 1850, as cited in Morrell, *op. cit.,* p. 23.
15. Young, Ann Eliza, *Life in Mormon Bondage,* pp. 219-220.
16. Meeks, *op. cit.,* p. 178.
17. Furniss, Norman F., *The Mormon Conflict 1850-1859,* pp. 48-51.
18. Bartholow, Robert, "The Physiological Aspects of Mormonism, and the Climatology, and Diseases of Utah and New Mexico," *Cincinnati Lancet and Observer,* 10(4):193-205, April, 1867; Bush, Lester E., Jr., "A Peculiar People: The Physiological Aspects of Mormonism, 1850-1875," *Dialogue,* 12(3):61-83, Fall, 1979.
19. Richards, *op. cit.,* p. 23.
20. Divett, Robert T., "Medicine and the Mormons," *Bulletin of the Medical Library Association,* 51(1):1-15, January, 1963, pp. 7-8.
21. Morrell, *op. cit.,* p. 18.
22. Vollum, E. P., "Special Report on Some Diseases in Utah," in U.S. Army Surgeon General's Office. Circular No. 8. May 1, 1875. *Report on Hygiene of the United States Army with Descriptions of Military Posts,* by J. S. Billings, p. 341.

Chapter Ten

1. Richards, Ralph T., *Of Medicine, Hospitals, and Doctors,* p. 13; Budge, S. M., "Early History of Medicine in Utah and Cache Valley," p. 1; Waters, Christine Croft, *Pioneer Physicians in Utah, 1847-1900.*

2. Morrell, Joseph R., *Utah's Health and You,* pp. 32-34.
3. Daines, Richard, "Heroes and Horse Doctors: Medicine in Cache Valley, 1857-1900," in Alder, Douglas D., ed., *Cache Valley: Essays on Her Past and People,* p. 69.
4. Young, Brigham, Discourse delivered in the Tabernacle 14 November 1869, *Journal of Discourses,* 13:155, 1871.
5. Vollum, E. P., "Special Report on Some Diseases in Utah," in U.S. Army Surgeon General's Office. Circular No. 8. May 1, 1875. *Report on Hygiene of the United States Army with Descriptions of Military Posts,* by J. S. Billings, pp. 340-346.
6. Meeks, Priddy, "Journal of Priddy Meeks," *Utah Historical Quarterly,* 10:212-213, 1942.
7. Terry, Keith Calvin, *The Contribution of Medical Women During the First Fifty Years in Utah,* pp. 3-4.
8. Smith, Ruth, "History of Disease and Medical Care in Cache Valley, 1860-1890," pp. 4-6.
9. Daines, *op. cit.,* p. 70.
10. Shipp, E. R., "Olive Oil," *Salt Lake Sanitarian,* 1(1):4, April, 1888.
11. Meeks, *op. cit.,* p. 215.
12. Noall, Clair, *Guardians of the Hearth,* pp. 33-34.
13. *Deseret News,* 20 January 1858, as cited in Morrell, *op. cit.,* p. 15.
14. Young, Brigham, Discourse in the Bowery, 17 August 1856, *Journal of Discourses,* 4:24, 1857.
15. Gillespie, L. Kay, *Cancer Quakery in the State of Utah.*

Chapter Eleven

1. Garrison, Fielding H., *An Introduction to the History of Medicine,* p. 425. This encyclopedic and classic history of medicine is the source of much of the material in this chapter. However, the concept of the swampy mountain meadow as a description of the growth of various medical sects in that of the author, not Dr. Garrison.
2. Risse, Guenter B., "Calomel and the American Medical Sects During the Nineteenth Century," *Mayo Clinic Proceedings,* 48:61, 1973; Berman, Alex "The Heroic Approach in 19th Century Therapeutics," *Bulletin of the American Society of Hospital Pharmacists,* 11:326, September-October, 1954.
3. Young, Brigham, Discourse delivered in the New Tabernacle, 11 July 1869, *Journal of Discourses,* 13:141-142, 1871.
4. *Deseret Weekly News,* 23 February 1870, cited in Morrell, Joseph R., *Utah's Health and You,* pp. 38-39.

Chapter Twelve

1. Bush, Lester E., Jr., "Brigham Young in Life and Death: A Medical Overview," *Journal of Mormon History,* 5:79-103, 1978, p. 80.
2. *Ibid.,* p. 80.
3. *Ibid.,* p. 80.
4. *Ibid.,* pp. 80-81.
5. *Ibid.,* p. 81.
6. *Ibid.,* p. 82.
7. *Ibid.,* p. 83.
8. *Ibid.,* p. 83.
9. *Ibid.,* p. 84.

10. Young, Brigham, Discourse in the Bowery, 17 August 1856, *Journal of Discourses,* 4:24, 1857; Discourse delivered in the Tabernacle, 8 August 1869, *Journal of Discourses,* 14:108-109, 1872.

11. Young, *ibid., Journal of Discourses,* 4:24, 1857.

12. Young, Brigham, Discourse delivered to meeting of Weber County Relief Societies, 19 July 1877, *Journal of Discourses,* 19:67, 1878.

13. Tyler, Daniel, *A Concise History of the Mormon Battalion in the Mexican War, 1846-1847,* p. 146; Clark, John R., *Messages of the First Presidency,* 1:302.

14. Offenses Against Public Health; Acts, Resolutions and Memorials Passed at the Several Annual Sessions of the Legislative Assembly of the Territory of Utah 1850-1855, Chapter XXXII, Title IX, Sections 106, 107, cited in Wilcox, Linda P., "The Imperfect Science: Brigham Young on Medical Doctors," *Dialogue,* 12(3):27, Fall, 1979.

15. Clark, *op. cit.,* 2:98.
16. Wilcox, *op. cit.,* p. 28.
17. *Ibid.,* p. 28.
18. *Ibid.,* p. 30.
19. *Ibid.,* p. 30.
20. *Harpers Weekly,* v. 13, 2 October 1869, cited in *ibid.,* p. 30.

21. Young, Brigham, Remarks made at the Tabernacle, 17 February 1861, *Journal of Discourses,* 9:125, 1862.

22. Young, Brigham, *Journal of Discourses,* 13:141-142, 1871; *Journal of Discourses,* 13:155, 1871; *Journal of Discourses,* 14:1080109, 1872.

23. Young, Brigham, Discourse delivered in the New Tabernacle, 11 July 1869, *Journal of Discourses,* 13:141-142, 1871.

24. Personal correspondence with Dr. Lester Bush, Jr.

25. Young, Brigham, Discourse delivered in the Old Tabernacle, 31 August 1875, *Journal of Discourses,* 18:71-72, 1877.

26. Young, Brigham, Discourse delivered at the 42nd Semi-Annual Conference, 9 October 1872, *Journal of Discourses,* 15:225-226, 1873.

27. *Ibid.*
28. Bush, "Brigham Young," *op. cit.,* pp. 87-88.
29. *Ibid.,* p. 89.
30. *Ibid.,* p. 90.
31. *Ibid.,* pp. 90-91.
32. *Ibid.,* pp. 92-93, 97-99.
33. *Ibid.,* pp. 100-102.
34. Personal discussion with Preston Nibley; also cited by *ibid.,* p. 103.

Chapter Thirteen

1. Pizer, Irwin H., "Medical Aspects of the Westward Migration, 1830-60," *Bulletin of the Medical Library Association,* 53(1):1-14, January, 1965, p. 4.

2. Wilcox, Howard G., "Deseret's First Hospital," *Utah Medical Bulletin,* December 1976, pp. 2-3; Richards, Ralph T., *Of Medicine, Hospitals, and Doctors,* pp. 231-232.

3. Richards, *ibid.,* p. 232.

4. "Hospitals of Utah," in Carter, Kate B., comp., *Heart Throbs of the West,* 1:331-354, 1947, pp. 340-342.

5. Richards, *op. cit.,* pp. 24-50.
6. "Hospitals of Utah," *op. cit.,* p. 339.

7. Richards, *op. cit.*, pp. 51-72.
8. "Hospitals of Utah," *op. cit.*, pp. 342-343.
9. *Ibid.*, pp. 334-335; Richards, *op. cit.*, pp. 232-234.
10. "Hospitals of Utah," *ibid.*, pp. 339-340.
11. Richards, *op. cit.*, pp. 26-27.
12. Divett, Robert T., "Medicine and the Mormons," *Bulletin of the Medical Library Association*, 51(1):1-15, January, 1963, p. 11; Richards, *ibid.*, pp. 73-76.
13. Richards, *ibid.*, p. 31.
14. *Ibid.*, pp. 76-88.
15. "Splendid Institution," *Deseret News*, 6 January 1905.
16. Richards, *ibid.*, p. 31.
17. Morrell, Joseph R., *Utah's Health and You*, pp. 62-63.
18. Divett, *op. cit.*, p. 4; Richardson, Phyllis J., "Thomsonian Influences in Early Mormon Utah History," pp. 11-13, unpublished article, personal copy in author's files, an additional copy of file in Church Archives.
19. Clark, John R., *Messages of the First Presidency*, 2:72.
20. *Ibid.*, 2:191.
21. *Ibid.*, 2:192.
22. *Ibid.*, 3:123-124.
23. Morrell, *op. cit.*, pp. 70-71.
24. Waters, Christine Croft, *Pioneering Physicians in Utah 1847-1900*, p. 140.
25. Morrell, *op. cit.*, pp. 49-55.
26. *Ibid.*, pp. 77-164.
27. *Ibid.*, p. 100; *Deseret News*, 29 June 1870.
28. *Ibid.*, p. 100; *Woman's Exponent*, 15 August 1878.
29. *Ibid.*, pp. 101-105; Randall, Annette, "The Vaccination Controversy in Utah, 1900-1901," unpublished article in files of Leonard J. Arrington, used with his permission.
30. Morrell, *op. cit.*, p. 102; *Deseret News*, 17 May 1900.

Chapter Fourteen

1. Terry, Keith Calvin, *The Contribution of Medical Women During the First Fifty Years in Utah*, p. 45.
2. *Ibid.*, p. 33; *Deseret News*, 6 June 1855, p. 13; Morrell, Joseph R., *Utah's Health and You*, p. 20. It should be noted that medicine and surgery are separate professions in Great Britain, the physician having the title and degree of doctor, but the surgeon, considered of lower status, having only a Bachelor of Surgery degree, and being addressed as "Mister" rather than "Doctor."
3. Noall, Claire, *Guardians of the Hearth*, pp. 97, 120.
4. *Ibid.*, p. 120; Bush, Lester, Jr., "Brigham Young in Life and Death: A Medical Overview," *Journal of Mormon History*, 5:79-103, 1978, p. 94.
5. Richards, Ralph T., *Of Medicine, Hospitals, and Doctors*, p. 90.
6. Terry, *op. cit.*, p. 35.
7. *Ibid.*, p. 46.
8. *Ibid.*, p. 34.
9. *Ibid.*, p. 37.
10. Noall, *op. cit.*, p. 105.
11. Morrell, Joseph R., *Utah's Health and You*, p. 115.
12. Noall, *op. cit.*, p. 105.
13. *Ibid.*, p. 122; Terry, *op. cit.*, p. 49.

14. Noall, *ibid.*, pp. 133, 144; Terry, *ibid.*, p. 53.
15. Terry, *ibid.*, p. 52.
16. Divett, Robert T., "The Medical College of Utah at Morgan," *Bulletin of the Medical Library Association*, 48(1):1-10, January, 1960; "Utah's First Medical College," *Utah Historical Quarterly*, 31(1):51-59, Winter, 1963.
17. Terry, *op. cit.*, p. 67.
18. *Ibid.*, p. 62.
19. Richards, *op. cit.*, p. 34.
20. Wilkinson, Ernest L. and Skousen, W. Cleon, eds, *Brigham Young University: A School of Destiny*, p. 145.
21. Chamberlin, Ralph V., *The University of Utah: A History of its First Hundred Years 1850 to 1950*, pp. 258-261.
22. Richards, *op. cit.*, p. 85.
23. Chamberlin, *op. cit.*, p. 363.
24. *Ibid.*, pp. 432-433.
25. *Ibid.*, pp. 487, 521.
26. *Ibid.*, pp. 412, 495.
27. Wilkinson, *op. cit.*, pp. 500-501.

Chapter Fifteen

1. Richards, Ralph T., *Of Medicine, Hospitals, and Doctors*, p. 76.
2. Arrington, Leonard J., "Centers of Mercy: The Development of the L.D.S. Hospital System," unpublished manuscript, p. 3; Morris, Bradley Earl, "The Involvement of the L.D.S. Church in Hospital Building and Operations," unpublished manuscript in files of Leonard J. Arrington, pp. 11-13.
3. Arrington, *ibid.*, pp. 3-4; Morris, *ibid.*, pp. 13-14.
4. Arrington, *ibid.*, p. 5; Morris, *ibid.*, pp. 14-16.
5. Arrington, *ibid.*, pp. 4-5; Morris, *ibid.*, pp. 16-19.
6. Arrington, *ibid.*, p. 6.
7. Information gathered from various issues of the American Hospital Association publication, *Hospitals: Guide Issue*.
8. Arrington, *op. cit.*, p. 6.
9. Budge, S. M., "Early History of Medicine in Utah and Cache Valley," talk given before Cache Valley Chapter, Utah State Historical Society, 24 March 1954, on file in Library, Utah State University; Arrington, *ibid.*, p. 5; Morris, *op. cit.*, pp. 19-20; Divett, Robert T., "Medicine and the Mormons," *Bulletin of the Medical Library Association*, 51(1):1-15, January, 1963, p. 13.
10. Arrington, *ibid.*, p. 6.
11. Divett, *op. cit.*, p. 13; Arrington, *ibid.*, p. 5; Morris, *op. cit.*, p. 20.
12. Morris, *ibid.*, p. 21.
13. *Ibid.*, pp. 21-22; Arrington, *op. cit.*, p. 7.
14. See note 7 above.
15. Arrington, *op. cit.*, p. 6.
16. Morris, *op. cit.*, pp. 22-26.
17. See note 7 above.
18. Morris, *op. cit.*, pp. 17-19.
19. Arrington, *op. cit.*, p. 8.
20. *Ibid.*, pp. 8-10; Morris, *op. cit.*, pp. 28-29.
21. *A Tradition of Excellence: LDS Hospital 1905-1980*, pp. 47-48.
22. Morris, *op. cit.*, p. 30.

23. *Ibid.*, p. 30.
24. "LDS Give Up Hospitals," *Deseret News,* 6 September 1974.

Chapter Sixteen

1. "LDS Give Up Hospitals," *Deseret News,* 6 September 1974.
2. Allen, James B. and Leonard, Glenn M., *The Story of the Latter-day Saints,* pp. 604-609.
3. Croft, David, "Church Divests Self of Hospitals," *Church News, Deseret News,* 14 September 1974.
4. *Ibid.*
5. Lyon, Joseph L. and Nelson, Steven, "Mormon Health," *Dialogue,* 12(3): 84-96, Fall, 1979, Summarizes these studies.
6. Lyon, Joseph L., et. al., "Cancer Incidence in Mormons and Non-Mormons in Utah, 1966-1970," *New England Journal of Medicine,* 294:129-138, 1976.
7. "LDS Scene," *Ensign,* 8(7):79, July, 1979.
8. Morrell, Joseph R., *Utah's Health and You,* pp. 118-119.
9. Mason, James O., "As a Doctor, I Doubted," (Mormon Journal) *Ensign,* 7(8):58, August, 1977.

Bibliography

This bibliography is more than a listing of items cited in the foregoing text. It is an attempt to provide a fairly comprehensive listing of printed materials and scholarly works on medicine and health care and the Mormons. It is divided into three sections. The first section covers items specifically on medicine and the Mormons. The second section covers items of Mormon history that contain materials of interest to students of Mormon medical history. The third section covers items of medical history that contain materials of interest to students of Mormon history. In the last two sections the items may have only brief materials, or are of background value, in understanding medicine among the Mormons. The bibliography is partially annotated where the author has felt that explanation is needed beyond bibliographic information, or information is necessary to explain why it is included, or why the item is of particular importance.

Mormon Medicine

"And They Were Healed," in Carter, Kate B., comp., *Our Pioneer Heritage,* 2:57-124, 1959.

B. [Bennett, John C.], "Doctor of Medicine," *Botanico-Medical Recorder,* 13:399, 1844-45.

"Cholera," *Frontier Guardian,* 25 July 1849.

"Church Issues Statement on Abortion," *Ensign,* 6(7):76, July, 1976.

"Dr. T. V. Morrow vs. Dr. J. C. Bennett," *Botanico-Medical Recorder,* 13:553-4, 13 September 1845.

"Early Utah Dentist: Clipping From the Deseret News August 24, 1850," *Utah Historical Quarterly,* 10:36, 1942.

"The Eclectics vs. Dr. Bennett," *Botanico-Medical Recorder,* 13:306-309, 19 July 1845.

"Gain C. Robinson Day Book, 21 July 1823 to 2 June 1826," located in the King's Daughters Library, Inc., Palmyra, New York. Contains information about Dr. McIntyre, Smith family physician.

"Graves Along the Trail," in Carter, Kate B., comp., *Our Pioneer Heritage,* 16:421-476, 1973.

"History of Willard Richards," in series "History of Brigham Young," *Millenial Star,* 27:118-20, 133-36, 150-52, 165-67, 1865.

"Hospitals of Utah," in Carter, Kate B., comp., *Heart Throbs of the West,* 1:331-354, 1941.

"LDS Give Up Hospitals," *Deseret News,* 6 September 1974.

"LDS Scene," *Ensign,* 8(7):79, July, 1979. Statement on vaccination.

"Nurse of the San Juan Frontier," in Carter, Kate B., comp., *Our Pioneer Heritage* 19:269-316, 1976.

P----S. "Physician Heal Thyself," *Times and Seasons,* 4(21):325-26, 15 September 1843.
"Pioneer Dentists and Druggists," in Carter, Kate B., comp., *Treasures of Pioneer History,* 5:69-128, 1956.
"Pioneer Medicine," in Carter, Kate B., comp., *Heart Throbs of the West,* 7:189-228, 1946.
"Pioneer Midwives," in Carter, Kate B., comp., *Our Pioneer Heritage,* 6:425-560, 1963.
"Pioneer Women Doctors," in Carter, Kate B., comp., *Our Pioneer Heritage,* 6:361-424, 1963.
"Ralph T. Richards. In Memorium," *Selected Writings by the Staff of the Latter-day Saints Hospital,* Circular No. 3, Summer, 1954.
S.A.L. "Communication," *Western Medical Reformer,* 5:12-14, 1845. Re: Dr. J. C. Bennett.
"Splendid Institution," *Deseret News,* 6 January 1905. Editorial re: LDS Hospital.
A Tradition of Excellence: LDS Hospital 1905-1980, Salt Lake, LDS Hospital, 1980.
Alter, J. Cecil "Addenda(s)," *Utah Historical Quarterly,* 10:37-54, 1942.
Arrington, Leonard J., "Centers of Mercy: The Development of the L.D.S. Hospital System," unpublished manuscript. 196?.
Baker, Pearl and Wilcox, Ruth, "Folk Remedies in Early Green River," *Utah Humanities Review,* April, 1948, pp. 191-192.
Barrett, Gwynn W.
    John M. Bernhisel: Mormon Elder in Congress, Doctoral Dissertation, BYU, 1968.
Barrett, Gwynn W., "Dr. John M. Bernhisel: Mormon Elder in Congress," *Utah Historical Quarterly,* 36:143-67, Spring, 1968.
Bartholow, Robert, "The Physiological Aspects of Mormonism, and the Climatology, and Diseases of Utah and New Mexico," *Cincinnati Lancet and Observer* 10(4):193-205, April, 1867.
Beecher, Maureen Ursenbach, "A Decade of Mormon Women—the 1870s," *New Era,* 8(4):34-39, April, 1978.
Behle, William H.
    Biography of Augustus C. Behle, M.D., Salt Lake, Edward Brothers, 1948.
Bennett, John Cook
    The Accoucher's Vade Mecum, Buffalo, Salisbury, Manchester & Co., 1837.
Bennett, John C.
    The History of the Saints; or, An Expose of Joe Smith and Mormonism, Boston, Leland & Whiting, 1842.
Bennett, John C., "Letter to Alva Curtis, March 28, 1846," *Botanico-Medical Recorder,* 14:127, 1846.
Bennett, John C.
    The Poultry Book, Boston, Phillips Sampson, 1856.
Bernhisel, David M., "Dr. John Milton Bernhisel, Utah's First Delegate in Congress," *Utah Genealogical and Historical Magazine,* 1:173-177, October, 1912.

Brooks, Juanita, "Mariah Huntsman Leavitt: Midwife of the Desert Frontier," in Fife, Austin; Fife, Alta; Glassie, Henry H., eds., *Forms Upon the Frontier,* Logan, Utah State University Press Monograph Series, 16(2), April, 1969, pp. 119-131.
Brown, Kenneth J., "Early Nineteenth Century Health Views and the Word of Wisdom (Section 89)," in *Sidney B. Sperry Symposium on the Doctrine and Covenants, January 27, 1979,* Brigham Young University, pp. 255-273.

Brown, Kris, "Pioneer Prescriptions," *Exponent II,* 3:16, September, 1976.
Brown, Lois Sears, "Caring and Curing," *Saga of the Sanpitch,* 8:9-11, 1976.
Brown, Lois Sears, "The Doctor's Baby Bag," *Saga of the Sanpitch,* 8:1, 1976.
Budge, S. M., "Early History of Medicine in Utah and Cache Valley," in *Proceedings of the Cache Valley Historical Society, 1953-54.* Copy in Special Collections, Utah State University Library.
Bunker, Gary L. and Bitton, Davis, "Mesmerism and Mormonism," *BYU Studies,* 15:46-170, 1974-75.
Bunker, Gary L. and Bitton, Davis, "Polygamous Eyes: A Note on Mormon Physiognomy," *Dialogue,* 12(3):114-119, Fall, 1979.
Burgoyne, Rodney W. and Burgoyne, Robert H., "Conflict Secondary to Overt Paradoxes in Relief Systems—The Mormon Woman Example," *Journal of Operational Psychiatry,* 8(2):39-45, 1977.
Bush, Lester E., Jr., "Birth Control Among the Mormons: Introduction to an Insistant Question," *Dialogue,* 5(2):12-44, Autumn, 1976.
Bush, Lester E., Jr., "Brigham Young in Life and Death: A Medical Overview," *Journal of Mormon History,* 5:79-103, 1978.
Bush, Lester E., Jr., "Mormon Elder's Wafers: Images of Mormon Virility in Patent Medicine Ads," *Dialogue,* 5(2):89-93, Autumn, 1976.
Bush, Lester E., Jr., ed., "Mormon Medical Ethical Guidelines," *Dialogue,* 12(3):97-106, Fall, 1979.
Bush, Lester E., Jr., "On Mormons, Moral Epidemics, Homeopathy and Death From Natural Causes," *Dialogue,* 12(4):83-89, Winter, 1979.
Bush, Lester E., Jr., "A Peculiar People: The Physiological Aspects of Mormonism, 1850-1875," *Dialogue,* 12(3):61-83, Fall, 1979.
Cannon, George Q., Discourse 27 May 1883, *Journal of Discourses,* 24:138, 1884.
Congressional Globe. 32nd Congress. 1st Session. 1852. Appendix, pp. 89-90. Register of accusation of murder of Dr. Vaughan.
Cook, Lyndon W., "Isaac Galland—Mormon Benefactor," *BYU Studies,* 19(3):261-284, Spring, 1979.
Cox, Nancy, "Some Sources Say that Frederick G. Williams of the Original First Presidency had Apostatized when Joseph Smith Died, but Other Sources Say Otherwise. What are the Facts?" *Ensign,* 19(1):48-49, January, 1980.
Croft, David, "Church Divests Self of Hospitals," *Church News, Deseret News,* 14 September 1974.
Daines, Richard, "Heroes and Horse Doctors: Medicine in Cache Valley, 1857-1900," in Alder, Douglas D., ed., *Cache Valley: Essays on Her Past and People,* Logan, Utah State University, 1976.
Divett, Robert T., "His Chastening Rod: Cholera Epidemics and the Mormons," *Dialogue,* 12(3):6-16, Fall, 1979.
Divett, Robert T., "The Medical College of Utah at Morgan," *Bulletin of the Medical Library Association,* 48(1):1-10, January, 1960.
Divett, Robert T., "Medicine and the Mormons," *Bulletin of the Medical Library Association,* 51(1):1-15, January, 1963.
Divett, Robert T., "Medicine and the Mormons: A Historical Perspective," *Dialogue,* 12(3):16-25, Fall, 1979.
Divett, Robert T., "Utah's First Medical College," *Utah Historical Quarterly,* 31(1):51-59, Winter, 1963.
Durham, Reed C., "Joseph Smith's Own Story of a Serious Childhood Illness," *BYU Studies,* 10:480-482, Summer, 1970.
Ericksen, Bess R., "Dreaded Epidemics Scourge the Pioneer Towns," *The Kinsman,* 31:13, Spring, 1978.

Esplin, Ronald K., "Sickness and Faith, Nauvoo Letters," *BYU Studies*, 15(4): 425-434, Summer, 1975.

Ewing, William B., "Anderson, Washington Franklin (1823-1903)," in Kelly, Howard A. and Burrage, Walter L., *American Medical Biographies*, p. 27.

Farmer, James L.; Bradshaw, William S.; and Johnson, F. Brent, "The New Biology and Mormon Theology," *Dialogue*, 12(4):71-75, Winter, 1979.

Fife, Austin E., "Birthmarks and Psychic Imprinting of Babies in Utah Folk Medicine," in Hand, Wayland D., ed., *American Folk Medicine: A Symposium*, University of California Press, 1976.

Fife, Austin E., "Pioneer Mormon Remedies," *Western Folklore*, 16:153-62, 1957.

Fitzpatrick, W. K., "Medical Memorabilia . . . Utah's First Medical School," *Rocky Mountain Medical Journal*, 68:21-23, January, 1971.

Gardner, Helen Richards, comp.
Levi Richards 1799-1876—Some of His Ancestors and Descendants, Logan, Utah, Unique Printing, 1973.

Gardner, John W. and Lyon, Joseph L., "Low Incidence of Cervical Cancer in Utah," *Gynecologic Oncology*, 5:68-80, 1977.

Gemmel, Belle Anderson, "History of Dr. Washington F. Anderson," 1932. Typewritten copy in Library of Daughters of the Utah Pioneers, Salt Lake City.

Gemmel, Belle A., "Utah Medical History: Some Reminiscences," *California and Western Medicine*, 36(1):44-47, 1932.

Gillespie, L. Kay
Cancer Quackery in the State of Utah, Salt Lake, State of Utah, Department of Social Services, Office of Comprehensive Health Planning, July 1, 1976.

Gillespie, L. Kay, "Quackery and Mormonism: A Latter-day Dilemma," *Society for the Sociological Study of Mormon Life Newsletter*, 1:3, 23 November 1977.

Gillespie, L. Kay, "Quackery and Mormons: A Latter-day Dilemma," *Dialogue*, 12(4):76-82, Winter, 1979.

Gillespie, L. Kay, "Quackery: Definitional Contexts and Comparisons," *Journal of the Utah Academy of Sciences, Arts and Letters*, 54:79-89, 1977.

Grant, Jedediah M., Discourse 17 December 1854, *Journal of Discourses*, 2:231-232, 1855.

Grant, Jedediah M., Discourse 11 March 1855, *Journal of Discourses*, 2:275-279, 1855.

Hand, Wayland D., "Folk Medical Magic and Symbolism in the West," in Fife, Austin; Fife, Glassie, Henry H., eds., *Forms Upon the Frontier*, Logan, Utah State University Press Monograph Series, 16(2), April, 1969, pp. 103-118.

Hastings, Donald W., et. al., "Mormonism and Birth Planning: The Discrepancy Between Church Authorities' Teachings and Lay Attitudes," *Population Studies*, 26(1):19-28, March, 1972.

Hayward, Ira N.
Dr. David Clare Budge; a Pioneer of Western Medicine, Salt Lake, Stevens and Wallis, 1941.

Heinerman, John
Joseph Smith and Herbal Medicine: A Brief Study of the Botanical Arts in Mormonism, Manti, Utah, Mountain Valley Publishers, 1975.

Heinerman, John, "Religions and Botanical Science: The Mormons and Thomsonian Medicine—An Experiment in Practical Religion," *The Herbalist*, 1(5):177-183, 1976.

Heinerman, John, "Religions and Botanical Science: The Supernatural in the World of Herbs," *The Herbalist*, 1(9):351-354, 1976.

Hogan, Mervin B., "The Eccentric and Erratic John Cook Bennett M.D.LL.D.," nearprint article, copy on file, Church Library, Salt Lake City, [1971?].
Holy Cross Hospital School of Nursing from Beginnings to End 1901-1973, Salt Lake City, 1973?.
Jarvik, Elaine, "Underground Health," *Utah Holiday,* 9(2):24-37, November, 1979.
Jarvis, George K., "Mormon Mortality Rates in Canada," *Social Biology,* 24:294-302, Winter, 1977.
Kimball, Heber C., "Journal of Heber C. Kimball," extract in *Times and Seasons,* 6(5):838-840, 15 March 1845.
Kimball, Heber C., "Letter of Heber C. Kimball," *Elders Journal,* 1(1):4-5, October, 1837.
Larson, Lora Beth, "The Dos in the Word of Wisdom," *Ensign,* 7(4):46-53, April, 1977.
Lyon, Joseph L., et. al., "Cancer Incidence in Mormons and Non-Mormons in Utah, 1966-1970," *New England Journal of Medicine,* 294-129-138, 1976.
Lyon, Joseph L., et. al., "Low Cancer Incidence and Mortality in Utah," *Cancer,* 39:2608-18, June, 1977.
Lyon, Joseph L. and Nelson, Steven, "Mormon Health," *Dialogue,* 12(3):84-96, Fall, 1979.
Marshall, H. L., Rees, Don M., "Malaria in Utah," *Rocky Mountain Medical Journal,* 45:469-72, June, 1948.
Mason, James O., "As a Doctor, I Doubted," (Mormon Journal) *Ensign,* 7(8):58, August, 1977.
Meeks, Priddy, "Journal of Priddy Meeks," *Utah Historical Quarterly,* 10:145-223, 1942.
Meeks, Priddy, "Medical Note," *Utah Historical Quarterly,* 21:361-62, October, 1953.
Middleton, George W.
  Memoirs of a Pioneer Surgeon, Salt Lake, Publishers Press, 1976.
Middleton, Richard P., "Highlights of Early Surgery in Utah," *Rocky Mountain Medical Journal,* 64:33-40, January, 1967.
Monnett, John D., "John C. Bennett—Opportunist," Term paper, Brigham Young University, 1971. Copy in Church Library, Salt Lake City.
Morrell, Joseph R., "Medicine of the Pioneer Period in Utah," *Utah Historical Quarterly,* 23:127-44, 1955.
Morrell, Joseph R.
  Utah's Health and You: A History of Utah's Public Health, Salt Lake City, Deseret Book, 1956.
Morris, Bradley Earl, "The Involvement of the L.D.S. Church in Hospital Building and Operations," unpublished manuscript, 1971? in files of Leonard J. Arrington.
Muncy, R. L., "Celestial Marriage: An Experiment in Polygyny," in his *Sex and Marriage in Utopian Communities in 19th Century America,* 1973.
Nielsen, Cantril, "Some Mormon Stress Points From a Psychiatric Perspective," *Measuring Mormonism,* 3:3-7, Fall, 1976.
Noall, Claire
  Intimate Disciple: A Portrait of Willard Richards, Salt Lake, University of Utah Press, 1957. A historical novel of the life of Willard Richards.
Noall, Claire
  Guardians of the Hearth: Utah's Pioneer Medwives and Women Doctors, Bountiful, Utah, Horizon, 1974.

Noall, Claire, "Medicine Among the Early Mormons," *Western Folklore,* 18:157-164, 1959.
Noall, Claire, "Mormon Midwives," *Utah Historical Quarterly,* 10:84-144, 1942.
Noall, Claire, "Superstitions, Customs, and Prescriptions of Mormon Midwives," *California Folklore Quarterly,* 3(2):102-114, April, 1944.
Noall, Sandra Hawks
　A History of Nursing Education in Utah. Doctors dissertation, University of Utah, 1969.
Offenses Against Public Health; Acts, Resolutions and Memorials Passed at Several Annual Sessions of the Legislative Assembly of the Territory of Utah 1850-1855, Chapter XXXII, Title IX, Sections 106, 107.
Palmer, William R., ed., "Memoirs of Alice Parker Isom," *Utah Historical Quarterly,* 10:55-83, 1942.
Palmer, William R., "Pahute Indian Medicine," *Utah Historical Quarterly,* 10:1-13, 1942.
Peay, Darlene M. and Adams, Ramona S., "Some Cultural Values of Mormons and Their Implications for Health Care of the Elderly," "Discussion of Peay's Paper." In Leininger, Madeleine M. and Carbol, Kay, eds., *Transcultural Nursing Care of the Elderly: Proceedings from the Second National Transcultural Nursing Conference,* Salt Lake, University of Utah College of Nursing, 1977.
Pendleton, Mark A., "Dr. Calvin Crane Pendleton," *Utah Historical Quarterly,* 10:34-36, 1942.
Poulson, Ezra James
　Happy Day, Life and Times of Edward I. Rich, M.D. 1869-1969, Salt Lake, Granite Publishing, 1970.
Poulson, Richard C., "Some Botanical Cures in Mormon Folk Medicine: An Analysis," *Utah Historical Quarterly,* 44(4):379-388, Fall, 1976.
Pratt, Orson, Discourse 2 November 1873, *Journal of Discourses,* 16:289-292, 1874.
Randall, Annette, "The Vaccination Controversy in Utah, 1900-1901," unpublished article in files of Leonard J. Arrington.
Reese, Robert E. and Osborne, George E., "Early Utah Materia Medica: Priddy Meeks," *American Journal of Pharmaceutical Education,* July, 1954, pp. 401-9.
Rich, Ezra C., "Reminiscences of My Early Years in Ogden," manuscript in Utah State Historical Society Library, Salt Lake.
Richards, Ralph T., "The History of Medicine in Utah," *Bulletin of the University of Utah* 36, June, 1946, 15 pp.
Richards, Ralph T.
　Of Medicine, Hospitals, and Doctors, Salt Lake, University of Utah Press, 1953.
Richardson, Phyllis J., "Thomsonian Influence in Early Mormon Utah History," unpublished article, copies in author's files and Church Archives.
Reals, William J. and Merlis, Sidney, "Mormon Winter Quarters: A Medical Note," *Bulletin of the Creighton University School of Medicine,* 4:46-49, November, 1947.
Riley, Marjorie Madsen, "Medical Wonders," *Saga of the Sanpitch,* 10:85-59, 1978.
Rose, Blanche, "Early Utah Medical Practice," *Utah Historical Quarterly,* 10:14-33, 1942.
Rose, Blanche
　The History of Medicine in Utah. Masters Thesis, University of Utah, 1939.
Salt Lake Sanitarian, volumes 1-3, 1888-1890.
Shipp, E. R., "Olive Oil," *Salt Lake Sanitarian,* 1(1):4, April, 1888.

Smith, J. E. and Kuntz, P. R., "Polygyny and Fertility in Nineteenth-Century America," *Population Studies,* 30:465-80, 1976.
Smith, N. Lee, "Herbal Remedies: God's Medicine?" *Dialogue,* 12(3):37-60, Fall, 1979.
Smith, Ruth, "History of Disease and Medical Care in Cache Valley, 1860-1890." Seminar Paper, Utah State University, 1957, copy in Special Collections, Utah State University Library.
Sorenson, Patricia H., "The Nurse: Marva Christiansen Hanchett of Sevier County," *Utah Historical Quarterly,* 45(2):163-172, Spring, 1977.
Story, Elizabeth J., "Her Magic Touch," *Saga of the Sanpitch,* 9:49-53, 1977.
Sylvester, Robert H.
   Dr. John Milton Bernhisel, Utah's First Delegate to Congress, Masters Thesis, University of Utah, 1947.
Terry, Keith Calvin
   The Contribution of Medical Women During the First Fifty Years in Utah. Masters Thesis, BYU, 1964.
Thornton, Arland, "Religion and Fertility: The Case of Mormonism," *Journal of Marriage and the Family,* 41:131-42, February, 1979.
Tyler, James J., "John Cook Bennett, Colorful Freemason of the Early Nineteenth Century," *Proceedings of the Grand Lodge of Ohio,* 1947.
Vollum, E. P., "Special Report on Some Diseases in Utah," in U.S. Army Surgeon General's Office. Circular No. 8, May 1, 1875. *Report on Hygiene of the United States Army with Descriptions of Military Posts,* by J. S. Billings, pp. 340-346.
Waters, Christine Croft
   Pioneer Physicians of Utah, 1847-1900. Masters Thesis, University of Utah, 1976.
White, Jean Bickmore, "First Woman State Senator," *Exponent II,* 2:12, June, 1976. Subject is Dr. Martha Hughes Paul Cannon.
Widtsoe, John A. and Widtsoe, Leah D.
   The Word of Wisdom: A Modern Interpretation, Salt Lake, Deseret Book, 1937.
Wilcox, Howard G., "Deseret's First Hospital," *Utah Medical Bulletin* December, 1976, pp. 2-3.
Wilcox, Linda P., "The Imperfect Science: Brigham Young on Medical Doctors," *Dialogue,* 12(3):26-36, Fall, 1979.
Willardson, Marzetta, "Aunt Zale and Her Little Brown Satchel," *Saga of the Sanpitch,* 8:6-9, 1976.
Williams, Frederick G., "Frederick Granger Williams of the First Presidency of the Church," *BYU Studies,* 12:243-61, 1971-72.
Williams, Nancy Abigail (Clement)
   Meet Dr. Frederick Granger Williams and His Wife Rebecca Swain Williams, Independence, Mo., Zions Printing, 1951.
Wilson, Angus K., "How Radiology Became Established in Utah," *American Journal of Roentgenology, Radium Therapy, and Nuclear Medicine,* 119:210-11, September, 1973.
Wilson, Jerry A., "John C. Bennett." Term Paper, Brigham Young University, 1971. Copy in Church Library, Salt Lake City.
Wirthlin, LeRoy S., "Discovery: Joseph Smith's Surgeon," *Ensign,* 8(3):58-60, March, 1978.
Wirthlin, LeRoy S., "Joseph Smith's Boyhood Operation: An 1813 Surgical Success," *BYU Studies,* 21(2):131-154, Spring, 1981.
Wirthlin, LeRoy S., "Nathan Smith (1762-1828) Surgical Consultant to Joseph Smith," *BYU Studies,* 17(3):319-337, Spring, 1977.

Young, Brigham, Discourse 17 August 1856, *Journal of Discourses,* 4:24, 1857.
Young, Brigham, Discourse 15 March 1857, *Journal of Discourses,* 4:282-284, 1857.
Young, Brigham, Discourse 17 February 1861, *Journal of Discourses,* 9:125, 1862.
Young, Brigham, Discourse 8 February 1868, *Journal of Discourses,* 12:158, 1869.
Young, Brigham, Discourse 11 July 1869, *Journal of Discourses,* 13:141-142, 1871.
Young, Brigham, Discourse 8 August 1869, *Journal of Discourses,* 14:108-109, 1872.
Young, Brigham, Discourse 14 November 1869, *Journal of Discourses,* 13:155, 1871.
Young, Brigham, Discourse 10 July 1870, *Journal of Discourses,* 14:72, 1872.
Young, Brigham, Discourse 9 October 1872, *Journal of Discourses,* 15:225-226, 1873.
Young, Brigham, Discourse 31 August 1875, *Journal of Discourses,* 18:71-72, 1877.
Young, Brigham, Discourse 19 July 1877, *Journal of Discourses,* 19:67, 1878.
Young, Whitney Blair
    A History of the University of Utah College of Medicine. Thesis for Medical Doctorate, University of Kansas, 1963.
Zeuch, Lucius H., "The Mormons and Their Medical History in Nauvoo," in his *History of Medical Practice in Illinois,* Volume I, Chicago, The Book Press, 1927, p. 141-144.

Mormon History

John Whitmer's History. Original in the Library of the Reorganized Church of Jesus Christ of Latter Day Saints. Typescript photocopy from Modern Microfilm Co., Salt Lake City. Has discussion of faith healing in early church.
Allen, James B. and Leonard, Glenn M.
    The Story of the Latter-day Saints, Salt Lake, Deseret Book, 1976.
Anderson, Mary Audentia Smith
    Joseph Smith III and the Restoration, Independence, Missouri, Herald House, 1952.
    Has story of John C. Bennett's attempts to gain membership in RLDS Church.
Anderson, Richard Lloyd
    Joseph Smith's New England Heritage, Salt Lake, Deseret Book, 1971. Contains material on health of Joseph Smith progenitors.
Bachman, Milton V., Jr.
    Joseph Smith's First Vision, 2nd ed., Salt Lake, Bookcraft, 1980. Describes conditions of early Palmyra and vicinity including medical conditions.
Bancroft, Hubert Howe
    History of Utah, Salt Lake Bookcraft, 1964. Reprint of original.
Carter, Kate B., comp.
    Heart Throbs of the West, Salt Lake, Daughters of Utah Pioneers, 1940-1951 12 volumes. Materials submitted by members of the DUP vary in quality. Unfortunately material is undocumented.
Carter, Kate B., comp.
    Our Pioneer Heritage, Salt Lake Daughters of Utah Pioneers, 1958-1977, 20 volumes. Same standards as *Heart Throbs of the West.*
Carter, Kate B., comp.
    Treasures of Pioneer History, Salt Lake, Daughters of Utah Pioneers, 1952-1957, 6 volumes. Same standards as *Heart Throbs of the West.*
Chamberlin, Ralph V.
    The University of Utah: A History of its First Hundred Years 1850-1950, Salt Lake, University of Utah Press, 1960.

BIBLIOGRAPHY

Clark, James R.
Messages of the First Presidency of The Church of Jesus Christ of Latter-day Saints, Salt Lake City, Bookcraft, 1965-1975, 6 volumes. Contains several messages dealing with faith healing and medicine.

Ferris, (Mrs.) B. G.
The Mormons at Home: With Some Incidents of Travel From Missouri to California 1852-3, New York, Dix and Edwards, 1856. Contains comments on Council of Health meeting and on doctors leaving Utah.

Fitzpatrick, D. C.
The King Strang Story, Saint James, Michigan, National Heritage, 1970. Contains material on John C. Bennett's affiliation with Strang.

Flanders, Robert Bruce
Nauvoo: Kingdom on the Mississippi, Urbana, University of Illinois Press, 1965.

Ford, Thomas
History of Illinois, Chicago, S. C. Griggs, 1854.

Furniss, Norman F.
The Mormon Conflict 1850-1859, New Haven, Yale University Press, 1960.

Gentry, Leland H., "The Danite Band of 1838," *BYU Studies* 14(4):421-450, Summer, 1974. Contains material on Dr. Samson Avard.

Godfrey, Kenneth W.
Causes of Mormon, Non-Mormon Conflict in Hancock County, Illinois, 1839-1846. Doctoral Dissertation, BYU, 1967.

Hafen, LeRoy, ed.
The Westerners Denver Posse Brand Book, Denver, Colorado State Historical Society, 1948-1949.

Jennings, Warren A., "The Army of Israel Marches Into Missouri," *Missouri Historical Quarterly,* 62(2):107-135, January, 1968.

Jenson, Andrew
Latter-day Saint Biographical Encyclopedia, Salt Lake City, 1901.

Journal of Discourses, Volumes 1-26, 1854-1886.

Kane, Thomas L.
The Mormons, Philadelphia, 1850. Describes health conditions of Nauvoo refugees.

Kimball, Stanley B., "The Anthon Transcript: People, Primary Sources and Problems," *BYU Studies,* 10:325-352, 1969-70. Considers relationships of Church with Dr. Samuel Latham Mitchill.

Latter-day Prophets and the Doctrine and Covenants, Doxey, Roy W., comp. Salt Lake City, Deseret Book, 1978. 4 volumes.

Mack, Solomon
A Narrative of the Life of Solomon Mack. Tells of his health and accidents.

Morcombe, Joseph E.
History of the Grand Lodge of Iowa, 1910. Discusses relationship of Nauvoo Lodge in establishment of Iowa Lodges and part played by Dr. John C. Bennett.

Perkins, Keith W., "A House Divided: The John Johnson Family," *Ensign,* 9:54-59, February, 1979. Relates one of the first faith healing miracles.

Porter, Larry C., "Alvin Smith: Reminder of the Fairness of God," *Ensign,* 8(9): 68-69, September, 1978. Discusses death of Alvin Smith and his doctor.

Porter, Larry, "The Joseph Knight Family," *Ensign,* 8(10):39-46, October, 1978. Discusses first and possibly second faith healing miracles.

Pratt, Parley P.
Autobiography of Parley P. Pratt, 7th ed., Salt Lake City, Deseret Book, 1968.

Quaife, Milo M.
The Kingdom of Saint James, New Haven, Yale University Press, 1930. Discusses place of Dr. John C. Bennett in Strang church.

Quinn, D. Michael, "They Served: The Richards Legacy in the Church," *Ensign,* 10(1):24-29, January, 1980.

Rich, Russell R.
Ensign to the Nations: A History of the Church from 1846 to 1972, Provo, Brigham Young University Publications, 1972.

Rich, Russell R., "Where Were the Moroni Visits," *BYU Studies,* 10:255-258, 1969-1970. Discusses death of Alvin Smith.

Roberts, B. H.
A Comprehensive History of the Church of Jesus Christ of Latter-day Saints. Century I., Provo, Brigham Young University Press, 1965. 6 volumes.

Roberts, B. H.
The Mormon Battalion, it's History and Achievements, Salt Lake City, Deseret News, 1919.

Roberts, B. H.
The Rise and Fall of Nauvoo, Salt Lake City, Deseret News, 1900.

Smith, George A., "Historical Discourse, 20 June 1869," *Journal of Discourses,* 13:79, 1871. Discusses healing by anointing in Jackson County, Missouri.

Smith, Joseph
History of the Church of Jesus Christ of Latter-day Saints, edited by B. H. Roberts, 2nd ed., Salt Lake, Deseret Book, 1978. 7 volumes.

Smith, Joseph, "Manuscript History of the Church." Church Historian's Office, Salt Lake City.

Smith, Lucy [Mack]
Biographical Sketches of Joseph Smith, the Prophet, and his Progenitors for Many Generations, Liverpool, Orson Pratt and S. W. Richards, 1853. This book discusses the health of many of Joseph Smith's family.

Tyler, Daniel
A Concise History of the Mormon Battalion in the Mexican War, 1846-1847, Chicago, Rio Grande Press, 1964. Reprint of 1881 edition.

Whitney, Orson F.
History of Utah, Salt Lake City, George Q. Cannon & Sons, 1904. 4 volumes.

Wilkinson, Ernest L. and Skousen, W. Cleon, eds.
Brigham Young University: A School of Destiny, Provo, Brigham Young University, 1976.

Young, Ann Eliza
Life in Mormon Bondage, Philadelphia, Aldine, 1908. Mentions alleged murder of Dr. Vaughan.

Medical History

Aberbach, Alan D., "Samuel Latham Mitchill: A Physician in the Early Days of the Republic," *Bulletin of the New York Academy of Medicine,* 40:501-10, 1964.

Ackerknecht, Erwin H., "Diseases in the Middle West," in Illinois University. College of Medicine, *Essays in Honor of David J. Davis,* 1965, Lecture Nine, 1952, pp. 168-181.

Ackerknecht, Erwin H., "Malaria in the Upper Mississippi Valley, 1760-1900," *Bulletin of the History of Medicine,* Supplement No. 4, 1945.

BIBLIOGRAPHY

Angle, Paul M., "The Hardy Pioneer: How He Lived in the Early Middle West," in Illinois University. College of Medicine, *Essays in Honor of David J. Davis,* 1965. Lecture Six, 1949, pp. 132-146.

Ball, James Moores, "Samuel Thomson (1769-1843) and His Patented 'System' of Medicine," *Annals of Medical History,* 7:144-52, 1925.

Barrett, James T., "Cholera in Missouri," *Missouri Historical Quarterly,* 55(4): 346-47, July, 1961.

Benavides, E. F., "The Saints Among the Saints: A Study of Curandismo in Utah," *Utah Historical Quarterly,* 41:373-92, Fall, 1973.

Berman, Alex, "The Heroic Approach in 19th Century Therapeutics," *Bulletin of the American Society of Hospital Pharmacists,* 11:320-327, September-October, 1954.

Berman, Alex, "Neo-Thomsonianism in the United States," *Journal of the History of Medicine and Allied Sciences,* 11:133-155, 1956.

Berman, Alex, "The Thomsonian Movement and its Relation to American Pharmacy and Medicine," *Bulletin of the History of Medicine,* 25:405-428, 519-538, 1951.

Brewer, Paul W., "Voluntarism of Trial: St. Louis' Response to the Cholera Epidemic of 1849," *Bulletin of the History of Medicine,* 49(1):102-22, Spring, 1975.

Breiger, Gert H., "Health and Disease on the Western Frontier: A Bicentennial Appreciation," *Western Journal of Medicine,* 25(1):28-35, July, 1976.

Brieger, Gert H., "Therapeutic Conflicts and the American Medical Profession in the 1860s," *Bulletin of the History of Medicine,* 41:215-222, 1967.

Bryan, Leon S., "Blood-letting in American Medicine, 1830-1892," *Bulletin of the History of Medicine,* 38:516-529, 1964.

Cassedy, James H., "An Early American Hangover: The Medical Profession and Intemperance 1800-1860," *Bulletin of the History of Medicine,* 50(3):405-13, Fall, 1976.

Chambers, J. S.
The Conquest of Cholera: America's Greatest Scourge, New York, Macmillan, 1938.

Dark, Harris Edward, "Frontier Malaria Fighter," *Today's Health,* 44(5):28-29, 80-82, 85-86, May 1966.

Dennis, Frederick S., "Smith, Nathan (1762-1829)," in Kelly, Howard A. and Burrage, Walter L., *American Medical Biographies,* pp. 1073-76.

Donaldson, Gordon A., "The First All-New England Surgeon," *American Journal of Surgery,* 135(4):470-79, April, 1978. Article on Nathan Smith, Joseph Smith's surgeon.

Dunlop, Richard
Doctors of the American Frontier, New York, Doubleday, 1965.

Findley, Thomas, "Sappington's Anti-Fever Pills and the Westward Migration," *Transactions of the American Clinical and Climatological Association,* 79:34-44, 1968.

Francis, Samuel W., "Mitchill, Samuel Latham (1764-1831)," in Kelly, Howard A. and Burrage, Walter L., *American Medical Biographies,* pp.806-807.

Frazier, Claude A., comp.
Faith Healing: Finger of God? Or, Scientific Curiosity, New York, Thomas Nelson, 1973.

Garrison, Fielding H.
An Introduction to the History of Medicine, 2nd ed., Philadelphia, Saunders, 1928.

Goldstein, Beth, "Ginseng: Its History, Dispersion, and Folk Tradition," *American Journal of Chinese Medicine,* 3(3):223-34, July, 1975.

Hall, Thomas B.
Medicine on the Santa Fe Trail, Dayton, Ohio, Morningside Bookshop, 1971.

Haller, John S., Jr., "Samson of the Materia Medica: Medical Theory and the Use and Abuse of Calomel in the Nineteenth Century," *Pharmacy in History,* 13(1):27-33; 13(2):67-76, 1971.

Haller, John S., Jr., "Therapeutic Mule: The Use of Arsenic in the Nineteenth Century Materia Medica," *Pharmacy in History,* 17(3):87-100, 1975.

Hand, Wayland D., "The Folk Healer: Calling and Endowment," *Journal of the History of Medicine,* 26:263-75, July, 1971. This article by a Mormon folklorist.

Heffern, Richard
The Complete Book of Ginseng, Millbrae, California, Celestial Arts, 1976.

Holmes, Oliver Wendell
"Currents and Countercurrents in Medical Science," in *Medical Essays, 1842-1882,* New York, Houghton Mifflin, 1883, pp. 173-208.

Illinois State Board of Health
Medical Education and the Regulation of Practice of Medicine in the United States and Canada, Chicago, 1884. Appraises Dr. John C. Bennett's medical school at New Albany, Indiana.

Illinois University. College of Medicine.
Essays in Honor of David J. Davis, Chicago, 1965. A series of lectures on the history of medicine in the Middle West.

Jordan, Philip D., "Botanic Medicine in the Western Country," *Ohio State Medical Journal,* 40:143-6, 240-42, 1944.

Karolevitz, Robert F.
Doctors of the Old West, Seattle, Superior Publishing Co., 1967.

Kelly, Howard A. and Burrage, Walter L.
American Medical Biographies, Baltimore, Norman, Remington, 1920.

Kett, Joseph F.
The Formation of the American Medical Profession: The Role of Institutions, 1780-1860, New Haven, Yale University Press, 1968.

Kluger, Matthew J., "The History of Bloodletting," *Natural History,* 87(9):78-83, November, 1978.

Lathrop, Amy, "Pioneer Remedies from Western Kansas," *Western Folklore,* 20:1-22, 1961.

McLear, Patrick, "The St. Louis Cholera Epidemic of 1849," *Missouri Historical Quarterly,* 63(2):171-181, January, 1969.

Moore, Michael
Medicinal Plants of the Mountain West, Albuquerque, University of New Mexico Press, 1979.

Moore, R. Gordon, "Epidemics in Early Ohio," *Ohio State Medical Journal,* 71:798-802, November, 1975.

Pizer, Irwin H., "Medical Aspects of the Westward Migration, 1830-60," *Bulletin of the Medical Library Association,* 53(1):1-14, January, 1965.

Risse, Guenter B., "Calomel and the American Medical Sects During the Nineteenth Century," *Mayo Clinic Proceedings,* 48:57-64, 1973.

Robertson, David, "From Epidauros to Lourdes: A History of Healing by Faith," in Frazier, Claude A., comp., *Faith Healing: Finger of God? or, Scientific Curiosity,* p. 179-189.

Rosenberg, Charles E.
  The Cholera Years: The United States in 1832, 1849, and 1866, Chicago, University of Chicago Press, 1962.
Scheidemandel, Heinz H. E., "Did George Washington Die of Quinsy?" *Archives of Otolaryngology*, 102(9):519-21, September, 1976.
Shryock, Richard H.
  American Medical Research, New York, Commonwealth Fund, 1949.
Shryock, Richard Harrison
  Medicine and Society in America 1660-1860, Ithaca, New York, Cornell University Press, 1960.
Shryock, Richard H., "Quackery and Sectarianism in American Medicine," *Scalpel of Alpha Epsilon Delta*, May, 1949, pp. 91-96.
Shryock, Richard H., "Sylvester Graham and the Popular Health Movement," *Mississippi Valley Historical Review*, 18:172-183, 1931.
Smith, Nathan
  Medical and Surgical Memoirs, Baltimore, William A. Francis, 1831. Describes the surgical procedure used on Joseph Smith for osteomyelitis.
Snively, William D., Jr. and Furbee, Louanna, "Discovery of the Cause of Milk Sickness," *Journal of the American Medical Association*, 196:1055-60, June 20, 1966.
Stenn, Frederick, "The Pioneer History of Milk Sickness," *Annals of Medical History*, 9:23-29, 1937.
Stewart, Grace G., "A History of the Medicinal Use of Tobacco 1492-1860," *Medical History*, 11:228-68, July, 1967.
Thomson, Samuel
  A Narrative of the Life and Medical Discoveries of Samuel Thomson; Containing An Account of His System of Practice, and the Manner of Curing Disease with Vegetable Medicine, Upon a Plan Which is Entirely New; to Which is Added an Introduction to His new Guide to Health, or Botanic Family Physician, Containing the Principles Upon Which the System is Founded, With Remarks on Fevers, Steaming, Poison, etc., New York, Arno Press (Reprint of 1822 edition), 1972.
Transactions of the Medical Society of the State of New York, 1828, 1829, 1830. These transactions list Dr. Alexander McIntyre, the Smith family physician.
Vogel, Virgil J.
  American Indian Medicine, Norman, University of Oklahoma Press, 1970.
Waite, Frederick C., "An Attempt to Establish a Medical College in Wheeling in 1831," *West Virginia Medical Journal*, 42:316-319, December, 1946. Describes attempt by Dr. John C. Bennett to establish a medical school.
Waite, Frederick C., "The First Medical Diploma Mill in the United States," *Bulletin of the History of Medicine*, 20(4):495-504, November, 1946. Described Dr. John C. Bennett's medical school at New Albany, Indiana.
Waite, Frederick C., "Thomsonianism in Ohio," *Ohio Archeological and Historical Quarterly*, 49:322-31, 1940.
Waite, Frederick C.
  Western Reserve University Centennial History of the School of Medicine, Cleveland, 1946. Discusses medical school headed by Dr. John C. Bennett in a community near Kirtland.
Waller, Adolph E., "A Fictitious Medical Degree of the 1830s," *Bulletin of the History of Medicine*, 20:505-12, 1946. Describes diploma from Dr. John C. Bennett's New Albany, Indiana, medical school.

Wells, W. A., "Last Illness and Death of George Washington," *Virginia Medical Monthly*, 53:629-642, 1927.

Wilcox, Howard G., "Redskin Remedies: Contributions of the American Indian to Patent Medicines," *Rocky Mountain Medical Journal*, 71(1):29-33, January, 1974.

Willius, F. A. and Keys, T. E., "The Medical History of George Washington (1732-1799)," *Proceedings of the Staff Meetings of the Mayo Clinic* 17:92-96, 107-112, 116-121, 1942.

Winkler, Allan M., "Drinking on the American Frontier," *Quarterly Journal of Studies on Alcohol*, 29:413-45, June, 1968.

Young, James Harvey, "The Persistence of Medical Quackery in America," *Scientific American*, 60(1):318-326, January-February, 1972.

Index

A

accident rate, 121
accidents, 25
Accoucher's Vade Mecum, 74
administration to the sick, 11
Advisory Council of Hospital Administrators, 175
Afton, Wyoming, 171
ague and fever, *see* malaria
ague cakes (spleen tumors), 60
Albany, New York, 56
alcohol, 99
alcoholic beverages, 12, 47
alcoholism, 48
allopathic medicine, 130
American Bottoms, Illinois, 60
American frontier, 9
American Medical Association, 133
American revolution, 14
American Society for the Promotion of Temperance, 48
ammonia, 125
anesthesia, 131-132
angina pectoris, 149
anti-medicine attitudes, 110-111
antipathy to orthodox medicine, 116-117
antiseptis surgery, 132
antitoxins, 134
apoplexy, 136
apostles and faith healing, 41
appendicitis, 36, 134, 143
appendectomy, 155
Arkansas River, 102
Arrow Rock, Saline County, Missouri, 61
arsenic, 47, 103, 130
artificial heart, 167
asthenic (direct) debility, 15
attitude toward doctors, 180-181
attitude toward medicine, 21
autoinnoculation, 156

B

bachelor's degree nursing programs, 167, 168
bacteria, anaerobic, 132
bacteriology, 131
baptism for healing, 44, 45
baths, daily, 25
battle wounds in Civil War, 133
beeswax, 125
Bellevue Medical College, 160, 161
Bent's Fort (now Colorado), 108
bicarbonate of soda, 125
Big Cottonwood, Utah, 153
bile, 14
bilious colic, 36
bio-statistics, 25
birth rate, 122
bitter root, 122
Black Hawk War, 56
blackleg, 106
bleeding (phlebotomy), *see also* blood letting, 16, 31, 57
blistering agents, 103
blood, 14
blood letting (phlebotomy), *see also* bleeding, 47, 129
Board of Examiners, Salt Lake City, 152
Board of Health, 139, 152, 157
body, physical, 10
botanic medical societies, 20
botanic medicine, 124, 126-127, 153
botanic school of medicine, 123
Botanico-Medical School of Ohio, 79
bowel complaint, 125
brain fever (meningitis), 65
brandy, 125
Brigham Young University, 166, 167, 168, 173
Buffalo, New York, 56
burdock, 122
Burley, Idaho, 173
burns, 125
Buttermilk Fort, Millard County, Utah, 122

C

Cache Valley, Utah, 123-124, 172, 174
Cadet Nurse Corps, 167
Caldwell County, Missouri, 62
California, 154, 156
California gold rush, 108
California State Health Department, 154
calomel (mercurous chloride), 16, 31, 36, 47, 57, 103, 129, 133, 139
Camp Douglas, Utah, 116
Camp Douglas Post Dispensary, 146
Camp Floyd, Utah, 116
camphor, 125
cancer, 122, 179-180
canker sore, 122
carbonate of soda, 125
cardiovascular research, 167
carpenter and glazier, B. Young a, 135
Cassia County, Idaho, 173
Cassia Memorial Hospital, 173
cathartics, 103
catheterized, B. Young, 142
Catholic priests, 156
cayenne pepper, 99, 122, 124
curare, 18

changes in medicine, 129-134
charismatic healing, J. Smith, 42-43
charity hospital, 148
chastens, God—by disease, 11
chewing tobacco, 49
Cheyenne Indians, 109
chickens, Plymouth Rock, 81
childbirth, 123
children, 118
chiropractic medicine, 130
chiropractors, 127
chloroform, 132
cholera, 44, 55-59, 107-109, 133, 152
cholera infantum (infant diarrhea), 134, 155
Christian Church, early, 38-39
church advocates using good medicine, 127-128
church born during medical revolution, 14
church warns against health charlatans, 127-128
Church Commissioner of Health Services, 176
Church News, 127-128
cinchona, 18
cinchona bark, 61
Cincinnati, Ohio, 56
Circleville, Ohio, 69
City Cemetery, Salt Lake City, 145
Civil War, 132-133, 146
Clay County, Missouri, 62
Cleveland, Ohio, 56
coca, 18
coffee, 12, 47, 49, 50, 99
colds, 125, 141, 142
Colesville, New York, 39
College of Physicians and Surgeons, 161
colonies, LDS, 120
Colorado Tick Fever, 106
Columbia College, 34
Comanche Indians, 109
Commerce, Illinois, *see also* Nauvoo, Illinois, 42, 62-64, 87
Commissioner of Health, Salt Lake City, 155
Commonwealth Fund, 172
communities without doctors healthier, 140
Connecticut River Valley, 27
consulting groups, 178
consumption, *see also* tuberculosis, 26, 27
converts brought medical education, 159
Cottonwood Maternity Hospital, 171
Cottonwood LDS Hospital, 174
Council Bluffs, Iowa, 103
Council Grove (now Kansas), 102
Council of Fifty, 92
Council on Health, 115, 123, 152, 160
Cross Timbers, 102
culture, impact on health, 9
cupping agents, 103

D

Dartmouth Medical College, 27
dandelion, 122, 125
Danites, 86
Davies County, Missouri, 62
death rates, 59, 180
debility, 15
debt, Smith family, 24
Dee LDS Hospital, 169-170
definition of a good doctor, B. Young, 141
demon possession, 10, 25
Deseret Hospital, 148, 163, 165, 169, 177
Deseret News, 113, 150, 153, 157-158, 160, 177, 180
diarrhea, 107, 137
differences in accepting health care, 9
digestion, 131
diphtheria, 65, 107, 123, 133, 134
direct (asthenic) debility, 15
disease, consequence of sin, 25
disease, God chastens by, 11
disease, germ theory of, 11, 25
disease, humoral theory of, 14, 15
disease, nomenclature, 15
divestment of hospitals, 177-179
doctor, B. Young's definition of a good, 141
Doctor Groves Latter-day Saints Hospital, 149-152, 169, 170
doctors, American, trained in Europe, 15
doctors, in mobs, 97, 98
doctors, called to settlements, 120
doctors, no medical school graduates in settlements, 120
doctors, not expected to practice full time, 120
doctors, orthodox, in Cache Valley, 123
doctors, poison, 155
Doctrine and Covenants, (24:13-14) 39, 40; (35:9) 40; (42:43) 13, 46, 126; (42:43-44, 48-52) 40; (46:19-20) 40; (49:18-19) 46; (59:16-20) 46; (66:9) 41; (84:67-73) 41; (Sec. 89) 12, 50-51; (93:36) 159; (124:16-17) 75; (124:86-87) 43, 44; (124:98-100) 44; (130:18-19) 159
doctrine of signatures, 22
Duchesne County, Utah, 172
dysentery and diarrhea, 65, 107

E

earache, 125
Eclectic Medical College of Pennsylvania, 163
eclectic medicine, 130
edema arsenicals, 103
Edinburgh, Scotland, 15, 34
effluvia, 16
Egypt, 14
elements, four, 14

elocution, 163
emetics, 103
enemas, 57
Ensign, 181
epidemics, 16
epistles of the First Presidency, 139, 153, 154
ether, 131-132
evil, growing, doctors at childbirth, 141
evil spirits, 39, 42
extreme unction for death, 39

F

Fairfield, Illinois, 74
faith, if sufficient doctors not needed, 140
faith healing, 11, 38-45, 120, 126, 138, 150, 151, 152, 159, 181
famine, 152
fasting, 12
fear, of orthodox medicine, 127
federal funding entanglements, 178
fever, 53
fever and ague, *see* malaria
fever-sore (necrosis or osteomyelitis), 31
Fifteenth Ward, Salt Lake City, 150
Fillmore, Utah, 172
First Presidency, 169, 178, 180, 181
flaxseed-meal poultice, 123
flies, 25
fluid balance and cholera, 57
folk medicine, 124, 127
food workers, 156
Fort Armstrong (Rock Island), Illinois, 56
Fort Dearborn (Chicago), Illinois, 56
Fort Des Moines, Iowa, 63, 136
Fort Douglas, *see* Camp Douglas
Fort Laramie (now Wyoming), 105
Fort Leavenworth (now Kansas), 102, 103
Fowler's solution, 103, 104
Fremont General Hospital, 173, 174
Frontier Guardian, 108
frostbite, 121-122
funeral sermon, King Follett, 39

G

gangrene and calomel, 133
Garden Grove, Iowa, 101, 107
garlic, 125
gathering to Zion, dogma of, 177
general epistle of First Presidency, 109, 153, 154
germ theory of disease, 11, 25
ginger, 125
ginseng, 21-24
ginseng swindle, 21-24
glass, 25
glazier, B. Young a, 135

God's power, diseases demonstrate, 11
golden seal, 125
good doctor, B. Young's definition, 141
Grand River (now Kansas), 102
Great Basin, 120
Great Salt Lake Valley, Utah, 112
Greece, 14
Gross Isle, Canada, 55

H

handkerchief, healing token, 43, 45
Harmony, Pennsylvania, 39
Harper's Weekly, 139
healers were religious leaders, 38
healing, all ultimately comes from God, 11
healing, faith, 11
health conditions, in New England, 24
health examinations, 156
Health Missionary Corps, 179
Health Service Corporation of The Church of Jesus Christ of Latter-day Saints, 176, 179
heart disease, 179
heartburn, 125
herbal orientation, 13
herbalism, 126-127
herbalists, 12
herbs, native American, 17-18
herbs 38, 45-46, 104, 152
Herculaneum, Missouri, 91
heroic medicine, 15, 17, 129
Hill-Burton Funds, 173
History of the Saints, 78
hoarhound, 125
Holy Cross Hospital, 147
Holy Cross Hospital School of Nursing, 165
Holy Spirit, promptings of, 181
homeopathy, 130
hops, 125
horseradish, 107
hospital expansion world-wide considered, 178
hospitals, 144-152
hot drinks, 47, 51
humoral theory of disease, 14-15
humors, 14

I

Idaho Falls LDS Hospital, 171, 178
illnesses, most eventually heal themselves, 124
illnesses, B. Young says none in Salt Lake till doctors came, 139
immigrants to pass health exam, 153
Independence, Missouri, 61
Index-Catalogue, 134

Index Medicus, 134
Indian root, 122
Indians, and cholera, 108-109
indirect (sthenic) debility, 15
indigo-weed root, 125
inflammatory rheumatism, 122
influenza, 125, 131, 142
influx of allopathic Mormon doctors, 147
insane asylums, 145-146
Intelligence, 10
Intermountain Health Care, Inc., 179
ipecac, 18
Italian hemp root, 122
Ithaca, New York, 40

J

Jackson, County, Missouri, 41, 46
jalap, 16
James 5:14-15, pp. 11, 38, 45
jaundice, 125
Jerusalem artichokes, 107
Jewish people, 179
Journal of Discourses, 140
Judge Memorial Hospital, 166

K

Kanesville (Council Bluffs), Iowa, 108
Kaw Indians, 102
Keely Institute, 147
Keokuk, Iowa, 87
kidney, 122
Kiowa Indians, 109
Kirtland, Ohio, 40, 56, 60

L

lard, 125
Latter-day Saint practitioners, 13
Latter-day Saints Hospital, 149-152, 169, 170
laudanum, 125
laws, eternal, 10-11
laws, health, 138-139, 152
laws, requiring registration of midwives, 165
lay medical practitioners, 20, 125
lay priesthood, 138
laying-on-of-hands, 11
LDS Hospital, 149-152, 169, 170
LDS Hospital School of Nursing, 166-168
lead poisoning, B. Young exposed to, 135
Lebanon, New Hampshire, 28
Liberty, Missouri, 102
lobelia, 18, 57, 124
Logan, Utah, 123, 165
Logan LDS Hospital, 172
lung fever, 142

M

McBurney's Point, 155
McKay-Dee Hospital, 174
McMillan Bill, 158
malaria, 53, 60-65, 106
manure, cow or horse, 125
Massachusetts State Health Department, 154
measles, 65, 107, 123
meats, 12, 46
Medical College of Ohio, 163
Medical College of Utah at Morgan, 163-165
medical practitioners, lay, 20
Medical Repository, 34, 35
medical schools, proposed and rumored, 166, 167
Medical Society of the State of New York, 35
medications, home, 124
medicine, changes in, 129-134
medieval period, faith healing in, 39
men, should not deliver babies, 123
Mendon, Utah, 123
mentally disturbed, 145-146
mercurous chloride, *see* calomel
Mesopotamia, 14
Mexican War, 101-105
miasmas, 42
miasmata, 16
microbiology, 131
microscope, achromatic, 131
midwifery, 165
midwives, 120, 122, 123
milk, pasteurization, 156
milk leg inflammation, 125
milk sickness, 53-55
Millard Stake, 172
mineral medications, 129-130
Minidoka County, Idaho, 173
Minidoka Memorial Hospital, 173
mining development, 146
miraculous recoveries, 120-121
missionary church, 177
Missouri, 61
Missouri River, 108
Missouri Volunteers, 103
Mississippi Company, 105
Mississippi River, 60, 108
modesty, 12
Morgan, Utah, 163-165
Mormon Battalion, 101-105, 138
Mormons, nine die of cholera, 108
Mormons, use gentile hospitals, 147
Moroni's visit, 36
mortality rate, Utah's, 120
mosquitos, 25, 60, 102
mothers, expectant, washed with olive oil, 124
Mount Pisgah, Iowa, 101, 107

INDEX

Mount Pleasant, Utah, 172
mountain fever, 105-106, 123, 137-138, 144
mouth-to-mouth resuscitation, 137
mumps, 123, 135, 142
mustard, 125
mustard plaster, 123
mutton tallow, 125

N

Natchez, Mississippi, 91
National Formulary, 18, 127
Native American medicines, 17, 18
Native Americans, 34
naturopathic doctors, 127
naturopathy, 130
Nauvoo, Illinois, *see also* Commerce, 64-66, 68, 75-78, 99-101, 123, 136, 144
Nauvoo Board of Health, 152
Nauvoo Charter, 68, 75
Nauvoo City Council, 77
Nauvoo Expositor, 90, 92, 112
Nauvoo Legion, 68, 75, 77, 116
Nauvoo Lodge A & FM, 78
necessities, B. Young list of, 99
necrosis (osteomyelitis), 30
Neo-Thomsonianism, 79, 130
Neosho River (now Kansas), 102
New England, health conditions, 24
New England Journal of Medicine, 179
New Mexico, 156
New Orleans, Louisiana, 107
New Testament, faith healing in, 38
New York City, New York, 56, 91, 92
nomenclature, disease, 15
nursing school, 167-168, 173
nursing programs, bachelor's degree, 166-168

O

obstetricians, midwives licensed as, 165
Ogden, Utah, 147, 148, 169-170
Ohio, 19-20
oil, consecrated, 11, 12, 45
oil, sweet or olive, 124
onion, 125
opium, tincture of, 125
ordinances, health, 156
Orem, Utah, 172
orthodox doctors, 125
osteomyelitis, 30
osteopathy, 130
ovariotomy, 33

P

Palmyra, Missouri, 58, 59
panacea, ginseng thought to be, 21-22

Panguitch LDS Hospital, 173
parents, 138, 140-141
Parowan, Utah, 121
Parry's Monthly Magazine, 154
pasteurization, 156
pennyroyal, 102
pepper, 124
peppermint, 125
pestilence, 25
Pharmacopeia of the United States, 18
phlebotomy, 47, 129
phlegm, 14
phthisis (tuberculosis), 26, 122
physicians were religious leaders, 38
physicians, in Salt Lake Valley, 116
physiology, course in, 161
pine gum, 125
Pioneer Company, 105
plague, 25
Plymouth Rock chickens, 81
pneumonia, 123
poison doctors, 115
poisonous weeds, 152
Polk City, Iowa, 81
potato, 125
poultice, flaxseed meal, 123
The Poultry Book, 81
prayer, 12, 44, 45
prayer circle and faith healing, 44-45
prejudice against doctors, 139
Presiding Bishopric, 151, 169, 171
prevention of illness, 153
preventive medicine, 138
priesthood, 11
priesthood, Melchizedek, 11
priesthood and faith healing, 45
priesthood blessings, 120
priesthood healing, 138
priesthood, lay, concept of, 138
priests, Catholic, 156
Primary Association, 170, 171
Primary Children's Hospital, 170-171, 175
Primary Children's Medical Center, 181
priority for medical care, B. Young's, 140
prostate disease, B. Young had, 142
Providence, Utah, 123
Provo, Utah, 172
public health, 152
public health measures, in Nauvoo, 68
puerperal (childbed) fever, 131
purging, 16, 129

Q

quail, miracle of, 101
quality of Mormon health, 179-180
quarantine, 156
Quincy, Illinois, 63

quinine, 62, 103
Quorum of the Twelve, 178

R

railroad, coming of to Utah, 140
red pepper, 124
reformation, faith healing in, 39
reformed school of medicine, 79
Relief Society, 44, 45, 123, 148, 157, 160-162, 165, 166, 169, 171, 177
respiratory difficulties, B. Young's, 141
rheumatism, 25, 122, 142
rhubarb, 125
Richfield, Utah, 174
Richmond, Missouri, 58
Richmond, Utah, 123
Rocky Mountain Spotted Fever, 106
Roosevelt LDS Hospital, 172
rosin, 125
Rupert, Idaho, 173
Rush Medical College, 165

S

Sacramento, California, 109
saffron, 125
sage, 124
St. Anthony, Idaho, 173
St. Clairsville, Ohio, 69
St. Louis, Missouri, 56, 60, 108
St. Marks (Episcopal) Cathedral, 146
St. Marks Hospital, 146-147, 148-149
St. Marks Hospital School of Nursing, 165
St. Mary's Hospital, 147
saleratus, 99
Salt Lake City, Utah, 120
Salt Lake Herald, 164
Salt Lake Sanitarian, 124, 154-155
Salt Lake Valley, 120, 153
salve, 125
San Diego, California, 109
San Francisco, California, 109
San Pedro, California, 109
Sandwich Islands (Hawaii), 160
Sangamo Journal, 78
sanitation, 34, 154
Sanpete LDS Hospital, 172
Sanpete Valley, Utah, 172
Santa Fe Trail, 102
Sappington's Anti-Fever Pills, 100, 103, 112
sarsaparilla, 125
scarlet fever, 65, 123, 137
schism between doctors, 18
School of Obstetrics and Nursing, 165
School of the Prophets, 50
schools, medical, 15
scorbutic disease, *see also* scurvy, 63

scrofula (tuberculosis), 26
scurvy, 17, 106, 137
sengers (ginseng hunters), 23
Seventh-Day Adventists, 179
Shakers, 46
shortage, none of doctors, 120
Sick Detachment, Mormon Battalion, 105
sick should first try to heal themselves, 138
sickness in New England, 24
signatures, doctrine of, 22
sin, disease consequence of, 25
Sisters of St. Benedict, 174
slippery elm bark, 125
smallpox, 123, 153, 156-158
Smithfield, Utah, 123
snuff (tobacco), 49
soap, castile shavings, 125
Society of Health, Thomsonian, 152
soda, 125
son of God, man is literal, 10
Soul, 10
specialist, Utah's first medical, 162
Spirit, 10
spirits, evil, 10, 39
Star Valley LDS Hospital, 171-172
Star Valley, Wyoming, 171
state health commissions, 155-156
state health departments, 154
statehood, Utah, 155
steam sterilization in surgery, 134
steamboats, 61
sterilization, steam, 134
stethoscope, 130
sthenic (indirect) debility, 15
strichnine, 47, 130
sugar, 125
surgery, antiseptic, 132
surgery, primitive, 38
sweating, 125
sweet oil, 124, 125

T

tallow, mutton, 125
tea, 12, 47, 49, 99
temperance, 48
temple garments, 12, 44
temple ordinances, 44-45
temple prayer circle, 44-45
Thomsonian medicine, 138
Thomsonianism, 130
Times and Seasons, 110
tobacco, 12, 47, 48, 49, 102
Tremonton, Utah, 174
tuberculosis, 26-27, 122, 123
Tunbridge, Vermont, 21
turpentine, 125
typho-malarious fever, 106

typhoid fever, 27-33, 65, 106, 122, 133, 155, 156
typhous fever, 30
typhus, 30

U

Uinta Basin, Utah, 172
unction, extreme, for death, 39
"underground," 154
Union Pacific Hospital, 147
U.S. Center for Disease Control, 179
U.S. Dispensatory, 18, 127
University of the City of Nauvoo, 68
University of Louisville School of Medicine, 165
University of Michigan School of Medicine, 163
University of Pennsylvania, 91
University of Utah, 166-167
Utah Board of Health, 156
Utah, first health law, 138
Utah, health department urged, 154
Utah Historical Quarterly, 121
Utah-Idaho Hospital, 172
Utah, mortality rate high, 120
Utah State Legislature, 167
Utah State Mental Hospital, 172
Utah Territorial Insane Asylum, 146
Utah territorial officers, 1851, 114
Utah Valley, 175
Utah Valley LDS Hospital, 172
Utah War, 115-116

V

vaccination, 180
vaccination, anti-, bill, 158
vegetarians, 12
vital statistics, 156
vomiting, 125

W

Warm Springs, Salt Lake City, 148-149
Wasatch Front, Utah, 175
washing, anointing and faith healing, 12, 45
water, 25
water supplies, 156
Weber State College, 174
weeds, poisonous, 152
wells, 25
Wellsville, Utah, 123
western medicine, 14
Wheeling, (West) Virginia, 70-71
whiskey, 48
Williams Hospital, 144-145
Winter Quarters (now Nebraska), 105, 106

Woman's Exponent, 157
women, oppose tobacco use, 49
women doctors, 148
Women's Medical College in Philadelphia, 161-162, 163
Women's Medical College of Utah, 162
Word of Wisdom, 12, 47-52, 138, 180
work, hard, brings better health, 145
Wyoming, 105

X

x-ray, 134

Y

Yale College, 29
Yale University Beineke Library, 80
yellow dock, 122
yellow fever, 16, 34, 91

Z

Zion (Independence, Missouri), 61
Zion's Camp, 53-59

Name Index

A

Ackerknecht, Dr. Erwin H., 62
Adams, Dr. David, 113
Allred, John, 58
Allen, Col. James, 101, 103
Anderson, Sister, 170
Anderson, Dr. Washington, F., 113, 126, 133, 140, 143, 148, 161
Ashburn, Col. P. M., 103
Avard, Dr. Samson, 84-86

B

Bagley, Amanda S., 171
Baldwin, Sr., Samuel Clifton, 151
Bancroft, Hubert Howe, 67
Bard, Sr., Samuel, 34
Barker, Dr. Mary, 161
Barlow, Isaac, 63
Barney, Dr. Elvira S., 148, 163
Barrett, Matilda M., 148
Bartholomew, Sister, 147
Beatty, Dr. Theodore B., 155-158
Beaumont, Dr. William, 131
Beech, Dr. Wooster, 121
Behring, Dr., 134
Benedict, Dr. Francis Denton, 143, 147
Benedict, Dr. Joseph Mott, 143, 147
Bennett, Dr. John Cook, 60, 65, 67-82, 88, 112, 126, 132, 152
Bent, George, 108
Bernhisel, Dr. John M., 91-92, 96-97, 112, 113, 122, 126, 131
Beyrich, Carl, botanist, 103
Billings, Dr. John Shaw, 134
Bishop, Mr., 122
Boggs, Gov. Lilburn, 63
Brodie, Sir Benjamin, 30
Brown, Dr. John, 15
Budge, Dr. S. M., 120
Budge, Dr. William, 172
Burdell, Dr., 49
Bush, Dr. Lester, Jr., 106

C

Cannon, Dr. (poison doctor), 115
Cannon, Angus Munn, 148, 163
Cannon, George Q., 133, 157, 163
Cannon, Dr. Martha Hughes Paul, *see also* Paul, 156
Carter, John S., 58
Chamberlin, Dr. Ralph V., 166
Clay, Henry, 91
Clark, Jennette, 122

Connor, Gen. Patrick, 116, 146
Cooke, Philip St. George, 102-103, 105, 107
Costello, Dr. J. F., 164
Coward, Dr., 114
Cowdery, Oliver, 39, 47
Cullen, Dr. William, 15, 16
Curtis, Dr. Alva, 79

D

Daines, Richard, 124
Dee, Thomas D., 169-170
Dibble, Philo, 41
Dodge, Col. Henry, 102, 103
Doniphan, Gen. Alexander, 105
Drake, Dr. Daniel, 55, 62
Dyke, Lt., 104

E

Eberth, Dr. Carl Joseph, 134
Edson, Dr. Cyrus, 155
Ehrlic, Dr. Paul, 134

F

Felt, Pres., 170
Ferguson, Dr. Ellen R., 148, 163
Ferris, Mrs. B. G., 114
Fitz, Dr. Reginald Heber, 134
Follett, King, 39
Fordham, Eliza, 43
Foster, Dr. Robert T., 88-90, 112
Fowler, Dr. Allan, 147
France, Dr. William, 113, 160

G

Galland, Dr. Isaac, 63, 64, 86-88
Garrison, Dr. Fielding H., 129
Gilbert Algernon Sidney, 59
Graham, Sylvester, 47-48
Grant, Heber J., 170
Greenwood, Dr., 36
Groves, Dr. William H., 149, 169

H

H-----, Dr. (dentist), 114
Hall, Dr. Thomas B., 106
Hamilton, Dr. John F., 146
Hammond, Surgeon General William A., 133
Hancock, Joseph, 58
Hard, Liela, 151
Hardy, Dr. M. H., 154
Hedlock, Rheuben, 136
Heys, William of Leeds, England, 29
Higbee, Judge Elias, 88

218

NAME INDEX

Hildreth, Dr. Samuel P., 60
Hippocrates, 14
Hobbs, "Dr." Anna Pierce, 55
Hodge, Abraham C., 90
Holmes, Dr. Oliver Wendell, 17, 28, 131, 132
Holy Cross, Sister M., 147
Hotchkiss, Horace, 87
Hughes, Dr. Martha Paul, *see also* Cannon, 148
Hunter, John, surgeon, 28
Hunter, William, surgeon, 28
Huntington, Dimick B., 90
Hurlburt, Doctor Philastus, 97
Hurt, Dr. Garland, 115
Hyde, Orson, 42

J

Jackson, Andrew, 91
Jackson, Charles T., 148
Jartoux, Father, 22
Jenkins, E. Howard, 175
Jenner, Dr. Edward, 156
Johnson, Elsa, 40-41
Johnson, John, 40-41
Joyce, Dr. R. S., 170

K

Kane, Col. Thomas L., 100-101, 116
Kearny, Gen., 107
Kimball, Heber C., 42-43, 63, 136
Kimball, Sarah, 161
Klebs, Dr. Edwin, 134
Knight, Newell, 39, 41
Koch, Dr. Robert, 134
Kohler, Dr. Benjamin Rush, 164, 165
Kohler, Dr. Frederick S., 163-165

L

Laennec, Rene -T. -H., 130
Lafitau, Father Joseph Francois, 22
Latham, Dr. Samuel, 34
Law, William, 44, 89
Law, Wilson, 89
Lawson, Dr. Thomas, 103
Leavenworth, Gen. Henry, 102
Lemaire, Dr. Andre Alfred, 132
Lincoln, Abraham, 54
Lincoln family, 53
Lister, J. J., 131
Lister, Lord Joseph, 132
Louis, Dr. Pierre-Charles Alexandre, 131
Lyons, Dr. Joseph L., 179-180

M

McBurney, Dr. Charles, 155
McCauley, Dr. D. J., 164

McClure, Lt. George, 103
M'Intyre, Dr. Alexander, 35-36, 84
McIntyre, Dr. William, 103, 104, 105
Mack, Mrs. (Lucy Mack Smith's mother), 26
Mack, Lovina, 26
Mack, Lovisa, 26
Mack, Solomon, 25
Mack, Major Steven, 24
McKay, David O., 174
McKann, James, 121
Marks, William, 43-44, 90
Mason, Mr. James M., 164
Mason, Dr. James O., 176, 179, 181
Matthews, Benjamin, 153
Meeks, Dr. Priddy, 98, 112, 115, 121-122, 124, 125, 144, 152, 160
Miller, George, 69, 78
Mitchill, Dr. Samuel Latham, 15, 19, 34-35, 68, 83, 152
Mohammed, 49
Morrow, Dr. Thomas V., 79
Morton, Dr. William T. G., 132, 148
Moyle, Henry D., 174

N

Noble, Joseph B., 43

O

Olsen, Dr. Charles L., 180

P

P----S, 110
Page, John E., 43, 80
Parker, W. M., 163
Parkinson, Dr. W. B., 165
Pasteur, Louis, 132, 133
Paul, Dr. Martha Hughes, *see also* Cannon, 163
Peck, Electa, 40
Penn, Dr. George, 62
Pendleton, Dr. Calvin, 65, 98, 112, 121
Penrose, Charles W., 150, 157-158, 180
Penrose, Dr. Romania Bunnell Pratt *see also* Pratt, 157
Perkins, Dr. Cyrus, 32
Peterson, Anthony, 164
Pizer, Irwin, 144
Pope Clement VIII, 49
Porter, Mrs. Maud Dee, 170
Powers, Dr. H. J., 147
Pratt, Orson, 43, 85
Pratt, Parley P., 43, 47
Pratt, Parley P., Jr., 161
Pratt, Dr. Romania Bunnell, *see also* Penrose, 148, 161-163

R

Redden, Jackson, 90
Rich, Charles C., 109, 164
Rich, Dr. Emeline Grover, 164
Richards, Franklin D., 109
Richards, Hannah, 159
Richards, Dr. Heber John, 140, 160
Richards, Hepsibah, 95
Richards, Dr. Joseph S., 149, 151, 161, 162
Richards, Dr. Levi, 92-97, 112, 126
Richards, Levi Willard, 97
Richards, Dr. Phineas, 138
Richards, Dr. Ralph T., 120, 145, 151
Richards, Dr. Willard, 90, 92-97, 112, 113, 136, 138, 141, 152, 159
Rigdon, Sidney, 40, 64, 85, 89
Roberts, Dr. Margaret Shipp, *see also* Shipp, 165
Robinson, Dr. Gain C., 35
Robinson, Dr. King, 117-118
Rockwell, O. P., 88
Rockwood, A. P., 77
Roentgen, Dr. Wilhelm Konrad, 134
Rolapp, Judge Henry H., 170
Rowe, John, 55
Rush, Dr. Benjamin, 15, 16, 17, 33, 48

S

Sanderson, Dr. George B., 103-105, 112, 138
Sappington, Dr. John, 61-63, 65, 83, 103
Scanlon, Bishop Lawrence, 147
Semmelweis, Dr. Ignaz Philipp, 131
Sessions, Patty Bartlett, 112
Shipp, Doctors, 154
Shipp, Dr. Ellis Reynolds, 148, 154, 162-163
Shipp, Dr. M. Bard, 154, 162
Shipp, Dr. Margaret Curtis, *see also* Roberts, 154, 162-163
Shumway, Charles, 100
Silliman, Prof. Benjamin, 29
Simpson, Sir J. Y., 132
Skolfield, Dr. Jane, 151
Smith, Alvin, 30, 35-37, 46, 133
Smith, Lt. Andrew Jackson, 103
Smith, Cordelia T., 165
Smith, Don Carlos, 66
Smith, Dr. Elias, 19
Smith, George A., 41
Smith, Hyrum, 12, 30, 53
Smith, Joseph Sr., 21, 24, 27, 65, 85
Smith, Joseph, Jr.,
    all disease not of devil, 11
    herbal orientation, 13
    and typhoid fever, 27-33
    and faith healing, 39-41, 42-43, 64-65
    and Zion's Camp, 53, 54, 57, 58, 59
    and doctors, 83-98
    supports botanic medicine, 112
    sets apart midwives at Nauvoo, 123
    sees dangers in old school of medicine, 126
    used best medicines he could, 126
    and Frederick G. Williams, 138
    his attitudes affected church's attitudes, 135
    heals B. Young, 136
Smith, Lucy Mack, 21, 23, 26-27, 30-31, 63
Smith, Mary, 122
Smith, Dr. Nathan, 28-30, 33, 156
Smith, Samuel Harrison, 41
Smith, Sophronia, 30, 31
Smith, Dr. Theobald, 155
Smith, William, 80
Snow, Eliza R., 148, 160, 161, 162
Snow, Erastus, 85
Snow, Lorenzo, 157
Soxhlet, Dr. Franz von, 134
Spencer, Augustine, 90
Spencer, Orson, 90
Sprague, Dr. Samuel L., 133
Stevens, Mr., of Royalton, Vermont, 23, 24
Still, Dr. Andrew, 130
Stone, Dr., 32
Strang, James J., 79-80

T

Taylor, John, 43, 67, 85, 92, 97, 110-111, 154, 163
Thackeray, Helen Condie, 165
Thayer, Ezra, 58
Thomson, Dr. Samuel, 18-20, 47, 79, 83, 130
Thomson, Dr. Samuel, Jr., 47, 86
Tyndall, Prof. John, 133

V

Vaughan, Dr. J. M., 115
Vaughan, Dr. John R., 115
Vaughan, Dr. W. A., 155
Vollum, Dr. E. P., 118-119, 121

W

Waite, Dr. Frederick C., 71
Waltz, Miss, 151
Washington, George, 17
Waterhouse, Dr. Benjamin, 156
Wattis, William H., 170
Welch, Dr. William H., 33, 155
Wells, Daniel H., 77
Wells, Emmeline B., 148
Wells, Heber M., 155, 158
Whitmer, John, 41

NAME INDEX

Whitney, Newel K., 41
Widtsoe, Dr. John A., 179
Wight, Lyman, 11
Wilkes, Major Edmund, 146
Williams, Dr. Ezra, 144-145
Williams, Dr. Frederick Granger, 46, 84, 138
Wirthlin, Dr. LeRoy S., 32
Wonnacott, Clarence, 167, 175, 176
Woodruff, Wilford, 43, 106, 138, 153
Worthen, Dr. S. H., 171-172

Y

Young, Ann Eliza, 115
Young, Brigham
    advice on medication, 12-13
    herbal orientation, 13
    healed by J. Smith, 43
    circumstances of Word of Wisdom revelation, 50
    cousin of Drs. Levi and Willard Richards, 92, 93
    fled to Missouri, 94
    list of necessities for Westward journey, 99
    sends back help to Nauvoo, 101
    orders camps at Garden Grove and Mt. Pisgah, 101
    letter to Mormon Battalion, 104
    sick with mountain fever, 105-106
    sick with dysentery, 107
    letter to Franklin D. Richards, 109
    supports botanic medicine, 112
    on Dr. Sanderson, 112
    letter to Dr. David Adams, 113-114
    philosophy of medicine, 113-114
    orchestrated settlements, 120
    parents should care for families, 121
    assigned midwives to settlements, 123
    set apart midwives, 123
    sees dangers of orthodox medicine, 126
    friendship with Dr. W. F. Anderson, 126
    concern about imperfect medicine, 133
    priesthood blessing first step of healing, 133
    sends missionaries to medical schools, 133
    friendship with Dr. W. F. Anderson, 133
    his attitudes affected church's attitudes, 135
    childhood ailments, 135
    espoused botanic beliefs of J. Smith, 135
    "seasoned" to malaria, 136
    continuing illness, 136
    fell while jumping on ferry, 136
    had fit of apoplexy, 136
    scarlet fever, 137
    close to death, 137
    mouth to mouth resussitation, 137
    escapes scurvy, 137
    had diarrhea, 137
    apparently dead, 137
    mountain fever, 137-138
    cousin and friend of W. Richards, 138
    W. Richards taught him Thomsonianism, 138
    sick should first try to heal themselves, 138
    emphasized preventive medicine, 138
    strong advocate of Thomsonianism, 138
    wrote Mormon Battalion, 138
    addresses Board of Health, 139
    regarding calomel, 139
    prejudice against doctors, 139
    analogy of soul and body saving, 139
    attitude toward medicine, 139
    discourse on spiritual healing, health, medicine, 140
    doctors not needed with sufficient faith, 140
    never under necessity of calling doctor, 140
    liked doctors as friends, 140
    communities without doctors healthier, 140
    parents should learn medicine, 140
    Dr. W. F. Anderson close friend, 140
    called missionaries to medical school, 140
    priority for medical care, 140
    importance of parents in medical care, 140-141
    women having doctors in childbirth a growing evil, 141
    definition of a good doctor, 141
    remained youthful in appearance, 141
    respiratory difficulties, 141
    sick, can't attend W. Richards' funeral, 141
    sick, missed general conference, 142
    colds, 142
    influenza, 142
    catheterized, 142
    prostate disease, 142
    health degenerates, 142
    final illness, 142
    used opiates during final illness, 142
    conjecture over cause of death, 142-143
    cause of death per Dr. S. B. Young, 143
    Dr. W. F. Anderson assists during final illness, 143
    urges Mormons not to mine, 146, 147
    asked W. & H. Richards to teach health care, 159
    saints should learn about

orthodox medicine, 160
called missionaries to medical
schools, 160-161, 162
medicine a suitable field for women, 161
calls women to medical school, 161
J. Taylor sets apart B. Young—
called women, 163
Young, Joseph, 126
Young, Lorenzo Dow, 85
Young, Mrs. Lorenzo Dow, 122
Young, Miriam Works, 135
Young, Dr. Seymour B., 140, 142-143, 145-146, 148, 161, 162
Young, Zina D. H., 148, 160